JESUS

OTHER TITLES OF RELATED INTEREST
IN RELIGIOUS STUDIES

BIBLICAL STUDIES

David Barr, *New Testament Story*
Edwin D. Freed, *The New Testament: A Critical Introduction*
Benton White, *From Adam to Armageddon: A Survey of the Bible*

ETHICS

Ethel Albert et al., *Great Traditions in Ethics, 5th Edition*
Deborah Johnson/John Snapper, *Ethical Issues in the Use of Computers*
Robert Kruschwitz/Robert Roberts, *The Virtues: Contemporary Essays on Moral Character*
Richard Purtill, *Moral Dilemmas: Readings in Ethics and Social Philosophy*
James Sterba, *Ethics of War and Nuclear Deterrence*
Richard Nolan et al., *Living Issues in Ethics*
Pearsall, *Women and Values: Readings in Recent Feminist Philosophy*
Donald VanDeVeer/Christine Pierce, *People, Penguins, and Plastic Trees: Basic Issues in Environmental Ethics*

SELECTED TITLES IN THE WORLD RELIGIOUS TRADITIONS

Catherine Albanese, *America: Religions and Religion*
Kenneth Cragg, *House of Islam, 2d Edition*
Byron Earhart, *Japanese Religion, 3d Edition*
Sam Gill, *Native American Religions*
Thomas Hopkins, *The Hindu Religious Tradition*
Noel King, *African Cosmos*
Jacob Neusner, *The Way of Torah, 4th Edition*
Stephen Reynolds, *The Christian Religious Tradition*
Laurence Thompson, *Chinese Religion, 3d Edition*
Mary Jo Weaver, *Introduction to Christianity*

INTRODUCTION TO RELIGION

Roger Schmidt, *Exploring Religion*
Frederick Streng, *Understanding Religious Life*
Louis Pojman, *Philosophy of Religion: An Anthology*

OTHER BOOKS BY DENISE CARMODY AND JOHN CARMODY

Christianity: An Introduction
Shamans, Prophets, and Sages: A Concise Introduction to World Religion
Ways to the Center: An Introduction to World Religions, 2d Edition
Eastern Ways to the Center
Western Ways to the Center
How to Live Well: Ethics in the World Religions

JESUS
AN INTRODUCTION

Denise Lardner Carmody
John Tully Carmody

UNIVERSITY OF TULSA

Wadsworth Publishing Company
Belmont, California
A Division of Wadsworth, Inc.

Religion Editor: Sheryl Fullerton
Editorial Assistant: Cynthia Haus
Production Editor: Lisa Danchi
Print Buyer: Barbara Britton
Designer: Lisa Mirski
Copy Editor: Greg Gullickson
Compositor: G & S Typesetters, Inc.
Cover: John Osborne

Printed in the United States of America   54
1 2 3 4 5 6 7 8 9 10—91 90 89 88 87

Library of Congress Cataloging-in-Publication Data

Carmody, Denise Lardner, 1935–
   Jesus : an introduction.

   Bibliography:
   Includes index.
   1. Jesus Christ—History of doctrines.   2. Jesus
Christ—Person and offices.   I. Carmody, John, 1939–
II. Title.
BT198.C29   1987   232'.09   87-6103
ISBN 0-534-08016-2

For
BILL SHEA
and
HELENE LUTZ

Contents

Preface

This book is a comprehensive introduction to Jesus suitable for use in college courses. We have been moved to present it because we have searched in vain for a text that would cover the data we have found most useful in courses on Jesus.

Specifically, we have gathered information on the different understandings of Jesus available in the New Testament, on the historical evolution of Christian doctrine regarding Jesus, on leading issues of present-day christology, and on how Jesus compares with other great religious figures such as Buddha and Confucius. These four topics have created the four central chapters of our text. Certainly other topics—for example, the Jesus of Christian devotion through the centuries, the Jesus of art and literature, or the Jesus of various detractors—could also have been included, but spatial limitations and our sense of priorities made these four topics the crux.

Despite this limitation of its scope, the book remains quite dense. We therefore advise teachers to illustrate selected topics with fuller treatments—a detailed study of the Gospel of Mark, or the christology of Martin Luther, or feminist theologians' criticisms of traditional christology, or the comparison of Jesus and Buddha, for example. Teachers might also supplement the materials of the text with slides that suggest how Jesus was portrayed in Eastern iconography, or in medieval European cathedrals. They might offer hearings of recent musical interpretations of Jesus, such as *Jesus Christ Superstar* and *Godspell*, or of Handel's *Messiah* and Bach's *St. Matthew's Passion*. Such novels as *Man of Nazareth*, by Anthony Burgess, and *The Last Temptation of Christ*, by Nikos Kazantzakis, illustrate the problems of trying to imagine the consciousness of Christ. Such classical devotional works as *The Imitation of Christ*, by Thomas à Kempis, and *The Spiritual Exercises*, by Ignatius Loyola, illustrate how Jesus was worshiped through the centuries. We have concentrated on ideas and doctrines. The supplements that we suggest therefore head in the direction of images and affections.

To students our main suggestion would be to take the reading in fairly small doses. Physically, it is possible to read a chapter such as the one on the New Testament in an hour. Realistically, one will only master the wealth of the christological materials in the New Testament by reading each section of that chapter several times and correlating the main points with the key texts under discussion.

In our Introduction and Conclusion, we have tried to deal in balanced fashion with the methodological problems that attend the study of Jesus and with the modest yield that any such study may finally claim. In general, our approach is detached or relatively objective, but we have indicated the admiration Jesus has raised in many observers, and we have not hidden our own admiration.

It is a pleasant task to thank Bill Shea and Helene Lutz for being friends to whom one could dedicate a book on Jesus without fear of misunderstanding; to thank Sheryl Fullerton of Wadsworth Publishing Company for suggesting this project and overseeing its development; and to thank the following readers who offered helpful criticism or advice: Gene Gallagher, Connecticut College; David Graf, University of Miami; and Richard Keady, San Jose State University.

1

Introduction

Why Study Jesus in College?

Frequently people who teach religious studies in state universities are asked, "How is it that religion courses are offered at your school? Doesn't that violate the separation of Church and State?" The long answer to this two-part question involves the history of religious education in this country, with its delicate balancing act of trying to honor the obvious importance of religion to the majority of Americans without imposing the particular beliefs of any one religious group on a given state or on the country as a whole.[1] The short answer is that many colleges and universities, both public and private, have realized that religion is an important cultural phenomenon that deserves a place in any curriculum of humanistic or social-scientific courses. As well, these schools have recognized that there are ways of studying religion that do not require a commitment of faith and so can be objective or evenhanded.

Against this background, the question of studying Jesus in college becomes relatively straightforward. Just as the Buddha, Muhammad, Confucius, and other religious leaders have influenced a great deal of human history and so merit study, so does Jesus. We would have a very different country and world had there been no Jesus of Nazareth. The Western way of dividing history (B.C./A.D.) reflects his great impact, as do our Western ways of thinking about nature, human dignity, and the significance of birth and death. The followers of Jesus spread across the globe,

bringing his gospel and holding him up as the model of human perfection. Sometimes they were a blessing to the people to whom they
preached, and sometimes they caused a great many problems, but almost
everywhere they made a significant difference. Even Africa and Asia,
the continents that have remained least Christianized, felt the strong
impact of Christian missionaries, Christian colonizers, and Christian
entrepreneurs.

That is what one might call an historical reason for studying Jesus.
Because Jesus launched a movement that greatly shaped subsequent
world history, he is a worthy subject of objective, scholarly analysis. A
second, more philosophical reason for studying Jesus is the teaching or
world view that he and his followers have laid out. Jesus stands with the
Buddha, Confucius, Plato, Marx, and a handful of others as a teacher
who has given humanity some of its most important ideas about how
the world is constituted, what finally is good and what finally is evil. So,
just as it would make sense to study the ideas of Confucius or Buddha,
Plato or Marx, Muhammad or Lao-tzu, because they have shaped so
many human lives, it makes sense to study Jesus, the teacher of billions
even today. College is a place for examining the great ideas that have
shaped the past and still challenge us today. It is a place for learning not
only about other times and cultures, but also about one's own time, one's
own self. Since Jesus continues to influence people today through the
many Christian churches, his ideas are fit matter for college study.

We assume that these initial explanations of a course or a textbook
about Jesus are obvious enough, but perhaps a little further documentation is warranted. The 1984 American presidential election, which was
the big news while we were writing much of this book, witnessed a great
resurgence of Church-State issues. Abortion was a major issue, and most
of the time candidates had to contend with a complicated variety of religious stands that lay behind different groups' views on abortion. For
example, many of the most militant anti-abortionists or right-to-lifers
justified their vehemence on religious, or even specifically Christian,
grounds. In their eyes abortion was murder, and not to stand up for the
rights of the innocent unborn was to contribute to a horrible evil. On
the other hand, many of those who described themselves as pro-choice
justified their stand in terms of the sacredness or inviolability of private
conscience. Our American tradition, they argued, has been not to im-
pose a uniform public law or morality in matters so personal and private
as abortion. Others in the pro-choice bloc were frankly alienated from
religion. In their view the churches were one of the major hindrances to a
free and responsible control of human fertility. These critics said that
the churches, by their patriarchalism and dogmatism, wanted to keep
women in a subordinate status and the family under male control.

Apart from the specific issue of abortion, religion also dogged the
1984 presidential campaign as a more general concern. Charges flew that

if Reagan won, conservative religious groups such as the Moral Majority would have a big say in determining the new Supreme Court justices. The countercharges from the Republicans took the tack that critics of the involvement of right-wing religious groups in politics were being antireligious and one-sided. The American tradition had never meant the muzzling of religious people or of anyone else. In our tradition, all citizens have had the right to express their views and to lobby decently for them. Moreover, the religious right continued, who led the antiwar movement in the late 1960s and the prior civil rights movement? Who are the leaders of the nuclear disarmament movement today? If it is legitimate for liberal religious people to pressure for changes in civil rights, foreign policy, and nuclear arms policy, why is it illegitimate for conservative people to pressure for the changes they think are in the country's best interests?

These charges and countercharges admit of few easy solutions. Most fair-minded people come down someplace in the middle, not wanting religious leaders of any stripe, liberal or conservative, to dictate national policy, but also not wanting any group, religious or irreligious, barred from the debates over public policy. One of the reasons this middle-of-the-road or both/and position predominates in the overall Christian camp is the ambiguity of Jesus' own views on politics. Apart from the enigmatic statement that one ought to render to Caesar the things that are Caesar's and render to God the things that are God's (Matthew 12 : 17), Jesus said little explicitly about politics. What was implicit in his teachings and general attitudes (for example, in his not joining a political group like the Zealots, or in his going out of his way to establish friendships among the poor and outcast of his society) is a matter of interpretation and considerable debate.

Nonetheless, even when Jesus himself is only far in the background, the discussion of Church-State relations in the United States, like the discussion of a Christian Socialist or a Christian Marxist political regime in a country like Nicaragua, moves in tracks first laid down by Jesus. For the white people who founded the United States often were motivated by a desire for religious liberty, while some of the Sandinistas (and their Christian analogues in other countries involved in social upheaval) see the New Testament as a document for human liberation.

To be sure, these influences of Jesus matter less to many people than the comfort and challenge they find in their personal relation to him as Lord. When we study Jesus we must be aware not only of his influence on history and politics but also of the probably more profound effect he has had on individual believers, people who went to him in need and prayed for his help. This part of Jesus' influence largely passes outside what academic scholarship can evaluate, entering the realms of personal faith, mystery, and even mysticism. But since it dovetails with the more public sides of faith, we cannot overlook it.

Humanistic Ways of Studying Jesus

In introducing the study of Jesus with the question of why such study might be appropriate in a college course today, we have inevitably suggested some of the ways that one might go about estimating Jesus' significance. By and large, the ways of approaching Jesus that win most favor from academic scholars are what one might call humanistic methods. These are nothing novel or peculiar to the study of Jesus. They are simply the historical, literary, psychological, sociological, and other methods that one would use to study any ancient documents or famous personalities. If we call them humanistic, it is only to distinguish them from the theological or faith-motivated methods that predominate in the Christian churches. The methods that most academics employ do not require faith in Jesus of Nazareth as one's personal Savior. They do not require that one confess that Jesus is the Christ, or the Lord, or the Son of God. They simply take Jesus the way they would take Mahatma Gandhi or Martin Luther King, Jr., or Mother Teresa of Calcutta: as a fellow human being, subject to the limitations of space and time, mortality and ignorance, that afflict all the rest of us. Moreover, they assume that Jesus, like Gandhi, King, and Mother Teresa, is the product of a particular background, a particular cultural milieu, the stresses and strains of his given place and time. What might be peculiar to Jesus as more than human, as a God-man or a uniquely gifted prophet, falls outside what humanistic methods can handle and so must be left to personal faith or individual intuition.

We shall describe theological or faith-motivated methods of approaching Jesus in the next section. Here we merely want to clarify the advantages and the limitations of the academic approaches that we are calling humanistic. Sometimes churchpeople inveigh against these methods, making *humanism* a term of reproach, even of contempt. The humanist then is coupled with the atheist or the agnostic and viewed as at best ignorant, as at worst an enemy of faith or a minion of Satan. We have no such understanding of *humanism* in mind. In our usage, the term simply denotes the things that one can say about Jesus, or any other potential object of veneration, without making personal commitments to the rightness of his cause or the holiness of his person.

Humanism of this sort neither admits nor denies such personal commitments. If they occur, they take one beyond humanism, and they may bring either evil or good. If they do not occur, the issue of Jesus' further significance remains moot. If a humanist finally decides not to accept the claims for Jesus' special status, not to make the commitments of faith or belief, this need not distort the historical or literary study of Jesus. Indeed, it need not cast suspicion on those who have decided positively for Jesus and given him their faith.

So, humanistic ways of studying Jesus take him the way they would take any other world-historical figure, and this justifies the study of Jesus in a nondenominational or pluralistic setting. The humanistic scholar does no special pleading, either for Jesus or against Jesus. Jesus may emerge as a most admirable figure who quite justifies all the devotion that his followers have lavished upon him, or he may emerge as a person quite limited by the circumstances of his own time and place. One scholar may bring forward reasons for thinking that Jesus was deluded about his mission, while another scholar may bring forward reasons for thinking that Jesus' relationship with God or the ultimate Mystery of life was unique. Either way, their arguments, to be humanistic, must be public or available to all other students of Jesus. In other words, they must not depend upon a prior commitment to Jesus but rather must come from a study of texts or historical movements that any other student of Jesus could replicate.

This is the ideal, of course, and we are not going to claim that in actual practice things always proceed so unemotionally or purely. In actual practice, just about every person who comes to the study of Jesus has some prejudices and personal baggage. One person may have grown up in a pietistic Christian church and so think of Jesus as the best of human beings or even as the Son of God. Another person may have grown up in a similar situation and think of Jesus as part of the mythology that he or she threw off when becoming an adult. A third person may have grown up without any religion but be feeling pressure from personal problems to find answers to the great questions of good and evil, death and God. All of these people are bound first to look at Jesus through the lens they bring. From the outset, then, they all have the problem of gaining objectivity: awareness of their initial prejudices and some control over them.

When they are on top of their game, humanistic scholars deal with these issues of prejudice, personal involvement, and other obstacles to an objective or fair study of Jesus as a matter of course. What nowadays is called **hermeneutics** * is part and parcel of good humanistic studies. Hermeneutics deals with the whole process of interpreting texts or other documents, and so inevitably it deals with questions about the interaction between people of the past, who speak through the records we have about them, and people of the present, who are trying to know the past. Neither a completely other-oriented approach, which would pretend that a student had no prejudices or personal baggage, nor a completely self-oriented approach, which would neglect the text to concentrate only on the student's impressions, can satisfy the requirements of a thorough hermeneutics. Only a peaceful awareness of the dialogue or interaction between text and reader, between people of the past and present-day people trying to understand the past, can do the job.[2]

* Terms in boldface appear in the glossary.

Theological Ways of Studying Jesus

By contrast with humanistic ways of studying Jesus, what we are calling theological ways begin with faith. They assume an initial acceptance of Jesus and from this assumption proceed to investigate different aspects of Jesus' life, teaching, present relevance, and so on. Classically, Christian theology has been understood as "faith seeking understanding." For such influential Christian theologians as St. Augustine and St. Anselm, who developed this classical notion, faith was both the first moment in the theological enterprise and the constant foundation. In their view, because God is always greater than what limited human beings can understand, faith is a more comprehensive act than understanding. Even the theologian, directed by divine revelation and nourished by religious tradition, must confess that the divine mystery overspills the human mind. So theology is a modest enterprise, designed more to clarify or elaborate faith than to give it critical foundations. The understanding that theology can generate is precious, and it feeds a legitimate hunger of the mind, but this is ultimately less crucial than the hunger of the heart, of the integral human personality, which faith alone can satisfy.

How, though, has this traditional conception of the relation of faith to reason or understanding worked out in practice? In practice, faith has become the horizon of theologians' scholarly analyses. For theologians, scholarly work has meant probing aspects of God or religion that they had accepted as living truths in their own lives. So, for example, one came to Jesus having already accepted him as one's Lord and Savior. Or one came to the New Testament with a bias in its favor, with an inclination to regard its words as sources of special help (light from the Holy Spirit, revelation from God, and so on). This did not have to distort or vitiate one's scholarly work, but it was bound to color it. A theologian could probe historical data or perform literary analyses dispassionately, using the best of contemporary techniques, but the assumption always remained that such techniques were significant mainly on the level of literal meaning or empirical information. The deeper, more ultimate level of personal significance (such questions as death and evil, fulfillment and vocation) could not be left in the hands of historians or literary analysts. It was too whole or profound to be decided by anything less than an overall, global testing of claims such as the Christian claim that committing oneself to Jesus was the way to a meaningful and happy life.

Thus theological approaches to Jesus became ways of trying to enrich or illuminate faith, the basic relationship or commitment to Jesus that stamped the Christian as a believer. As long as one was actually proceeding theologically, the value or authority of Jesus and the Christian tradition never came into serious question. From the outset one assumed that Jesus was uniquely valuable, truthful, powerful, and the like;

for he was the locus of one's salvation, the personal place where one found the world most beautiful or coherent. Edward Schillebeeckx, whose massive volumes *Jesus* and *Christ*[3] will be one of our major resources, makes this plain from the beginning of his analyses of the early Christian documents. It was their faith in Jesus as the locus of salvation that shaped all the writers of the New Testament. In all ways, the New Testament writings were faith-inspired, theological accounts. They never were humanistic or uncommitted, never were disturbed by doubts about the adequacy of Jesus' teaching or work.

Throughout the history of the world religions, Eastern and Western, what we are calling theological approaches have predominated. In Jewish, Muslim, Buddhist, Hindu, Confucian, Taoist, and Shinto studies, the typical writer has stood within the tradition, has worked as a believer and practitioner. So, for example, the **abhidhamma** literature of Indian Buddhism, which seems the driest of psychological analyses (dealing with the meaning of Buddhist doctrines, or the practice of meditation, or the implications of Buddhist ethics), actually is conceived as but a means to the better living of one's Buddhist commitment. Similarly, Islam has generated a wealth of legal commentary that strikes many readers as dry to the point of distraction. In the minds of the Muslim lawyers, however, their labors were completely directed to the better living of the commitment to Allah and the program of Muhammad that made one a "submitter," a walker on "the path that is straight."

The same is true for most of the literature that we call Christian. In New Testament, **apostolic, patristic, conciliar,** medieval, and Reformation times, the great Christian writers began with an assumption of faith. Only with modernity, from the seventeenth century on, do we find the rise of a body of literature critical of faith and desirous of approaching religious matters by bracketing a faith-commitment. Indeed, much of what we now mean by *modernity* is precisely this bracketed outlook, this distancing of one's studies or analyses from one's personal commitments. In crude forms, the modern mentality often was antireligious, bracketing traditional religious faith but actually being driven by atheistic convictions. In sophisticated forms, the modern mentality has been more evenhanded, applying its critical (probing, testing, judgmental) stance to all sorts of presuppositions, atheistic as much as theistic.

In response to the increasing sophistication of the modern critical mentality, Christian theologians have developed more nuance. Without taking away the priority of faith or denying the greater significance of faith in the end, they now tend to be very careful about the way that faith inclines them to evaluate particular data or phenomena. So, for instance, Edward Schillebeeckx scrupulously details the interactions between faith and experience, faith and history, and faith and received traditions that he finds at work in the different New Testament interpretations of

Jesus. He also deals at some length with general problems of hermeneutics, trying to walk a thin line that will allow both fidelity to Christian faith (on the bigger or more central issues of Jesus' significance for salvation) and fidelity to the best of contemporary scholarship (on the technical questions of where a particular text came from or what a given story likely first meant).

The result of this recent theological effort to grow more sophisticated and work out some accommodation with the critical mentality sponsored by modernity is that current studies of Jesus and New Testament topics tend to be very complicated. Just about any text or story has a half-dozen stages to its development, a dozen questions attending its significance. In dealing with these stages or questions, a humanistic scholar and a theologian often will proceed almost identically. For the middle parts of their analyses, when questions of initial assumptions or ultimate significance are not much in play, they can work side by side. But the framework in which they later will set their findings, as well as any ethical or religious lessons they will draw, tend to take them back to the issue of faith or nonfaith, theological or humanistic scholarship.

We have laid all this out in some detail so as to alert the reader to the complexity or richness of the methodological problems involved in attempting today a responsible study of Jesus. Unless one is to ignore current scholarship, both humanistic and theological, one has to think hard about assumptions, conclusions, rules for interpretation, the interaction of faith and reason, the interaction of data and judgment, and much more. By and large we shall spare the reader the burden of dragging all this up in each biblical or historical study that we undertake. By and large we shall proceed straightforwardly, saying what we find a given source to suggest about Jesus and how we evaluate that suggestion. But we would be derelict in one of our duties if we allowed any reader to think that the current study of Jesus was not fraught with immense critical problems. For every text, every assertion, every belief, there is level upon level.

This Book

Our approach in this book will be more humanistic than theological, although frequently we will report the findings of theologians or scholars working from Christian faith. We are seeking an overview of Jesus, what he most likely was in himself and what he has meant to various kinds of people through the ages. We are not assuming that Jesus was divine or that he is the most important revelation of how human beings ought to live, as a theological work would assume. We are leaving readers free to make of Jesus what personal significance they will. On the other hand, we are not backing away from the claims that many of our sources make for Jesus, and the total documentation on which we draw probably comes more from inside the Christian community of faith than from outside. The result, we hope, will be a balanced view of Jesus, adequately suggesting how he has looked both to insiders and to those outside the Christian orbit.

More precisely, we begin our study of Jesus by consulting the views of the New Testament (our most primary source). All of the New Testament authors have **christologies** or interpretations of Jesus' decisive significance, and the sum of the New Testament views has been Christianity's charter or constitution. The later church councils that defined christological dogma presented themselves as interpretations or updatings of the faith laid out in the New Testament, while even present-day Christian interpreters are constrained by the gospels and epistles.

To deal with the New Testament's views of Jesus, we begin with Mark, the gospel that shows many signs of having been the earliest account of Jesus' story. Focusing intensely on Jesus' sufferings, Mark raises serious questions about the kind of **messiahship** Jesus envisioned. Mark also challenges his Christian readers to stand by their suffering Lord, not to imitate the disciples who abandoned Jesus when it came to mounting the cross. The second very early source, which along with Mark furnished Matthew and Luke much of their material, is the collection of traditions that scholars call **Q** (from the German **Quelle** or "source"). No one has in hand a copy of Q—it is an hypothesis rather than a solid fact that such a document or oral collection existed—but the majority of New Testament scholars speak of themes distinctive to Q and so invite our investigation of Q's christology.

In the remainder of our chapter on New Testament views of Jesus, we fill out the circle of early understandings. Thus we consider how Matthew, Luke, and John, the other gospel writers, present the traditions of their churches. We spend two sections on the views of Paul and his followers that are available in the Pauline epistles, and then we conclude with studies of the christologies of Hebrews, Revelation, and the minor epistles.

Having looked at the first Christian understandings of Jesus, we move on in Chapter 3 to the development of christology through the subsequent Christian eras. Thus we consider the views of the early theologians known as the apologists, who endeavored to explain Christian faith to Jews and Greeks outside the church; the views of the church fathers who labored prior to the great church Council of Nicaea (325); and the opposing views of Arius and Athanasius that set the agenda for Nicaea. After Nicaea, the Council of Chalcedon (451) completed the architecture of classical christology, so we next discuss the views of the two men who set the agenda for Chalcedon, Nestorius and Cyril of Alexandria. To summarize these developments, we consider what we call the Orthodox tradition, meaning by that both the interpretation of Jesus that the church was employing against heretics after Chalcedon and the sense of Jesus that Eastern Christianity has maintained throughout most of its history.

To deal with Western developments, we consider the influential views of Augustine and Thomas Aquinas, the paramount medieval theologians, and then the emphases brought forward by Protestant reformers such as Luther and Calvin. We follow this with a section on the christological crises occasioned by modern Western philosophy and historiography. To conclude, we examine two recent responses to modernity, Protestant neo-orthodoxy and Roman Catholic liberation theology.

Chapter 4, dealing with contemporary issues, brings our survey into the present. Some of these issues arise mainly inside the church, such as the relation of Jesus to the church bureaucracy that has grown up. Other issues take us across the lines that divide churchpeople from outsiders: the relation of Jesus to peacemaking, to the poor, to ecology, or to a salvation that would embrace all human beings of good will. Fundamentalism—the tendency to interpret scripture literalistically—is an issue that concerns both churchpeople and outsiders, as is sexuality. The contemporary interest in spirituality prompts consideration of Jesus' teachings on prayer, while the contemporary interest in political change prompts consideration of Jesus' prophetic stance. Finally, we take up the issue of **eschatology,** or the once-and-for-allness of Jesus Christ. In what sense do Christians think Jesus ushered in the consummation of history? In what sense does history still await fulfillment (perhaps from Jesus' return)?

For three chapters, then, we will follow a fairly straight line from the New Testament to the present era. Chapter 5 will break with this pattern, comparing Jesus to a series of other world-religious leaders. Our reason for pursuing this comparative matter is twofold. First, we believe that such a study sheds valuable light on Jesus, suggesting what was unique to his experience and message as well as what he held in common with one or more other religious geniuses. Second, recently followers of Jesus have entered into serious dialogue with followers of other traditions—Buddhists, Muslims, Jews, Hindus—and inevitably in such contexts comparisons between Jesus and other "founders" arise. Consequently, in Chapter 5 we shall place Jesus alongside the Buddha, Confucius, Lao-tzu, Zoroaster, Socrates, Krishna, Karl Marx, Muhammad, and Mahatma Gandhi, hoping that the overall result will be the reader's better sense of how Jesus stands in the context of global religious history.

Chapter 6, our summary and conclusion, will revisit the sources that we have studied, explain the modesty that befits most study of Jesus, try to pin down the reason for Jesus' appeal across so many different centuries and cultures, and then gingerly indicate the further questions, both personal and social, that honest investigations of Jesus raise.

Summary

We began our introduction to the study of Jesus by asking why such a study should take place in college. The first answer was that Jesus has influenced so much of history that placing him in the curriculum makes good sense. Just as the impact of the Buddha on history justifies courses on the Buddha and Buddhism, so the impact of Jesus justifies courses on Jesus and Christianity. A second justification for studying Jesus is the cogency and depth of his ideas, which still shape hundreds of millions of people. If it is sensible to study Plato and Marx, Confucius and Muhammad, because of the depth and influence of their ideas, it is sensible to study Jesus. Third, the knotted question of the place of religion in American public life, which the 1984 presidential election spotlighted, suggests another rationale for a course on Jesus. One would not have the culture that presently obtains in the United States without his influence.

Still, the legitimacy of studying Jesus in college does not completely determine the methods appropriate to such a task. We therefore considered the two main kinds of approaches to Jesus (or any other religious figure), which we called the humanistic and the theological. Humanistic approaches do not assume faith, and they employ the ordinary techniques of modern historical, literary, sociological, psychological, and other kinds of research. Ideally, the humanistic scholar has no bias concerning a subject such as Jesus, no initial prejudice for or against. Insofar as they work toward this ideal reflectively, humanistic scholars usually focus on hermeneutics. For the typical students approaching a course on Jesus, hermeneutics leads to the caution not to let one's experiences or emotional needs color one's reading or interpretation.

Theological ways of studying Jesus do start with an assumption of faith. Theology classically is "faith seeking understanding," and the traditional sense has been that one's scholarship never should supplant the commitment one makes at the outset of an investigation or the surrender one makes at the end. The theologian may employ the investigative techniques that secular scholars have developed, but these must remain in the service of an appreciative approach to the subject matter. Such a theological attitude has predominated in most religious researches, both Christian and non-Christian, throughout history. Only with the rise of modernity and its critical mentality have humanistic approaches become commonplace.

Our own approach will be humanistic, not requiring faith in Jesus as a precondition. Inevitably, however, most of our materials will derive from theological sources. Thus our first three studies, dealing with the interpretations of Jesus available in the New Testament, the historical development of orthodox christology, and contemporary christological discussion, will largely consider Christian sources. Chapter 5, in which we compare Jesus to other religious founders or figures of world-historical import, will break the linear pattern of chapters 2 through 4. As well, it will deal extensively with non-Christian sources. Chapter 6, our conclusion, will review the sources and probe such intriguing questions as the cause of Jesus' wide appeal and the challenges Jesus now sets before fair-minded observers.

––––––––––––––––––– **STUDY QUESTIONS** –––––––––––––––––––

1. Is the legitimacy of studying Jesus in college the same as the legitimacy of studying the Buddha?

2. How is it possible for humanistic ways of studying a figure such as Jesus not to be prejudiced for or against him?

3. How do theologians who use historical or literary techniques distinguish the impact of such techniques from the impact of their own assumption of faith?

4. Why do we include a chapter that compares Jesus to other great religious or world-historical figures?

––––––––––––––––––––––– **NOTES** –––––––––––––––––––––––

[1] See Sydney E. Ahlstrom, *A Religious History of the American People.* New Haven: Yale University Press, 1972.

[2] See Paul Ricoeur, *Essays on Biblical Interpretation,* ed. Lewis S. Mudge. Philadelphia: Fortress, 1980.

[3] Edward Schillebeeckx, *Jesus.* New York: Seabury, 1979; *Christ.* New York: Seabury, 1980.

2

New Testament Views of Jesus

Mark

The Gospel of Mark probably came into something close to its present form about 70 C.E. ("Common Era" = A.D.). It was the first of the **synoptic** Gospels, and both Matthew and Luke used it. Mark seems to have arisen from churches in Palestine, and behind it lies a strong interest in the mission of early Christianity to the **Gentiles.** In the interpretation of Pheme Perkins, two themes dominate this gospel: who Jesus is and what it means to be a disciple of Jesus.[1]

The author of Mark approaches these two themes convinced that he (granted the patriarchalism of the times, it is probable that the author was male, although we cannot say this for sure) must present a paradox. On the one hand, Jesus was powerful and authoritative. On the other hand, he kept much of his identity and mission hidden or secret, and he agreed to undergo great suffering. This paradox of a powerful yet hidden and suffering leader ought to move Christians to ponder deeply the model they have been given. If the meaning of Jesus has to be read out of his rejection and suffering, Christian life is bound to be a costly discipleship. That is the gist of Mark's message.

The background for Mark's message (indeed, for the whole New Testament) is the religion of Israel, Jesus' people. From the time of Abraham, their "father," the Jews had thought of themselves as bonded to their God. Under Moses they had entered into a covenant with God, pledging themselves to obey laws designed to make them holy and so more worthy of God. The prophets had called the people back to this vocation, stressing social justice and purity of heart. In the centuries immediately prior to Jesus, hopes had grown that God would send a kingly leader to rescue Israel from foreign rule and give Jews a golden prosperity. For early Christians such as Mark, Jesus was the fulfillment of these Jewish hopes, although quite paradoxically. The glory that Jesus brought, the new set of possibilities symbolized by the Kingdom of God that dominated Jesus' preaching, came not through political or military victory but through suffering and death.

The key designation that Mark uses to describe Jesus is Son of man. This is a very complicated notion with considerable Jewish history behind it. The most important overtones, for Mark's purposes, come from Daniel 7 : 13 – 14: "I saw in the night visions, and behold, with the clouds of heaven there came one like a son of man, and he came to the Ancient of Days and was presented before him. And to him was given dominion and glory and kingdom, that all peoples, nations, and languages should serve him; his dominion is an everlasting dominion, which shall not pass away, and his kingdom one that shall not be destroyed."

Another set of overtones to Son of man made it equivalent to *a human being*. Mark remembers Jesus as having used Son of man of himself, and Mark's interpretation (of the meaning that the phrase should have for Christians) is that the very lowliness of Jesus as thoroughly human (mortal, vulnerable, set upon by enemies and finally crucified) is the paradoxical form that his power and heavenly glory (the wondrous status suggested by Daniel 7 : 13 – 14) assumed. It was in his very rejection that Jesus manifested the saving power of God and his own unique status. To be a disciple of Jesus, therefore, is to confront head-on his rejection and paradoxical sort of grandeur.

A key text in Mark's Gospel is 8 : 27 – 33. There Mark describes Jesus' kind of messiahship and the unreadiness of Jesus' disciples (the companions of Jesus during his earthly ministry) to accept this: "And Jesus went on with his disciples, to the villages of Caesarea Philippi, and on the way he asked his disciples, 'Who do men say that I am?' And they told him, 'John the Baptist; and others say, Elijah; and others one of the prophets.' And he asked them, 'But who do you say that I am?' Peter answered him, 'You are the Christ.' And he charged them to tell no one about him. And he began to teach them that the Son of man must suffer many things, and be rejected by the elders and the chief priests and the scribes and be killed, and after three days rise again. And he said this plainly. And Peter took him, and began to rebuke him. But turning and seeing his disciples, he rebuked Peter, and said, 'Get behind me, Satan! For you are not on the side of God, but of men.'"

To Mark's mind, Peter is the spokesman for the early disciples (as he was the leading figure of the Church after Jesus' Resurrection, perhaps because he regathered the disciples after they had dispersed at Jesus' crucifixion). Peter shows both the assets and the liabilities of many Christians' faith. On the one hand, he perceives Jesus' special status as the anointed one who has long been anticipated as God's deliverer for Israel. On the other hand, he interprets Jesus in all too human a fashion, being unwilling to face the rejection and suffering that Jesus' mission entails. The prediction of his passion that Mark puts in Jesus' mouth is written after the event, so Jesus' destiny may not have been so clear to him as Mark suggests. Still, Mark presents an earthly or historical Jesus who quickly realized that his mission would not succeed in worldly terms but would entail his worldly destruction.

Mark may have been writing in a time or locale where Christians were hard put upon, and so where fidelity to a suffering Lord was an important test of faith. In this regard, his unflattering picture of Jesus' disciples, who all scatter when it comes to the pinch and Jesus is arrested, is meant to highlight the demands of Christian faith. Believers must do better than those who lived with the historical Jesus did, and not misunderstand him.

To the later Christian Church, the Gospel of Mark therefore bequeathed a very challenging portrait of Jesus. The christology we meet in this Gospel refuses to take Jesus for granted or dilute his mysteriousness. The Markan Jesus is not a person who reveals himself easily. He has considerable skepticism about human motivation, and he prefers to speak through his deeds. In preaching the good news of the **Kingdom of God,** Jesus has given people enough to draw near and study him. Those who are well motivated will want to know more about who he is and what he demands. In healing the sick and casting out demons, the Markan Jesus is on the offensive against the destructive forces that threaten human beings' lives. Mark never detracts from Jesus' dignity or spiritual power. Always his Jesus is authoritative, in control. Despite this, the forces of evil do Jesus great injury. Religious leaders such as the Pharisees reject his message and plot to harm him, and eventually Jesus' enemies are able to arrange his crucifixion and death. Jesus therefore seems to be in the middle of a great battle or power-struggle. Will his God and Kingdom prove stronger than Satan and the forces of sin, or will the opposition triumph over him?

The Resurrection of course gives us the final verdict, but by stressing Jesus' authority Mark has hinted at a positive outcome. It is by refusing to be deflected from his mission, even when it threatens his physical life, that Jesus emerges as the victorious Lord and Savior. The climax of Mark's account of Jesus' crucifixion, in fact, comes when Jesus is utterly defeated in worldly terms. The centurion standing by the cross represents what Mark thinks any honest witness of Jesus would conclude: "And Jesus uttered a loud cry, and breathed his last. And the curtain of the temple was torn in two, from top to bottom [symbolizing the end of an old order of worship and service of God centered on the Jewish Temple in Jerusalem]. And when the centurion, who stood facing him, saw that he thus breathed his last, he said, 'Truly this man was the Son of God!'" (15:37–39). This links up with the way that Mark begins his Gospel: "The beginning of the gospel of Jesus Christ, the Son of God" (1:1).

For Mark, Jesus is both a suffering Messiah and the Son of God (one especially blessed by God) whose final reality is as full of power and glory as the Son of man depicted by Daniel. Indeed, Jesus is precisely the fusion of suffering and glory, a glorious emissary from God who went so deeply into our human condition that he suffered an ignominious death. That was the profundity of God's work in Jesus. To offer the sort of salvation human beings most need, God's Messiah had to endure gross human evil. The good news of Mark's Jesus, therefore, is that evil is not the final word. Jesus' God is always greater.

Q

Q is a strange element in the New Testament, a somewhat ghostly source. Scholars postulate it because of the block of materials that Matthew and Luke have in common (and do not derive from Mark, their other common source), but most of the current picture of the Q community (the community behind this stratum of the synoptic materials) is a matter of conjecture. The following is typical of current scholarly conjectures: "There is no absolutely certain way to date Q, other than to say that it was put in writing before Matthew and Luke used it. Yet, because of its apocalyptic orientation, and the almost unanimous belief that it entirely emanates from a type of early Jewish apocalyptic Christianity found in Palestine or southern Syria, most judge it to have been written within the first two generations after the death of Jesus. There is also no way to determine any individual who put Q into writing. In short, whatever is said about Q and the type of Christian community it represents must be said on the basis of internal analysis of the material."[2]

Apocalypticism is also strong in Mark, so the two earliest New Testament sources reveal a taut expectation in the primitive Christian communities: the Lord will soon return, history is about to come to completion. The tenor of many of the passages that New Testament analysts ascribe to Q is also what we might call **prophetic.** Out of the tradition of the Israelite prophets, the writers of Q call their times to account. Jesus is set against the background of Israel's regular resistance to the demand of the prophets that the nation repent and become worthy of its covenant with the holy God. So, for example, we find the following Q passage in Luke (the Gospel apparently most shaped by Q): "O Jerusalem, Jerusalem, killing the prophets and stoning those who are sent to you. How often would I have gathered your children together as a hen gathers her brood under her wings, and you would not! Behold, your house is forsaken. And I tell you, you will not see me until you say, 'Blessed is he who comes in the name of the Lord'" (13:34–35).

The Jesus of Q confronts the leaders of his people (the religious establishment symbolized by "Jerusalem"). He links their rejection of him with a long history of rejecting previous emissaries from God. (In fact, it is dubious how many prophets Israel actually killed over the years. Nonetheless, the idea that the people regularly resisted religious reform [return to justice and pure cult] was a stock notion among all those who loved the classical prophets.) Whether the reference to the house of Jerusalem being "forsaken" suggests an editing of this text after 70 C.E. and the Roman destruction of the Holy City is debatable. Many passages in the New Testament do reflect this crisis in Jewish history. But the general tone of Q rings out clearly: Jesus challenged the religious establishment, suffered for his holy mission, and triumphed through the Resurrection. He will soon return to render full justice, to both those who believe in him and to his enemies. (This return is sometimes called the **Parousia**.)

Among those whom Q holds responsible for Jesus' rejection the Pharisees, a lay group zealous for strict observance of the Covenant Law, stand out. So, for example, Luke 11:42 makes them the target of Jesus' woe: "But woe to you Pharisees! for you tithe mint and rue and every herb, and neglect justice and the love of God; these you ought to have done, without neglecting the others." The Pharisees, then, are seen by Q as legalists—people who cling to the letter of the Law (the Jewish **Torah**) but miss the substance. Jesus is rejected, in other words, by people who do not know the heart of the religious matter. (More dispassionate, modern scholarship tends to speak of the Pharisees less negatively.) Because they are closed at heart, the Pharisees and their like will miss out on the messianic banquet that Q associates with the return of the Lord: "And men will come from east and west, and from north and south, and sit at table in the kingdom of God" (Luke 13:29). Jesus had preached the dawning of God's Kingdom or Reign, apparently thinking of it as a time when things would be as human beings yearn for them to be: just, kindly, prosperous—the way the world would be were God fully in charge, were human beings not perverse. Q ardently expects the full shining of the Kingdom in the near future, when Jesus will return to pass judgment and throw a great party.

Behind Q lies the Wisdom literature of the Old Testament and the contemporary Jewish tendency to think of "Wisdom" as a sort of solid entity coexisting with God. The Q community conceives of Jesus as the enfleshment of God's Wisdom, its dramatic coming into history. Thus Q is especially interested in Jesus' teaching, which it considers the enlightenment proper to the eschatological time just prior to the consummation of history. Scholars tend to picture the Q community as filled with wandering, charismatic preachers who went about proclaiming the teachings of Jesus, the Wisdom of God, and predicting the swift end of history at the Lord's return.

The view of the Christian community that we find in Q fits in with Q's apocalyptic character. The twelve leading disciples (symbolic of the twelve tribes that constituted biblical Israel) are not so much the foundation of the Church as judges who will preside over the end-time that is soon to come. So, for instance, we find the following Q section in Luke 22:28–30: "You are those who have continued with me in my trials; and I assign to you, as my Father assigned to me, a kingdom, that you may eat and drink at my table in my kingdom, and sit on thrones judging the twelve tribes of Israel." Christians, epitomized in their leaders, may expect not only the joyous feasting of the Parousia but also a share in its rendition of judgment. The followers of Jesus have succeeded the twelve tribes of Israel and constitute the new community of salvation.

It took some time for these notions to work themselves out. In the early years after Jesus' death, most of his followers still thought of themselves as loyal Jews and did not want to dissociate themselves from traditional Israel. But we can see in Q the beginnings of a separationist mentality. Traditional Israel, in the person of its chief priests and Pharisees, had rejected Jesus and was continuing to oppose Jesus' followers. Leadership and judgment therefore were passing out of traditional Israel. Jesus was coming to be considered the crucial figure; faith in Jesus or rejection of Jesus was becoming the prime criterion for God's favor or dismissal.

Edward Schillebeeckx has added another characterization of the Q community and its christology, one with which we can conclude our study. In his view, the early Christian sense of the activity of the risen and exalted Christ was especially strong in the Q community.[3] After the Resurrection, all the churches struggled to understand the meaning of God's extraordinary intervention on Jesus' behalf. Certainly it set a seal on Jesus' teaching and mission, giving Jesus God's ratification. But Jewish thought of the period used the notions of resurrection and exaltation to express the idea of being with God definitively. That is, these notions had become ways of conceiving of how good people, who often suffer in history, gain recompense and reward. If a person dies without such recompense and reward, God seems a pale entity, no proper Lord of History. The Israelite God was nothing if not Lord of History, so Jewish thought in the century or so preceeding Jesus and the first Christians had begun to speak of God's exalting of holy people such as Enoch or Elijah: taking them up into the divine sphere (heaven), where they would be free of death and suffering and would be properly rewarded.

Resurrection had much the same original significance, although it was not necessarily linked with exaltation. The original sense of resurrection was that God would restore to bodily existence good or just people who had been treated badly by their times. This was another way that a Lord of History could triumph over evil and render justice to his saints. Implied in both resurrection and exaltation was a pattern of humiliation or abject defeat followed by God-given vindication and success. The Jewish speculative temper in the decades prior to Jesus produced many variations on this theme. Thus the various apocalyptic writings, along with the writings of the Qumran community of **Essenes** who lived near the Dead Sea, offer several models on which the gospel writers might have drawn. If the Q community was composed mainly of Jewish Christians of apocalyptic temper, it too probably drew on the contemporary scheme of defeat/victory.

Matthew

The Gospel of Matthew was written later than both Q and Mark. A likely date is after 70 C.E. (Matthew 22:7 mentions the fall of Jerusalem), perhaps about 85 C.E. From the themes of this Gospel we can infer that Matthew's community probably was composed mainly of Jewish Christians. Some scholars conjecture that Antioch in Syria was the center of the Matthean church.

At any rate, Matthew uses materials from the Q collection and from Mark to fashion his own distinctive christology. The Gospel is carefully structured into five main parts, each concluded by a "wrap-up" such as 7:28–29: "And when Jesus finished these sayings, the crowds were astonished at his teaching, for he taught them as one who had authority, and not as their scribes." Matthew is greatly concerned to present Jesus as the authoritative new teacher who succeeds Moses as the main interpreter of Torah. Indeed, the overall christology of this Gospel delights in explaining how Jesus was the fulfillment of Jewish prophecy, the Messiah that the Scriptures had long predicted would one day come. The Gospel's five sections (chapters 3–7, 8–10, 11–13, 14–18, and 19–25) perhaps are meant as a new five books or Christian **Pentateuch,** in which the Law attributed to Moses is now superseded by the teaching of Christ.

From the outset, the Gospel of Matthew stresses the marvelous powers that Jesus displayed. Thus Howard Clark Kee, from whom we borrowed the division of the five Matthean "books" that we sketched above, says of Matthew: "Although all the Gospel writers present a picture of Jesus marked by marvelous powers on his part and by miraculous events that accompany his ministry, Matthew lays greater stress on this than do the other evangelists. The birth story consists almost entirely of divine disclosures through dreams and miraculous occurrences, chief among which is the supernatural conception of Jesus in the virgin's womb. Only slightly less wonderful is the guiding star that led the Magi to the birthplace. All these miracles are told in distinctive passages. Matthew has reproduced nearly all the miracle stories found in his sources, Mark and Q. At times he has abridged them; at other times he has expanded them. On occasion his modification has had the effect of heightening the miraculous element, such as when the ruler's daughter is not merely at the point of death, but dead (cf. Mark 5:23 with Matt. 9:18), and when the blind man at Jericho in Mark 10:46 becomes two men (Matt. 20:30). But for the most part, Matthew's changes in the miracle stories serve his theological objectives by concentrating on the faith of the persons healed, or on the authority of Jesus, or on the demands of discipleship."[4]

The power that Jesus displays in his marvelous healings is for Matthew but one sign of his newness. He was holy and singular from the outset, as the narrative of his conception (1:18–25) is meant to show. On the other hand, Matthew has Jesus concerned to perfect Jewish Law and prophecy rather than completely destroy or abrogate them. For all that he is new and marvelous, Jesus represents a continuity between Israel and the Church. In all likelihood the community for which Matthew was writing (Jewish Christians) was trying to harmonize two allegiances. Much in the traditions of Israel would have appealed to this group (we know that in the earliest years after Jesus' death his followers continued to go to the Temple in Jerusalem to pray, continued to keep the Jewish laws, and functioned much as a Jewish synagogue). Thus Matthew was at pains to make Jesus the fulfillment of God's past history with Israel. What had begun with Moses, developed with the prophets, and come to beg further perfecting had received its next phase and form from Jesus of Nazareth.

Jesus therefore emerges in Matthew as a great teacher of righteousness. As such, he transposes an old Jewish interest into a new Christian theme. For Matthew Jesus is the Christ, the anointed emissary from God, come to proclaim and enact the Reign of God in which a righteousness more excellent than that of the scribes and Pharisees will flourish. As is appropriate to a Gospel written mainly for Jewish Christians, Matthew's characterizations of Jesus draw heavily on the Jewish Scriptures. The notion that Jesus is the Messiah, like the notions that he is the Son of David, or the Son of man, or the Son of God, all derive from the Jewish Scriptures. Most of them originally were terms of intimacy or chosenness indicating that an individual enjoyed God's favor or had a special mission from God. These connotations remain when Matthew applies such titles to Jesus, but they are taken up into what for him is a higher order. Because Jesus had brought the Reign of God, and because his Resurrection had sealed his authority, Jesus was the Messiah, or the Son of God, in a definitive sense. Others might have partaken of some of the qualities of these roles, but Jesus alone fulfilled them. Indeed, Jesus broke through their connotations, representing God more fully than even the most exalted Old Testament titles could.

We see this fuller claim for Jesus advanced in such Matthean texts as 14:28–33: "And Peter answered him, 'Lord, if it is you, bid me come to you on the water.' He said, 'Come.' So Peter got out of the boat and walked on the water and came to Jesus; but when he saw the wind, he was afraid, and beginning to sink he cried out, 'Lord, save me.' Jesus immediately reached out his hand and caught him, saying to him, 'O man of little faith, why did you doubt?' And when they got into the boat, the wind ceased. And those in the boat worshiped him, saying 'Truly you are the Son of God.'"

The point to Matthew's stress on Jesus' miraculous powers in this story, as in so many others, is Jesus' unique closeness to God. The confession that Jesus is the Son of God is repeated in 16:16, where it is instructive that Matthew adds to the Markan Peter's avowal that Jesus is the Christ. So when Jesus asks who the disciples say that he is, Peter answers, "You are the Christ, the Son of the living God." Matthew has Jesus praise Peter for this answer and proclaim that it comes not from flesh and blood but from Jesus' Father in heaven. Indeed, this faith that Jesus is the Christ and Son of God leads to Peter being called the rock on which Jesus will build his church.

The confession of Jesus that Matthew would have his readers make is therefore nothing apart from faith. Only a wholehearted openness to Jesus and reliance upon him will give anyone access to Jesus' full meaning. But the wonders that Jesus works and the sublimity of his teaching are in Matthew's eyes more than sufficient warrant for making the act of faith that will disclose Jesus' fuller significance. In the context of Matthew's times, and quite in keeping with his Jewish heritage, faith and the power of God fit hand in glove.

This is worth underscoring today, when we tend to read stories such as Matthew's accounts of Jesus' miracles with a literalist mentality. In all probability, the gospel writers such as Matthew assumed when they wrote about Jesus' sayings and doings that people would take their writings symbolically. So, for instance, most present-day New Testament scholars think that Matthew's account of Jesus' birth was meant more to declare Jesus' lineage as the Messiah and his holy relation to God than to depict literally his family tree or the events leading up to his birth.[5] Similarly, scenes such as Jesus' walking on the water and summoning Peter to do the same are less descriptions of prodigies that Jesus worked than further ways for Matthew to say that this man was singularly holy, singularly empowered to bring salvation. The world in which Matthew lived and wrote knew of many wonder-workers and miracles. Most of what the Gospels picture Jesus doing would not have been unique. What was unique was the overall power of Jesus' person, teaching, and activities to mediate salvation or bring the Kingdom of God.

Summarily, then, Matthew stresses that Jesus is the fulfillment of Israelite hopes for a deliverer, the one who brings salvation and the perfecting of the Jewish Law.

Luke-Acts

Luke, like Matthew, assembled his Gospel of Jesus from Mark, Q, and materials special to himself. As with Matthew and all the other New Testament writers, Luke's view is peculiarly his own, the product of the particular church that he served and the understanding of Jesus that he had developed. Scholars currently opine that the Gospel of Luke probably arose about the same time as Matthew (about 85 C.E.), but from a Gentile rather than a Jewish Christian church. The places of origin considered most likely are either Antioch in Syria or someplace in Asia Minor (current-day Turkey).

We have seen that Luke is the Gospel that seems to follow the order of Q most closely. It also makes its own the great variety of materials assembled in Q: narratives, parables, oracles, beatitudes, prophetic pronouncements, wisdom words, and exhortations.[6] The general structure into which Luke fits these materials and the materials from his other sources is fairly clear. He begins with a prologue (1:1–4), moves to an infancy narrative (1:5–2:52), has a section on the preparation for Jesus' public ministry (3:1–4:13), describes the ministry of Jesus in Galilee (4:14–9:50), gives an account of Jesus' journey to Jerusalem (9:51–19:27), narrates Jesus' ministry in Jerusalem (19:28–21:38), narrates Jesus' passion (22:1–23:56a), and concludes with an account of Jesus' Resurrection (23:56b–24:53).[7]

The Gospel of Luke is, however, but the first book in a two-volume account of Jesus and the early Church. If we want the full span of Luke's christology, we have to take into account the Acts of the Apostles. Speaking of this whole Lukan christology, Joseph A. Fitzmyer says: "The key figure in Lucan salvation-history is Jesus Christ himself, for he is the one in whom God's activity in human history is now manifested. He is not only the one who proclaims; he becomes himself the object of the proclamation. Moreover . . . for all of Luke's emphasis on the word of God and its spread to the end of the earth, the main thing that his two-volume work proclaims is Jesus of Nazareth: 'Salvation comes through no one else, for there is no other name under the heavens given to human beings by which we must be saved' (Acts 4:12). Luke sees Jesus not only as 'the climax of God's activity in Israel' (E. Franklin, *Christ the Lord*, 7), but as the very center of salvation-history itself."[8]

In developing his presentation of Jesus as the center of salvation-history (the story of God's action in time to heal human ills and grant human beings fulfillment), Luke paints with a skillful brush. His portrait of Jesus' humanity is the most artistic of all the gospel writers'; the most memorable of Jesus' **parables** (the prodigal son, the good Samaritan) are found in Luke. The Lukan Jesus is sensitive, compassionate, keenly aware of the emotional overtones to any situation. Luke mutes somewhat the violence or harshness of the Markan and Q materials that he uses, although not to the point of distorting the conflicts that Jesus faced or his cruel death on the cross. The connection of Jesus' lineage with Adam, the first human being (3:38), shows Luke's concern to relate Jesus to all of humanity, rather than just Israel. The spread of the Church to the Gentiles that Acts narrates is in keeping with this universalist theme: Jesus is the Savior of all human beings.

In treating Luke's presentation of Jesus' special, perhaps more than human, status, Fitzmyer deals with five different aspects or emphases. First, Luke's account of Jesus' virginal conception by the power of the Holy Spirit (1:34–35) implies that from the beginning of his existence Jesus was someone very special. Second, Luke stresses that Jesus' ministry proceeded under the special inspiration of the Holy Spirit. The Spirit descends in the shape of a dove at Jesus' baptism by John the Baptist (3:22), presides over Jesus' retreat into the wilderness to be tempted (4:1), and anoints Jesus' spirit with joy at God's providence: "In that same hour he rejoiced in the Holy Spirit and said, 'I thank thee, Father, Lord of heaven and earth, that thou hast hidden these things from the wise and understanding and revealed them to babes; yea, Father, for such was thy gracious will'" (10:21).

Third, Luke agrees with the other evangelists that Jesus had a special relationship with God the Father, something more intimate than what other human beings, however pious, might attain. Fourth, Luke lays considerable emphasis on Jesus' Resurrection, trying for a balance between assurances that the resurrected Jesus was no ghost (24:37, 24:43) and assurances that what happened after Jesus' death was unique: no mere resuscitation from the dead or return to a natural, earthly existence; rather, the manifestation of Jesus' having entered into the glory of the heavenly Father. Fifth and last, it is Luke who lays greatest stress on Jesus' ascension to the Father.

These five ways of singling Jesus out or separating him from the ordinary run of human beings fold into Luke's rather dynamic account of Jesus' career. The first phase stretches from Jesus' virginal conception to his baptism. Here a main theme is that Jesus is born as the one who will fulfill the hopes of faithful Jews such as Simeon: "Now there was a man in Jerusalem, whose name was Simeon, and this man was righteous and devout, looking for the consolation of Israel, and the Holy Spirit was upon him. And it had been revealed to him that he should not see death before he had seen the Lord's Christ. And inspired by the Spirit he came into the temple; and when the parents brought in the child Jesus, to do for him according to the custom of the law, he took him up in his arms and blessed God and said, 'Lord, now lettest thou thy servant depart in peace, according to thy word; for mine eyes have seen thy salvation which thou hast prepared in the presence of all peoples, a light for revelation to the Gentiles, and for glory to thy people Israel'" (2:25–32).

The second phase of the Lukan Jesus' career stretches from his baptism, which is a sort of commission or vocational clarification, through to his ascension. This is the crux of salvation-history, the period in which God established the Kingdom and gave all time a new center. Brief though it was in months, it was the decisive passover from confusion about human destiny to unshakable success. Third, Luke sees the career of Jesus continuing in the ongoing history of the Church. From the time of his ascension to the Father until the Parousia when he will return to consummate history, Jesus is active and influential. He is not so much gone from the earth or his followers as with them in a new, spiritual mode. The final period of Jesus' career will be the Parousia or return itself, when what Jesus achieved in principle during his earthly life, and continued to foster from heaven, will reach its final climax.

In contrast to the christologies of Paul and John, therefore, Luke lays little stress on any preexistence of Jesus before his conception. For Luke the story begins with the angel's annunciation to Mary that she shall conceive the Son of the Most High; it will come to conclusion when history greets the Son at the Parousia. The titles that Luke gives Jesus, in addition to Son of the Most High, stress both Jesus' fulfillment of Jewish hopes and his achievement of salvation for all human beings. Thus Luke makes it plain that Jesus is the Messiah or Christ, explaining much of what happened to Jesus as the inevitable consequence of his role as the anointed one of God: "Was it not necessary that the Christ should suffer these things and enter into his glory?" (24:26). Luke also calls Jesus Lord, Savior, Son of God, Son of man, Servant, Prophet, and King. Obviously, therefore, Jesus represents a richness or fullness of blessing and mission from God that Luke cannot convey in a single title. Rather, Jesus gathers together all the main threads of Israelite history, and all the main needs of human beings everywhere, to make salvation a most comprehensive act. Salvation is the healing of human ills, the fulfillment of human hopes, the forgiveness of sins, the communication of God's peace, the imparting of true (divine) life, and the pouring out of God's Spirit. It could not be fuller, richer, or more joyous.

John

The Gospel of John most likely appeared after the other three Gospels, and the Johannine Epistles even later. A rough date for the Gospel of John is about 90 C.E. Both the Gospel and the Epistles draw on traditions different from Q and the Synoptics. A popular hypothesis is that the Johannine churches centered in Ephesus and were the products of a rather complicated development among Jewish Christians, originally from Palestine, and Gentile converts, perhaps from the Ephesus area. One part of the original Jewish Christian component of the Johannine churches apparently interpreted Jesus as the successor to Moses. Like Moses, Jesus had been with God and become God's chief mode of revelation. Raymond Brown has worked out a rather full hypothesis of how the Johannine church may have developed,[9] and in his view the cause of its several splits (first from the Jewish synagogue, then from Johannine Christians who eventually became **Docetists** or **Gnostics**) was christological disputes.

Of the Johannine christology Brown writes: "The christology of GJohn [Gospel of John] may be the highest in the NT. Mark presents Jesus as the Son of God already at the baptism and so throughout the whole public ministry. Matthew and Luke picture Jesus conceived through the Holy Spirit without a human father, and so there is never a moment of his earthly life when he is not the Son of God. But no Synoptic Gospel proposes the incarnation of a being who came down from God, i.e., a preexistent Son of God. Paul is often thought to have had a preexistent christology, although that is not certain. However, even if Paul did refer to a type of preexistence, it was in highly poetic terms patterned on the OT hymnic portrait of divine Wisdom, with no clear indication of a preexistence *before creation*. Hebrews 1:2 moves into a precreation sphere but still remains poetic. GJohn too in the Prologue refers to preexistence before creation in a hymn patterned upon the OT Wisdom motif . . . ; but GJohn goes beyond the poetic hymn genre by introducing the preexistence motif into Jesus' own statements (8:58; 17:5)."[10]

The first text that Brown cites (8:58) appears in the first half of John's Gospel, which many analysts refer to as the "book of signs" (2:1–12:50). The theme in this portion of the Gospel is Jesus' many indications of his special status as the definitive revealer of God. Such striking deeds as turning the water into wine at the wedding feast at Cana (2:1–11) and feeding the multitude (6:1–59) are presented by John as evidence that Jesus was the Word of God enfleshed. (The signs also reflect the sacramental life of the early Christian community, especially its celebration of **baptism** and the **Eucharist**.)

In this context of having shown Jesus doing remarkable things that ought to stir up faith in his person and mission, John leads up to the affirmation of Jesus' divinity that Brown cites (8:58). An argument with "the Jews" (John's designation for those of Jesus' compatriots who would not believe in him) brings Jesus finally to affirm that he is greater even than Abraham, the father of the Jews. Indeed, it brings Jesus to speak the sort of words that the Judaism of his time reserved exclusively for God: " 'Truly, truly, I say to you, if any one keeps my word, he will never see death.' The Jews said to him, 'Now we know that you have a demon. Abraham died, as did the prophets; and you say, "If any one keeps my word, he will never taste death." Are you greater than our father Abraham, who died? And the prophets died! Who do you claim to be?' Jesus answered, 'If I glorify myself, my glory is nothing; it is my Father who glorifies me, of whom you say that he is your God. But you have not known him; I know him. If I said, I do not know him, I should be a liar like you; but I do know him and I keep his word. Your father Abraham rejoiced that he was to see my day; he saw it and was glad.' The Jews then said to him, 'You are not yet fifty years old, and have you seen Abraham [who lived about 1800 years earlier]?' Jesus said to them, 'Truly, truly, I say to you, before Abraham was, I am.' So they took up stones to throw at him; but Jesus hid himself, and went out of the temple" (8:51–59). When Jesus says, "I am," he calls to mind God's self-naming in Exodus 3:14. The Jews understand this, and so want to stone him for blaspheming—for claiming that he is equal to God.

The general context of the second text that Brown cites, 17:5, is the second half of John's Gospel, which often is called "the book of glory." In this part of the Gospel, John more nakedly depicts Jesus' share in the glory or luminous aura of the Godhead, teaching through Jesus' several "farewell discourses" the intimacy between Jesus and the Father, and between Jesus and the Spirit. John 17:5 comes in the midst of Jesus' address to the Father: "When Jesus had spoken these words, he lifted up his eyes to heaven and said, 'Father, the hour has come; glorify thy Son that the Son may glorify thee, since thou hast given him power over all flesh, to give eternal life to all whom thou has given him. And this is eternal life, that they know thee the only true God, and Jesus Christ whom thou hast sent. I glorified thee on earth, having accomplished the work which thou gavest me to do; and now, Father, glorify thou me in thy own presence with the glory which I had with thee before the world was made'" (17:1–5). There is no question in John's mind, therefore, but that Jesus preexisted with the Father, sharing the divine glory long before he took flesh—indeed, before creation.

This "high" christology of the Gospel of John, which concentrates so much on Jesus' divinity, was probably the decisive New Testament influence on the classical christological **dogmas** developed from the Council of Nicaea on.[11] Within the Gospel itself, Jesus' preexistence as the Word or Son of the one God both draws on Old Testament precedents and supplies the foundation for the roles that John has Jesus play. The Old Testament precedents include the notion of a divine "Word" that coexisted with God, much as the Torah and the Spirit of God were conceived as always having existed alongside God, and of a similarly eternal Wisdom. For John, therefore, Jesus is the enfleshment of God's Word, Son, and Wisdom. He comes to reveal what flesh can of God's own being.

He also comes to save human beings from sin and communicate divine life to them. The condition of both salvation and divinization is faith, and the substance of both is love. Thus the glory that Jesus discusses in John 17 is mediated by his being raised up on the cross. The "hour" that has come is the paradoxical time of his triumphing by dying. The Johannine triad of light, life, and love stands in contrast to the darkness, death, and hate of a world that resists God, that does not want God's saving revelation because it would have to be converted from its sinful deeds.

After the writing of the Gospel of John, experts conjecture, some members of the Johannine community pushed Jesus' divinity so far that they jeopardized his humanity. Thus a schism arose in the Johannine church. The Johannine Epistles stem from a controversy about Jesus' humanity and represent the side that later was adjudged orthodox. The First Letter of John, for instance, from the very beginning insists on Jesus' having been really human—visible, palpable: "That which was from the beginning, which we have heard, which we have seen with our eyes, which we have looked upon and touched with our hands, concerning the word of life—the life was made manifest, and we saw it, and testify to you, and proclaim to you the eternal life which was with the Father and was made manifest to us" (1 : 1−2).

Those who deny that Jesus really came in the flesh, who want a salvation untainted by human weakness, suffering, and the like, play false to both history and faith. For the author of 1 John they are children of the Antichrist, a Satanic figure. They would denature salvation, reducing it to the mythologies of the many religions in the first century that spoke of savior figures and secret knowledges in purely symbolic, unhistorical terms. Paradoxically enough, the New Testament school that most insisted on Jesus' divine preexistence with the Father also most insisted on the historical, enfleshed character of God's Savior. The Synoptics did not have to insist on this, because no one in their orbit denied Jesus' humanity. The Johannine school had to and did.

Paul

In the sixth decade of the first century C.E., the apostle Paul wrote a number of letters to young Christian churches. Although Paul was not himself one of Jesus' original band of disciples, his conversion from being a persecutor of the Church to an ardent missionary was later looked on as giving him rank equal to the original eyewitnesses. The conversion experience, narrated several times in Acts (9 : 1−22, 22 : 4−16, 26 : 9−18; see also Galatians 1 : 13−17), puts a premium on Jesus' identification of himself with the Church. The resurrected Christ is one with his Church, so that to persecute the Church is to persecute him. This initial experience meant a great deal to Paul as he later pondered the nature of the Christian community. Along with the Johannine notion (John 15) that Jesus and his disciples are related as vine and branches, sharing a single life, the Pauline notion of the Church as Christ's body has been extremely influential.

The first letters of Paul, from the early and mid 50s, to the Thessalonians, Galatians, and Corinthians, reveal an initial expectation that the Christ would soon return—that the Parousia would soon occur—and then show an increasing concentration on current Church life. By the time one gets to 2 Corinthians, Paul has somewhat shifted his emphasis from Jesus' return to Jesus' current presence to the Church in the Spirit. Thus Paul's christology is taut with a tension between what already has been given in the Spirit and the full realization of the Kingdom that is yet to come.

James D. G. Dunn has put this tension as follows: "In the first-century Christianity most clearly represented in Paul we see the same kind of eschatological tension, between the already of the grace already given and the not yet of a kingdom inheritance still to be realized. Not only so, but this post-Easter eschatological tension is also understood as a function of the Spirit: in the Pauline churches the Spirit is understood precisely as the first installment of that kingdom inheritance which guarantees its full realization in the resurrection of the body (Rom. 8.10f., 15–23; I Cor. 6.9–11; 15.45–50; II Cor. 4.16–5.5; Gal. 4.6f., 5.16–24; Eph. 1.13f.). More important, the Spirit thus experienced is experienced as the Spirit of Jesus—the power of the crucified and risen one which manifests itself precisely as it did in him, as power in weakness, as life through death. . . . That is to say, there is a certain merging or fusing of the role of the Spirit with the exalted Christ (I Cor. 15.45) so that the presence and work of the Spirit is determined and defined by its relation to Christ, that is, by whether or not it manifests the same character as was manifested in the ministry of Jesus."[12]

Two great texts from Paul spring to mind. The first, on the character that was manifested in the ministry of Jesus, is a famous hymn from Philippians, probably used by Paul toward the end of the 50s but no doubt itself considerably older: "Have this mind among yourselves, which is yours in Christ Jesus, who, though he was in the form of God, did not count equality with God a thing to be grasped, but emptied himself, taking the form of a servant, being born in the likeness of men. And being found in human form he humbled himself and became obedient unto death, even death on a cross. Therefore God has highly exalted him and bestowed on him the name which is above every name, that at the name of Jesus every knee should bow, in heaven and on earth and under the earth, and every tongue confess that Jesus Christ is Lord, to the glory of God the Father" (2 : 5 – 11).

This hymn has the pattern of humiliation and exaltation that we previously saw the Synoptics borrowing from contemporary Jewish literature. In Paul's mind, Christ is in the form of God, as Adam was, but Christ's humility and obedience reverse the fall away from God that Adam's pride and disobedience caused. Christ therefore is the new Adam (Romans 5:14–21), and from his exalted station in heaven he pours forth the Spirit that is the sign and substance of the new life where grace abounds over sin. Through Adam's sin all die. By Christ's obedient love all can live, exulting in the very life of God. The Spirit is the firstfruits or down payment on the divine promise blazing forth in Christ's exaltation or Resurrection.

The second great text is the whole of the eighth chapter of Romans. There Paul reflects on the riches of the life that comes with the Spirit. Those possessing Christ's Spirit, the Spirit of the Father who raised Jesus, no longer live a fleshly, sinful, and mortal life. They are in the grasp of the grace of the immortal God and are headed for heavenly glory. So 8:9–11 assures the Romans: "But you are not in the flesh, you are in the Spirit, if in fact the Spirit of God dwells in you. Any one who does not have the Spirit of Christ does not belong to him. But if Christ is in you, although your bodies are dead because of sin, your spirits are alive because of righteousness. If the Spirit of him who raised Jesus from the dead dwells in you, he who raised Christ Jesus from the dead will give life to your mortal bodies also through his Spirit which dwells in you."

This same Spirit presides over the prayer of Jesus' followers, interceding for them with sighs too deep for words. It brings the conviction of salvation and victory home, establishing in their marrow great faith and hope that in all things God works for their good. So the religious goal, the psychological effect, of faith in Jesus the Christ and experience of his Spirit is an unshakable trust that nothing can separate the true believer from God's love: "For I am sure that neither death, nor life, nor angels, nor principalities, nor things present, nor things to come, nor powers, nor height, nor depth, nor anything else in all creation will be able to separate us from the love of God in Christ Jesus our Lord" (8:38–39).

We see in Paul, therefore, the "enthusiasm," the sense of being filled with Christ's Spirit, that played such an important role in the early Christians' understanding of Jesus. Jesus was not someone stuck back in the past, however heroic, but a present force both powerful and splendid. The sense of the Spirit that Acts records at Pentecost (Acts 2) gave all the early churches, but perhaps especially the Pauline churches, an enormous vitality. Thus the discussion of charismata or gifts that occurs in 1 Corinthians 12–14 has the outpouring of the Spirit as its context. The quickly developing sacramental system of the Christian community, which emphasized the beginnings of a new life (of being buried with Christ and rising with him) at baptism and the nourishment of this life in the Eucharist, makes much more sense when one takes these symbolic actions as expressions of a life-giving Lord and Spirit. What some of the early Church fathers called a **mystagogy** has its seeds in the earliest initiations into the dynamic workings of Christ and the Spirit throughout the community. Thus, much of the "inside" of the primitive christology, its roots in the lived religious experience of the early believers, is suggested to us by the writings of Paul and his followers.

As most commentators point out, Paul's christology is remarkable for its disinterest in the earthly Jesus. Virtually nowhere does Paul use any of the traditions about the historical sayings or doings of Jesus, the ministry that Jesus performed prior to being exalted to Lordship. Toward the end of his very readable study of Paul, Lucas Grollenberg offers an opinion as to why this should be so: "Might it be, then, that everything that Jesus had said and done to reveal God's love during his earthly life had paled into insignificance for Paul in the light of the cross and resurrection? This suggestion seems to me to have much to commend it. Perhaps Paul was also afraid that stories about Jesus' miraculous cures might distract people from the most important things of all: cross, resurrection and the new life in the Spirit; moreover, to hand on Jesus' teaching might lead Christians to regard it as a new Torah, with a righteousness of its own [and so to contradict the central conviction of Paul that all righteousness comes only through faith]. Could this be why Paul did not bother to use the gospel material, and preferred to keep his distance from it?"[13] We do not have the historical materials to settle this question, but Grollenberg's interpretation is quite persuasive.

Pauline Writings

Romans, which scholars usually date from 58 or 59 C.E., is the last of the Epistles from Paul's own hand. Subsequent to Paul's death in Rome several years later, disciples or church leaders wrote several other letters that eventually got into the New Testament canon under Paul's name. The most important of these are Colossians and Ephesians, and studying them will fill out our sense of the Pauline christology.

Colossians is a somewhat mysterious letter. Scholars cannot agree either on when it was written (between 63 and 90 C.E.) or on who the Colossians were (the actual Christian community at the town of Colossae in Phrygia or another group). Despite this uncertainty about the historical details of the letter, few scholars dispute its significance. In Colossians, as in Ephesians, we see the Pauline school broadening and deepening its speculation about the significance of Christ, to the extent that Jesus Christ finally becomes a cosmic presence.

The most famous passage in Colossians, like the famous passage from Philippians that we studied, probably was a Christian hymn that predated the Epistle in which we now find it. It is another exultant appreciation of Christ's lordship and heavenly status: "He is the image of the invisible God, the first-born of all creation; for in him all things were created, in heaven and on earth, visible and invisible, whether thrones or dominions or principalities or authorities—all things were created through him and for him. He is before all things, and in him all things hold together. He is the head of the body, the church; he is the beginning, the first-born from the dead, that in everything he might be preeminent. For in him all the fullness of God was pleased to dwell, and through him to reconcile to himself all things, whether on earth or in heaven, making peace by the blood of his cross" (1:15–20).

Present-day scholars situate this hymn against the backdrop of Jewish speculation about Wisdom. Thus Joseph Burgess explains: "The hymn was used by the churches in southern Asia Minor. The first stanza stresses creation and the second redemption. The 'image of the invisible God' (1:15) does not mean simply the 'reflection' of God, for Hellenistic terminology requires that in an 'image' what is represented is present (Wisdom is the 'image' of God. Wis. Sol. 7:25–26). Since Christ represents the 'invisible God,' he is not part of creation, but God's revelation and God's instrument. Thus something else is meant here than in 3:10, where the new man is to be renewed after the image of the creator. As the context demonstrates in 1:15–16 and in 1:18 bc, 'the first-born of all creation' does not mean in Arian [heretical] fashion that Christ is part of creation, even though he is the first-born. In Hellenistic Wisdom speculation the same kind of terminology was used to describe Wisdom as the one who was created 'at the beginning' and 'before all things' (Prov. 8:22; Sir. 1:4; 24:9). In similar terms the hymn depicts Christ's superiority over the whole cosmos."[14]

Prompted by their experience of what they considered to be Jesus' dynamic presence to them in the Spirit, the writers of hymns such as these struggled to understand Jesus' lordship. He had been raised at the Resurrection into the sphere of God. This seemed a confirmation or ratification not simply of his holiness or authority from God but also of his teaching. The **Hellenistic** milieu that commentators mention was the contemporary form of Greek culture in the midst of which both Jews and early Christians did their theologizing. Many of the most influential early Christian thinkers apparently were converts from Judaism who spoke Greek rather than Aramaic. Frequently these Hellenistic Jewish converts were well versed in the speculations about Wisdom that had absorbed the generations both prior to Jesus and after his death. It was a rather natural move, therefore, to ask whether this Wisdom-speculation didn't fit Jesus and clarify his exalted status. When they focused on Jesus as the great teacher—or even as the new Torah—that God had revealed, such early Christian theologians were enticed to make Jesus preexistent, as the Wisdom that played before God (Proverbs 8:22–31) had been. The hymn no doubt expresses this sort of appreciation of Jesus, making him the one in whom creation itself occurred and holds together.

It is hard to know how physically to take such a notion, but some

exegetes do not hesitate to interpret Colossians as making Christ a cosmological principle—the center and binding force of physical creation: "Paul uses the strange phrase: 'In him all things hold together.' This means that not only is the Son the agent of creation in the beginning and the goal of creation in the end, but between the beginning and the end, during time as we know it, it is he who holds the world together. That is to say, all the laws by which this world is order and not chaos are an expression of the mind of the Son. The law of gravity and the rest, the laws by which the universe hangs together, are not only scientific laws but also divine."[15]

As we shall see in the next chapter, the idea that the Logos or Word of God partook in the design of creation, so that Jesus was the **Pantokrator,** became a mainstay of christological speculation, especially among the Eastern church fathers. For the hymn in Colossians, the **soteriological** aspects of Jesus' exaltation bulk as large as the cosmological aspects. Jesus is the axis of a process of reconciliation that brings alienated humanity back to God and makes it possible for all kinds of human beings—Jews and Gentiles, sinners and just—to come into harmony. He is as well a principle of reconciliation that embraces the entire cosmos: in his resurrection a new creation was born. But the idea is not purely concerned with admiring the theological build of nature. It is equally concerned with praising God for having given space and time the Wisdom to overcome its divisions and the power to rejoin its God.

The Epistle to the Ephesians probably is later than the Epistle to the Colossians, perhaps even as late as the last decade of the first century C.E. It may have been sent to the actual community of Christians at Ephesus on the southwest coast of Asia Minor, or it may not—such matters concerned the early Church less than the content of a teaching letter; what was sent to one group soon became the property of all. The leading christological text of Ephesians (1 : 15 – 23) is similar to Colossians 1 : 15 – 20 in being dazzled by the cosmic implications of Jesus the Christ. However, it is more **ecclesiological** than Colossians, relating the cosmic Christ to his body the Church: "For this reason, because I have heard of your faith in the Lord Jesus and your love toward all the saints, I do not cease to give thanks for you, remembering you in my prayers, that the God of our Lord Jesus Christ, the Father of glory, may give you a spirit of wisdom and of revelation in the knowledge of him, having the eyes of your hearts enlightened, that you may know what is the hope to which he has called you, what are the riches of his glorious inheritance in the saints, and what is the immeasurable greatness of his power in us who believe, according to the working of his great might which he accomplished in Christ when he raised him from the dead and made him sit at his right hand in the heavenly places, far above all rule and authority and power and dominion, and above every name that is named, not only in this age but also in that which is to come; and he has put all things under his feet and has made him the head over all things for the church, which is his body, the fulness of him who fills all in all" (1:15–23).

Ephesians goes on to soteriological themes, and it develops a nuptial analogy for the relation of Christ and the Church. Perhaps its most distinctive teaching, however, at least for our purposes, is the notion that Christ is the "fulness" of God, the **pleroma** of what human beings can know of God or receive of divine life. Thus the author prays that his readers "may have the power to comprehend with all the saints what is the breadth and length and height and depth, and to know the love of Christ, which passes knowledge, that you may be filled with all the fulness of God" (3:18–19). The limited, earthly Jesus has been left far behind.

Hebrews

The Epistle to the Hebrews, which actually is a sermon rather than a letter, arose before 96 C.E. For some time it was attributed to the apostle Paul, but stylistic differences from Paul's known writings make his authorship of Hebrews unlikely. The heavily Jewish symbolism and modes of argument suggest a source well trained in contemporary Jewish theology. As well, they suggest an original audience composed mainly of Christian converts from Judaism. We know that Hebrews was circulating before 96 C.E. because 1 Clement, a noncanonical early Christian writing that appeared about 96 C.E., quotes it. Beyond that, we know nothing about which churches' christologies it represents or who finally wrote it.

The characteristic teaching of Hebrews about Christ stresses that Christ was a high priest, the successor and fulfillment of the various priestly mediators of the Jewish covenant, especially the line descended from Levi. Reginald Fuller offers the following orientation to this characteristic teaching: "We now come to the central doctrine of Hebrews and its signal contribution to Christology. Was the author the first to use this title [high priest]? Some have thought that 3:1 ('high priest of our confession') indicates that the baptismal confession of the community already contained the title. This, however, is doubtful. . . . If the whole epistle, as we have claimed, is an extended midrash [rabbinical commentary] on Psalm 110, this will mean that the document in its entirety is related to that text, and to the exposition of Christ's high priesthood. This is obvious in the central section (5:1–10:39), and fairly obvious in the major exhortation (11:1–12:29). It is less obvious in 1:1–4:16. But there are, to begin with, three references to Christ as high priest in these opening chapters (2:17, 3:1, 4:14)."[16]

Fuller's interpretation of Hebrews as a commentary on Psalm 110 reminds us that the early Christian community thought of the Hebrew

Bible (or the Greek translation known as the Septuagint) as its Scripture. The psalms no doubt played an important role in early Christian worship, and the whole Hebrew Bible was the first place to which Jesus' followers would go for their sense of the prior stages of salvation that Jesus had brought to fulfillment. Psalm 110 is relatively brief, so we may quote it in full: "The Lord says to my Lord: 'Sit at my right hand, till I make your enemies your footstool.' The Lord sends forth from Zion your mighty scepter. Rule in the midst of your foes! Your people will offer themselves freely on the day you lead your host upon the holy mountains. From the womb of the morning like dew your youth will come to you. The Lord has sworn and will not change his mind, 'You are a priest for ever after the order of Melchizedek.' The Lord is at your right hand; he will shatter kings on the day of his wrath. He will execute judgment among the nations, filling them with corpses; he will shatter chiefs over the wide earth. He will drink from the brook by the way; therefore he will lift up his head."

The psalm originally was what scholars call a royal psalm, meant to be sung at the coronation of a king. Much of the imagery pertains to the enthronement of a Jewish leader and the assurance that God will bless his reign. For the early Christians, however, the application to Jesus leapt out in the first verse. In raising and exalting Jesus, God had placed him at the divine "right hand," establishing Jesus' intimacy with the power and throne of heaven. Christians had enough enemies to be glad that God's exaltation of Jesus would make Jesus' foes his footstool. The reign of Jesus on earth, like the Kingdom of God that Jesus had preached, was something to be anticipated joyfully.

The verse that preoccupies Hebrews, however, is 110:4: "The Lord has sworn and will not change his mind, 'You are a priest for ever after the order of Melchizedek.'" Genesis 14:18 describes Melchizedek as the priest-king of Salem ("Peace") who brings out bread and wine and blesses Abram (Abraham): "And Melchizedek king of Salem brought out bread and wine; he was priest of God most High. And he blessed him and said, 'Blessed be Abram by God Most High, maker of heaven and earth; and blessed be God Most High, who has delivered your enemies into your hand!'" (Genesis 14:18–19). For the author of Hebrews, Jesus is the high priest who comes like Melchizedek without lineage (as though directly from heaven). Jesus is a king and priest of God's shalom or peace, and the sacrifice that Jesus' followers make in memory of him is with bread and wine. Finally, Jesus, like Melchizedek, is superior to Abraham, the father of the Jews. Jesus is superior because he brings a new covenant and familial relation to God, one that is more intimate and possessed of a purer faith. Melchizedek is superior in that one blesses an inferior, not a superior.

Hebrews makes use of Psalm 110:4 in several passages, as part of its general depiction of Jesus as the priest of a new, eternal covenant perfected in Jesus' once-and-for-all self-sacrifice on the cross. In exercising this priesthood Jesus has assured believers a full penetration into the holiness of the Temple of God (the divine presence symbolized by the holy of holies, the innermost precincts of the Jerusalem Temple): "We have this as a sure and steadfast anchor of the soul, a hope that enters into the inner shrine behind the curtain, where Jesus has gone as a forerunner on our behalf, having become a high priest for ever after the order of Melchizedek. For this Melchizedek, king of Salem, priest of the Most High God, met Abraham returning from the slaughter of kings and blessed him; and to him Abraham apportioned a tenth part of everything. He is first, by translation of his name, king of righteousness, and then he is also king of Salem, that is, king of peace. He is without father or mother or genealogy, and has neither beginning of days nor end of life, but resembling the Son of God he continues a priest for ever" (6:19–7:3).

Hebrews then goes on to elaborate the superiority of Melchizedek to Abraham, arguing that Levi, a later descendant of Abraham (and the source of the Jewish priesthood) paid tithes to Melchizedek and so acknowledged his superiority: "One might even say that Levi himself, who receives tithes [in recent Jewish history], paid tithes through Abraham, for he was still in the loins of his ancestor when Melchizedek met him" (7:9–10).

The argument that Hebrews uses here, and throughout, depends on **types.** What went before is a prefigurement of what came after in Jesus. Abraham and Melchizedek both foreshadowed aspects of Jesus' faith-relation to God and sacrificial priesthood. Jesus is the fulfillment of everything that they, and the other heroes of Jewish faith, accomplished and promised. The great thing that Jesus does for all who believe in him is accomplish the goal that Jewish priesthood sought but could not accomplish: the complete forgiveness of sins.

Through his very weakness, humaneness, and complete identification with sinners, Jesus served as a perfect high priest and won God's exaltation: "Since then we have a great high priest who has passed through the heavens, Jesus, the Son of God, let us hold fast our confession. For we have not a high priest who is unable to sympathize with our weaknesses, but one who in every respect has been tempted as we are, yet without sin. Let us then with confidence draw near to the throne of grace, that we may receive mercy and find grace to help in time of need. For every high priest chosen from among men is appointed to act on behalf of men in relation to God, to offer gifts and sacrifices for sin. He can deal gently with the ignorant and wayward, since he himself is beset with weakness. Because of this he is bound to offer sacrifice for his own sins as well as for those of the people. And one does not take the honor upon himself, but he is called by God, just as Aaron was. So also Christ did not exalt himself to be made a high priest, but was appointed by him who said to him, 'Thou art my Son, today I have begotten thee'; as he says also in another place, 'Thou art a priest for ever, after the order of Melchizedek.' In the days of his flesh, Jesus offered up prayers and supplications, with loud cries and tears, to him who was able to save him from death, and he was heard for his godly fear. Although he was a Son, he learned obedience through what he suffered; and being made perfect he became the source of eternal salvation to all who obey him, being designated by God a high priest after the order of Melchizedek" (4:14–5:10). It is hard to overestimate the influence that texts such as these had on both later Christian christology, which frequently focused on Jesus' mediation of forgiveness for sins, and on the self-conception of the Christian priesthood, which soon became the main line of power-bearers in the Church.

Revelation

Revelation is a Christian apocalypse. Quite likely it was written between the years 70 and 95 C.E. It speaks of Rome as Babylon, a Jewish usage that arose after the Roman destruction of Jerusalem in 70 C.E., and the early church father Irenaeus says that it was in circulation at the end of the reign of the Roman emperor Domitian (95–96 C.E.). Many Jewish apocalypses had arisen in the generations before Revelation. Borrowing this literary form, the author sought to console Christians who were suffering various dissatisfactions by writing a faith-inspired disclosure of how Christ would come to vindicate them.[17] The heavy debt to the symbolism of the Hebrew Bible suggests a Jewish Christian author, while the circle of churches addressed in chapters 2 and 3, along with the author's claim that he is writing from the island of Patmos (1:9), suggest that the document was first meant for the churches in Asia Minor.

We may begin our study of the christology of Revelation by noting some of the titles that the author uses for Jesus Christ. In 1:5 Jesus is "the faithful witness, the first-born of the dead, and the ruler of kings on earth." In 1:6 he is praised for being the one "who loves us and has freed us from our sins by his blood and made us a kingdom, priests to his God and Father." He is worthy of glory and dominion for ever and ever (1:6). He is coming with the clouds to punish the wicked (1:7). He is the Son of man, Daniel's glorious heavenly figure, standing in the midst of the Church (the seven golden lampstands): "Then I turned to see the voice that was speaking to me, and on turning I saw seven golden lampstands, and in the midst of the lampstands one like a son of man, clothed with a long robe and with a golden girdle round his breast; his head and his hair were white as white wool, white as snow; his eyes were like a flame of fire, his feet were like burnished bronze, refined as in a fire, and his voice was like the sound of many waters; in his right hand he held seven stars, from his mouth issued a sharp two-edged sword, and his face was like the sun shining in full strength" (1:12–16). When the author falls at the feet of this visionary figure, Jesus tells him not to fear. For Jesus is the first and the last, the living one. He died but now is alive forevermore. He holds the keys of Death and Hades.

This wealth of titles and imagery, from just the first chapter of Revelation, makes it plain that the author is packing into the person or reality of Jesus everything divine and messianic. Moreover, the supernal character of this Jesus clearly depends on his resurrected status. He is the one who died but now is alive forevermore. He has power over death and hell, power to lock people into those domains or keep them out. He is both judge and redeemer, both the first cause (alpha) and the last end (omega). Blazing with light and power, he gives the churches their reason to be and their reason to hope.

Chapters 2 and 3, the letters to the various churches of Asia Minor, spill out more titles and images of Christ, as if from an inexhaustible treasury. In 2:18 he is the Son of God. In 3:1 he has the seven spirits of God and the seven stars. In 3:7 he is the holy one, the true one, who has the key of David. In 3:14 he is the amen, a faithful and true witness (martyr), and the beginning of God's creation. Moreover, in each of the letters Jesus is depicted as capable of rewarding his faithful followers who persevere and punishing the faithless who fall by the wayside. Basically, his reward amounts to bringing the faithful follower to heaven or the realm of God, where Jesus himself reigns. Thus the final letter, to the church of Laodicea, concludes: "He who conquers, I will grant him to sit with me on my throne, as I myself conquered and sat down with my Father on his throne" (3:21).

Through the rest of Revelation, which is a highly structured work, Jesus, the victorious-resurrected-exalted Christ, keeps his heavenly location. He is with God the Creator in glory, as a central actor in both the drama of vindication that is going to be played out by heaven's action on behalf of the faithful Christians on earth and in the liturgy or ongoing worship that seems to be the main occupation of heaven. His main designation in this later context is the Lamb, the **paschal** victim whose blood was the price of the salvation of humankind. For this redemptive activity he is constantly hymned by the heavenly citizenry: "Worthy is the Lamb who was slain, to receive power and wealth and wisdom and might and honor and glory and blessing" (5:12). The Lamb will marry the Church, celebrating heavenly nuptials. He will be the lamp of the heavenly Jerusalem, obviating the need for any sun or moon (or temple) (21:22–23).

In the context of the great battles between heaven and the Satanic forces of this earth—Rome, Babylon, and the great beast—Jesus is the Lord of lords and King of kings (17:14). These titles, which seem to radiate from a more basic title that makes Jesus the Word of God, are like the apparel of a mighty warrior: "Then I saw heaven opened, and behold, a white horse! He who sat upon it is called Faithful and True, and in righteousness he judges and makes war. His eyes are like a flame of fire, and on his head are many diadems; and he has a name inscribed which no one knows but himself. He is clad in a robe dipped in blood and the name by which he is called is The Word of God. And the armies of heaven, arrayed in fine linen, white and pure, followed him on white horses. From his mouth issues a sharp sword with which to smite the nations, and he will rule them with a rod of iron; he will tread the wine press of the fury of the wrath of God the Almighty. On his robe and on his thigh he has a name inscribed, King of kings and Lord of lords" (19:11–16).

Finally, Jesus is the Lord (Aramaic: Mar) whom the author of Revelation, and in his company many of the Christian churches, beg to come (at the Parousia). This request ("Maranatha") caps the ardent longing of Revelation for release from present sufferings, for the execution of justice that feels so long delayed. Revelation wants the full outpouring of the victory that Jesus won through his death and resurrection. It wants what has been achieved in principle to expand and fill the earth. Then the persecutors of the faithful and just will receive a deadly comeuppance. Then things will be as they ought to be, and the splendor of God will shine in the heavenly Jerusalem.

Ultimately, therefore, the christology of Revelation spotlights the justice that the resurrection of Christ empowers believers to expect. Now reigning in heaven, the Lord will soon judge the nations and vindicate his elect. The worship that goes forward in heaven so gloriously, with such riches and song, will find a fitting mirror in the rescue of Christians from earthly trials, the full establishment of God's Kingdom on earth. The Christ of Revelation is the Messiah, yes, and the Risen Lord, but in more militant terms than we find elsewhere in the New Testament. Apocalypticism often deals with cosmic battles, and Revelation is no exception. Jesus therefore is the great warrior, fighting for justice and truth, who will completely crush Satan and his earthly minions, such as the great whore Rome. The author's certainty of Jesus' victory in the cosmic battle is rooted in the victory Jesus already has won over Satan and death. The Resurrection broke the spine of everything ungodly, placing in heaven the firstborn of a new race destined to enjoy the splendor of God and spend an eternity singing God's praises. Balancing the martial imagery, therefore, is the finer religious imagery of pure worship. The last act of religion, and the first act, is praising God for being God: absolutely holy and good.

The Pastorals and 1 Peter

Toward the end of the first century C.E., when Church structures began to solidify and the Christian community put off some of its apocalyptic character to accommodate to Christ's delay (and to its own consequent need to situate itself in the world), a group of writings called the Pastorals emerged. They focused on the charge of the pastor to guard the deposit of faith handed down from the apostles and to establish or maintain right order in the local community. First and Second Timothy and Titus long were attributed to Paul, but most current biblical scholarship rejects that authorship. A principal reason is the difference between the christology of the Pastorals and the christology of Paul.[18]

For example, the regular designation for Christ in the Pastorals is Savior, a designation that the letters surely from Paul's hand use most sparingly (for example, Philippians 3 : 30). Savior was a popular title for the gods of the Hellenistic mystery religions, which may indicate that the author of the Pastorals (if there was a single author) was dealing with people aware of the Hellenistic cults. (Savior also could be used in the cult of the Roman emperor.) The at least implicit point would have been to proclaim the greater salvation available in Christ. At times Christianity was forced to compete in the quite free market of Hellenistic religions. Thus Paul and the Pauline authors developed the sort of gnosis or privileged knowledge that Christian faith offered, in order to make Christianity competitive with the philosophies and cults that were preaching special (healing or saving) knowledge. The Pastorals, by focusing on Jesus' saving powers, would have been encouraging Christians, or any potential converts, to experience the power that faith in Jesus could bring.

A second christological accent peculiar to the Pastorals and not much in evidence in Paul is the idea of Christ's **epiphany.** This term also has the flavor of worship or cult, and it could apply either to Christ's first coming—the Incarnation—or to his second coming at the Parousia. In both cases he makes manifest, makes to "appear," the goodness and power of divinity. This manifestation is cause for great joy, because it works human beings' passover from hopelessness to hope. Thus 2 Timothy 1 : 8–10 counsels: "Do not be ashamed then of testifying to our Lord, nor of me his prisoner, but share in the suffering for the gospel in the power of God, who saved us and called us with a holy calling, not in virtue of our works but in virtue of his own purpose and the grace which he gave us in Christ Jesus ages ago, and now has manifested through the appearance of our Savior Christ Jesus, who abolished death and brought life and immortality to light through the gospel."

In Titus 2 : 13 the accent, by contrast, falls not just on the appearance of Christ that is past history but even more on the appearance that is yet to come: "For the grace of God has appeared for the salvation of all men, training us to renounce irreligion and worldly passions, and to live sober, upright, and godly lives in this world, awaiting our blessed hope, the appearing of the glory of our great God and Savior Jesus Christ, who gave himself for us to redeem us from all iniquity and to purify for himself a people of his own who are zealous for good deeds" (2 : 11–14). One might say, therefore, that the Pastorals picture Christian life as a time bracketed by two great appearances of the divine mercy in the person of Jesus

Christ. Looking backward, they recall the manifestation of the divinity in the flesh of the historical Jesus. Looking forward, they await the consummating manifestation of the Parousia. What they do not develop, as one would expect the author of Romans, for instance, to develop, is the present life of grace that Christians share with the Risen Christ and the outpoured Spirit.

In their charge to pastors (presbyters or bishops such as Timothy and Titus) to guard the traditional faith and shepherd their people to strict morals, the Pastorals reflect what some scholars have called "early Catholicism." By this they mean the institutionalization of the Church, its move away from a **charismatic** authority under the Spirit to something more human, formal, regulated. The Church hierarchy that soon developed, separating the clergy somewhat from the ordinary Christian laity, has roots in the Pastorals. On the other hand, the Church had to accommodate to the world, and it was beset with many differing interpretations of the Christ-event, some of them offensive to traditional faith (and thus heretical). Few scholars deny that it had to fashion lines of authority, ways of safeguarding the precious heritage now endangered. This could well be the main reason that the Christ celebrated in the Pastorals is less **pneumatic,** more susceptible of being captured in formulas that could provide a test for orthodoxy.

Still, not all of the formulas of the Pastorals are wooden or fashioned only as a test of orthodoxy. In many places these letters are quite poetic, in part because they borrow from hymns used in the liturgy. Thus 1 Timothy 3 : 16 has preserved the memorable lines, "Great indeed, we confess, is the mystery of our religion: He was manifested in the flesh, vindicated in the Spirit, seen by angels, preached among the nations, believed on in the world, taken up in glory." Second Timothy 2 : 11−13 shows the ethical follow-through that the Pastorals expected from such a lyric memory of Christ's grandeur: "The saying is sure: If we have died with him, we shall also live with him; if we endure, we shall also reign with him; if we deny him, he will also deny us; if we are faithless, he remains faithful— for he cannot deny himself." Insofar as many of these sentiments inform the christologies of the earlier New Testament writings, we should not think of the Pastorals as retracting what the Synoptics, John, or Paul had developed. Rather they had a different set of problems in mind, and so they tailored their faith to the sort of "appearance" and salvation they thought most helpful to planting their communities solidly in traditional doctrine and firming up a strict discipline.

First Peter, also from the end of the first century C.E., and also probably not by the apostle whose name it bears, may have arisen from Ephesus. Chapter 1, verses 19−21, offers a good example of 1 Peter's christological style. It reminds its readers that they have not been ransomed with silver or gold, "but with the precious blood of Christ, like that of a lamb without blemish or spot. He was destined before the foundation of the world but was made manifest at the end of times for your sake. Through him you have confidence in God, who raised him from the dead and gave him glory, so that your faith and hope are in God." The figure of the Lamb, familiar to us from Revelation, along with the depiction of Rome as Babylon in 5 : 13, also familiar from Revelation, suggests affinities between the author of 1 Peter and John of Patmos.

On the other hand, 1 Peter doesn't have the dazzling panoply of figures for the heavenly Lamb or resurrected Christ that we found in Revelation. Its suggestion that Christ came "at the end of times" stamps it as somewhat eschatological or apocalyptic: still expecting the last eon of history that Christ announced to be consummated soon. Verse 18 of chapter 3 stresses that Christ died for the sins of humankind, that humankind might come to God. When Christians are baptized, the resurrection of Christ works to bring them salvation (3 : 21). Jesus is now at the right hand of God, having subject to him the angels and heavenly powers (3 : 22).

Somewhat like Paul, the author of 1 Peter juxtaposes death and resurrection, making their conjoint action the axis of salvation. Like the author of Revelation, however, he is trying to buoy up believers who are suffering trials and tribulations, so he tends to stress Christ's sufferings or the price that was paid for believers' faith. Thus 2 : 20–25 argues: "If when you do right and suffer for it you take it patiently, you have God's approval. For to this you have been called, because Christ also suffered for you, leaving you an example, that you should follow in his steps. He committed no sin, no guile was found on his lips. When he was reviled, he did not revile in return; when he suffered, he did not threaten; but he trusted to him who judges justly. He himself bore our sins in his body on the tree, that we might die to sin and live to righteousness. By his wounds you have been healed. For you were straying like sheep, but have now returned to the Shepherd and Guardian of your souls." First Peter therefore makes Christ the suffering model whose emulation can see Christians through present trials and bring them home to God.[19]

Summary

We began our survey of the New Testament's views of Jesus with the synoptic sources: Mark, Q, Matthew, and Luke. Mark stresses the title Son of man, which names both the heavenly figure of Daniel 7 : 13–14 and the lowly humanity of an ordinary earthly person. The Markan Messiah, however, is a suffering figure, and those who cannot abide this sort of leader had best reconsider their Christian faith. The fusion of Jesus' suffering with a powerful authority makes him enigmatic, a fighter against Satan who both wins and loses. The Resurrection, however, seals the issue in victory. For Mark the centurion's confession (15 : 37–39) tells it all: "Truly this man was the Son of God."

Q, the source that scholars hypothesize was used by Matthew and

Luke (along with Mark and other sources peculiar to each) to fashion the second and third synoptic Gospels, comes from an apocalyptic early Christian community. The Jesus of Q is a powerful prophet whose rejection by his people fits the tradition of the sufferings of the classical prophets (for example, Jeremiah). The Pharisees are singled out for special blame, but Q gains some peace from contemplating the messianic banquet that Jesus will celebrate with his disciples at his return. Q draws on the Wisdom traditions of contemporary Jewish theology, making Jesus the newest and fullest form of God's Wisdom. Apparently this community experienced the presence of the Risen Lord vividly, and this surety of his victory allowed it to use the pattern of humiliation/exaltation to summarize its christology.

Matthew writes a proclamation of Jesus that is much concerned to show him as a great teacher, in the footsteps of Moses, who fulfills Jewish prophecy and perfects the Torah. Matthew gives much evidence of Jesus' supernatural powers, beginning with the story of Jesus' marvelous conception, in order to demonstrate Jesus' unique closeness to God. It is not the prodigies themselves that are important so much as their symbolization of the salvation, the bringing of the Kingdom, that God effected through Jesus. For Matthew's largely Jewish Christian audience, this would have been the crux: in Jesus God fulfilled all his covenantal promises.

Luke-Acts, directed toward a more Gentile Christian audience, is the most artistic rendering of Jesus' humanity. Luke sees Jesus as the key figure in a drama of salvation-history that will reach out to the ends of the known world. Many of Jesus' most memorable parables come from Luke, such as the good Samaritan and the prodigal son. Luke's Jesus proceeds under the guidance of the Holy Spirit and presently is active in the Church as a resurrected power.

In contrast to the Synoptics, John stresses Jesus' divine status as the preexistent Son or Word. In such texts as 8 : 58 and 17 : 5 John is at pains to make the identification of Jesus and God almost brutally clear to such adversaries as "the Jews." The Johannine Jesus brings to human beings the life of God, as symbolized in the eucharistic feeding of the multitudes. In the second half of the Gospel, known as the "book of glory," John depicts Jesus as most intimate with the Father and the Spirit, sharing their life and glory. Jesus' coming to bring divine life is also the forgiveness of human beings' sins. If people cling to him in faith they share the love-life of God, as branches share the life of the vine. First John, written after the Gospel and in part to counteract misreadings of the Johannine high christology, insists on the reality of Jesus' humanity, its palpable and historical quality.

The letters of Paul stress the Risen Christ present in the churches, so much so that they pay virtually no heed to the historical Jesus. The Spirit of Jesus given through the Resurrection is the inmost soul of the

Christian community. In the famous hymn of Philippians 2:5–11, Paul stresses the emptying or humiliation that Jesus accepted to work human beings' salvation. In the eighth chapter of Romans he stresses the unshakable confidence that the Spirit of Christ, groaning in the believer's prayer, ought to inspire: nothing can separate one from God's love in Christ Jesus.

The writings of Paul's disciples, such as Colossians and Ephesians, continue the development of a pneumatic christology. Colossians is famous for 1:15–20, which seems to teach a preexistence of Christ and a structural involvement in creation. Christ is the pleroma of God, the fullness that brought the reconciliation of human beings to their loving Maker. The background of speculation such as this seems to be the Wisdom theology of contemporary Jewish reflection. The Resurrection of Jesus showed that he belonged to the sphere of God, much as Wisdom had played before God at the foundations of the world. Ephesians, which lays more stress on Christ's fullness in the Church, is somewhat less physical in its christology, but its viewpoint, too, stretches out cosmically. Thus the love of God that the author prays for his readers is the height and breadth and length and depth of the divine reality.

With Hebrews we entered the different thought-world of Jewish speculation on priesthood. The author is concerned to display how Jesus is the great high priest—superior to Abraham, Levi, and all the Jewish rest—whose sacrifice has opened the holy of holies: atoned for sin and made possible great intimacy with God. Jesus comes in the line of Melchizedek, kingly priest of Salem, who blessed Abraham and received tithes from him. Jesus fulfills this Old Testament type, and he is a high priest fully united with his fellow human beings, tested and suffering as they are. From Hebrews Christians got much of their notion of the new sacrifice that Jesus had accomplished for the forgiveness of sins.

Revelation, a Christian apocalypse, has a wealth of titles for Jesus, most of them right from the Hebrew Bible. The glory or dazzling splendor of the resurrected Christ absorbs the author from the opening page. In the letters to the seven churches, Jesus is the possessor of all the powers requisite for salvation, the one able to reward with heaven or punish with remission back to the realm of Satan. The heavenly drama that occupies the main body of Revelation adds two further christological dimensions. Jesus the Lamb is the recipient of heavenly worship, and Jesus the Word of God will ride out to avenge God's suffering servants. Revelation ends with the prayer for Jesus' return that captures the book's tense mood: "Maranatha!"

The Pastorals stress that Jesus is the Savior who appeared to manifest God's goodness and who will return to manifest it more fully still. The expected goal of the exhortations in the Pastorals is fidelity to the promises that God has given in the death and Resurrection of Christ; one achieves this fidelity through clinging to solid, traditional doctrine and sound morals. First Peter offers the suffering Christ as the example that beleaguered Christians should keep in mind, and it emphasizes the high price paid for their salvation.

STUDY QUESTIONS

1. Why does Mark so greatly stress that Jesus was a suffering Messiah?
2. What sort of a prophet does Q show Jesus to have been?
3. What is the place of miracles in Matthew's christology?
4. How does Luke schematize history around the Christ event?
5. What is the balance in the Johannine christology between divinity and humanity?
6. Why does Paul pay so little attention to the historical Jesus?
7. In what sense does Colossians offer a "cosmic" christology?
8. How does Hebrews use Melchizedek as a type of Christ?
9. Why should the Lamb of Revelation receive glorious worship?
10. What is the epiphany of Christ that is so important to the Pastorals?

NOTES

[1] Pheme Perkins, *Reading the New Testament: An Introduction.* Ramsey, NJ: Paulist, 1978, p. 201.

[2] Norman Perrin and Dennis C. Duling, *The New Testament: An Introduction*, 2d ed. New York: Harcourt, Brace, Jovanovich, 1982, p. 100.

[3] See Edward Schillebeeckx, *Jesus.* New York: Seabury, 1979, p. 540.

[4] Howard Clark Kee, *Understanding the New Testament*, 4th ed. Englewood Cliffs, NJ: Prentice-Hall, 1983, p. 133.

[5] For a full discussion of all the infancy narratives, see Raymond E. Brown, *The Birth of the Messiah.* Garden City, NY: Doubleday, 1977.

[6] See Perrin and Duling, *The New Testament: An Introduction*, pp. 100–103.

[7] See Joseph A. Fitzmyer, *The Gospel According to Luke I–IX*, 2d ed. Garden City, NY: Doubleday, 1983, p. 134.

[8] Ibid., p. 192.

[9] See Raymond E. Brown, *The Community of the Beloved Disciple.* New York: Paulist, 1979, pp. 166–167.

[10] Raymond E. Brown, *The Epistles of John.* Garden City, NY: Doubleday, 1982, pp. 73–74.

[11] See Schillebeeckx, *Jesus*, p. 570.

[12] James D. G. Dunn, *Unity and Diversity in the New Testament: An Inquiry into the Character of Earliest Christianity.* Philadelphia: Westminster, 1977, p. 214.

[13] Lucas Grollenberg, *Paul.* Philadelphia: Westminster, 1978, pp. 173–174.

[14] Joseph Burgess, "Colossians," in *Ephesians, Colossians, 2 Thessalonians, the Pastoral Epistles,* ed. Gerhard Krodel. Philadelphia: Fortress, 1978, p. 53.

[15] William Barclay, *The Letters to the Philippians, Colossians, and Thessalonians,* rev. ed. Philadelphia: Westminster, 1975, p. 120.

[16] Reginald H. Fuller, "Hebrews," in *Hebrews, James, 1 and 2 Peter, Jude, Revelation,* ed. Gerhard Krodel. Philadelphia: Fortress, 1977, pp. 8, 10.

[17] See Adela Yarbro Collins, *Crisis and Catharsis: The Power of the Apocalypse.* Philadelphia: Westminster, 1984.

[18] See Reginald H. Fuller, "The Pastorals," in *Ephesians, Colossians, 2 Thessalonians, the Pastoral Epistles,* ed. Gerhard Krodel, pp. 97–121.

[19] See Gerhard Krodel, "First Peter," in *Hebrews, James, 1 and 2 Peter, Jude, Revelation,* ed. Gerhard Krodel, pp. 50–80.

3

The Jesus of
Postbiblical Theology

The Apostolic Fathers

As should be clear from the last chapter, the New Testament bequeathed a wealth of christologies to later Christian history. In the earliest period of this history, which we now take up, the different Christian churches did their reflecting on Jesus with a strong sense of being linked to the apostles who had actually seen Jesus and been instrumental in the founding of many churches. Such important apostolic fathers as Clement of Rome, Ignatius of Antioch, Hermas, Polycarp, and the authors of such influential early writings as the Didache, the Epistle to Diognetus, and the Epistle of Barnabas were pastors trying to develop what Christian faith ought to mean in the second century C.E.

Clement of Rome, writing to the Corinthians to try to restore order in their community, mainly moralizes about Christ. The Corinthians, in their prideful disputes, are out of step with their humble master: "Christ belongs to the lowly of heart, and not to those who would exalt themselves over His flock. The coming of our Lord Jesus Christ, the Sceptre of God's Majesty, was in no pomp of pride and haughtiness—as it could so well have been—but in self-abasement, even as the Holy Ghost had declared of Him, saying, 'Lord, who has believed what we have heard, and to whom has the Divine arm been revealed?'"[1] Clement does reaffirm the reality of Christ's Resurrection, but with nothing like the depth of penetration that Paul had offered the Corinthians in 1 Corinthians 15.

Speaking of the apostolic fathers as a whole, but singling out Ignatius of Antioch for special consideration, G. W. H. Lampe says: "The beginnings of Christology in these writers are still rudimentary. Ignatius merely sets the divine and human aspects of the person of Christ alongside each other, in terms which recall the foreshadowing of the later doctrine of the two natures in the opening words of St. Paul's Epistle to the Romans. Christ is 'one physician, of flesh and of spirit, generate and ingenerate, God in man, true life in death, Son of Mary and Son of God, first passible and then impassible, Jesus Christ our Lord.' According to the flesh, he was of the seed of David, but he is both Son of man and Son of God. The contrast between 'flesh' and 'spirit,' which we shall notice more fully in later writings, is virtually synonymous with a contrast between 'humanity' and 'deity.' Thus Ignatius says that the risen Christ ate and drank with his disciples as one of them in the flesh, though in the spirit he was united with the Father. So far as the deity of Christ is concerned, Ignatius insists on his personal pre-existence, and in the Johannine manner, on his continuous existence with the Father: 'Christ, who came forth from one Father and is with one, departed to one.'"[2]

Hermas, to whom is attributed a work entitled "The Shepherd," has a rather apocalyptic outlook and stresses ethics rather than speculative matters. Indeed, the main significance of Hermas lies in his views of repentance, which now figure in historical studies of the origin of the sacrament of **penance.** Concerning christology proper, Hermas seems confused about the relations between the Son or Word and the Holy Spirit, often identifying the two (or taking the Holy Spirit to be the divine principle in the incarnate Christ). This suggests a strongly pneumatic experience of Jesus the Risen Lord and the likely influence of speculation shaped by the Wisdom literature of the Hebrew Bible.

Polycarp, bishop of Smyrna in Asia Minor, does not develop a systematic christology, but he does write to the Philippians phrases reminiscent of 1 John. These are to the effect that anyone who denies that Jesus has come in the flesh is speaking like the Antichrist, denying the evidence of the cross and speaking filth from the gutter. For Polycarp, Jesus is the hope and pledge of the believer's righteousness. Because of Jesus' patient endurance, those who cling to him can gain true life. Thus, somewhat like 1 Peter, Polycarp's epistle urges Christians to endure their sufferings by looking to the model of Jesus.

The Didache or "Teaching of the Twelve" is an early Christian moral treatise that was long lost. Only in 1883 did the publication of the text, which had been found in a book (itself originally published in 1056) in a library in Constantinople, bring the Didache into the consciousness of scholars of early Christianity. The text, which probably is a compilation of short writings from several hands, tells us something about the moral tone of Christian life in either Syria or Egypt toward the end of the first century. Reminiscent of Deuteronomy 30:15–30, it speaks of two "ways," of life and of death, and tries to shepherd Christians onto the way of life. The Didache gives us a precious glimpse of early Christian worship, and thereby an insight into the eucharistic understanding of Christ that had developed by 100 C.E. or so: "In regard to the Eucharist— you shall give thanks thus: First, in regard to the cup: We give you thanks, our Father, for the holy vine of David your son, which you have made known to us through Jesus your Son. Glory be to you forever. In regard to the broken bread: We give you thanks, our Father, for the life and knowledge which you have made known to us through Jesus your Son. Glory be to you forever. As this broken bread was scattered on the mountains, but brought together was made one, so gather your Church from the ends of the earth into your kingdom. For yours is the glory and the power through Jesus Christ forever. Let no one eat or drink of the Eucharist with you except those who have been baptized in the name of the Lord; for it was in reference to this that the Lord said, 'Do not give that which is holy to dogs.'"[3]

The Epistle to Diognetus, which is an **apologia** for Christianity that argues its superiority to paganism and Judaism, has two central sections that bear on christology. The first makes Jesus Christ the revelation of divine truth that God sent down from heaven for the instruction of human beings. For the author, the remarkable thing about this revelation is its mode: not in power and might, but through humility and likeness to human beings, God sought to persuade (rather than compel) humanity to embrace the truth. The second section stresses the ordinary or non-magical character of God's revelation in Christ, emphasizing that the only access to such truth is by faith. God (the Father) has been remarkably long-suffering with humanity, and he even gave his Son as a ransom for sinful humanity (the holy for the wicked, the just for the unjust). To the author, this gift of the Son shows God's surpassing tenderness and mercy.

The Epistle of Barnabas, from about the same period as the Epistle to Diognetus (125–130 C.E.), is mainly interested in showing how Christ fulfilled Old Testament prophecies. Indeed, it is a full example of the typological **exegesis** we saw in Hebrews. Barnabas sees Christ as the Son of God who became manifest in the flesh to communicate God's revelation. Just as human beings cannot gaze directly at the blazing sun, so they cannot contemplate the naked divinity of God. By manifesting the divine truth in human terms, Jesus Christ accommodated to human weakness. Barnabas often has peculiar interpretations of Old Testament texts; for example, he makes Genesis 1 : 26 ("Then God said, 'Let us make man in our image, after our likeness.'") the speech of the Father to the Son. This of course implies an existence for the Son prior to creation. Barnabas also stresses the sufferings of Christ for the salvation of sinners.

The Apologists

The beginnings of speculative christology lie with the later second-century writers known as the apologists, who labored to make the case that Christianity was not only a decent religion but also the fulfillment of the best aspirations of its competitors. It was necessary to defend the decency of Christianity because some opponents were charging that one could not be a good Roman citizen and belong to the Christian religion. Two main arguments lay behind this charge. The first was that Christians could not worship the emperor and so be loyal subjects. The second was that Christians engaged in licentious rites. The apologists countered the first charge with a distinction: Christians could not proclaim the emperor divine, in the strict sense, but their faith urged them to be obedient and loyal to the **secular** authorities. Romans 13, which had shown the divine origin of the authority of the state, was a useful text in this regard. The apologists countered the charge of licentiousness by explaining such rites as the Eucharist and by making plain the high moral demands of their faith. If opponents thought that the Eucharist was a cannibalistic practice, involving a literal drinking of blood or eating of flesh, they obviously had been misinformed. If they thought that Christians practiced fornication or other immoral acts they knew nothing of the commandments and moral codes to which believers bound themselves.

Jesus certainly figured as a model and reference point in these discussions, but the weightier christological contributions of the apologists lie in the second area of their work, the effort to display Christianity as the fulfillment of the best aspirations of its competitor religions. These latter fell into two groups. By themselves in the first group were the varieties of Judaism that continued a vigorous life in the middle of the second century C.E. To the apologists these comprised a single religion, but we should remember that Judaism before, during, and after Jesus' time was never a monolith. Basically, the apologists argued that Christianity represented the truest Judaism. For them, Jesus fulfilled Old Testament prophecy. He was the true Jewish Messiah, and he brought to a new plane the revelation that God had made to the Jews. In trying to make this case, the apologists developed typological and **allegorical** interpretations of Old Testament prophecy, reading back from the Christ event. Thus the **servant songs** of Isaiah became prophetic predictions of Jesus' passion. The old covenants that God had made with Abraham, Noah, and Moses were taken as prefigurings of the new covenant established in the flesh of Christ.

To the pagan Gentiles the apologists argued that Christianity was implicit from the beginning of God's creation, and that the teaching of Jesus fulfilled the philosophical aspirations of such noble Greeks as Plato. The Christian doctrine of God, they said, squares perfectly with the testimony of nature. The order of nature points to a source or Creator both intelligent and benevolent. The regularity of nature, the lawful character it seems to exhibit (which the **Stoics** especially prized), implies a heavenly lawgiver. Christianity also teaches all of this, the apologists emphasized. Thus Romans 1:20 had insisted: "Ever since the creation of the world his invisible nature, namely, his eternal power and deity, has been clearly perceived in the things that have been made. So they [the ungodly who suppress the truth about the Creator] are without excuse."

The christological development for which Justin Martyr (about 100–165), perhaps the most important of the early apologists, is famous concerns the Logos. According to Justin it was the Logos, the divine Word, that spoke through both the Old Testament prophets and the best pagan philosophers. Jesus Christ, this Logos incarnate, therefore prepared for his coming by inspiring prefigurings of his teaching. Furthermore, the pagans, who did not enjoy the divine revelation recorded in the Old Testament, had a share in Christ the Logos through their human reason. It was this reason that the Stoics found in the laws of nature and that the pagan moralists stressed. To become mature and noble, they said, one has only to discipline oneself to follow the dictates of reason. So, for example, Marcus Aurelius (121–180) and Epictetus (about 55–135), two leading Stoic philosophers, worked out a bleak but elevated ethics derived from a rational analysis of human nature.

For Justin Martyr there is no reason or human virtue apart from the Logos that became incarnate in Christ. Alternately, all human beings who share in reason and follow its guidance of conscience may be correlated with Christ the Logos, even if by some standards they might be called atheists. (Justin sounds quite modern at this point, for such contemporary Christian theologians as the Roman Catholic Karl Rahner and the Protestant Paul Tillich have made similar analyses.) Summarily, Justin argued that there is a "seminal Logos" at work in all people to help them receive God's communication and understand something of the divinity.

In their focus on the Creator implied by nature and on Christ as the Logos, apologists such as Justin Martyr and Aristides of Athens, both of whom flourished in the middle of the second century c.e., worked hard to blend the traditions of the Old Testament with the concepts of contemporary Greek philosophy. They stressed the unchanging character of the one true God, and the mediation of this God's self-revelation through

Jesus. The prologue to John's Gospel (1:1–18) furnished them with elements of a Logos doctrine, speaking of a presence of the Word to God before creation. Such verses from the Psalms as 33:6 ("By the word of the Lord the heavens were made, and all their host by the breath of his mouth.") became proof-texts to buttress the teaching that Jesus was immanent in all of creation.

Like the apostolic fathers, the apologists never got fully clear the relation between Jesus as the Logos or Son and the Holy Spirit. Theophilus of Antioch, writing toward the end of the second century (and tending to praise Old Testament religion in contrast to paganism), was the first to use the term *Trinity* for the Christian godhead. For him the three aspects or names of the Christian godhead are Father, Logos, and Wisdom. (The influence of the Book of Wisdom from the Jewish Bible is apparent.) In actual practice, the apologists tended to meld Logos and Wisdom, Son and Spirit, in that they might take either as the inspiration of the prophets or the cause of the best ideas of the pagan philosophers. Finally, by comparison with both the writings of the New Testament and the emphases of later patristic thought, the apologists placed little stress on Christ's redemptive work. They typologized the cross and repeated stock phrases about Jesus' sufferings, but they didn't probe redemption very deeply. Their main task, as they saw it, was to make Jesus the fulfillment of both Judaism and Hellenistic philosophy.

The Ante-Nicene Fathers

The line between the apologists who first took up the work of making the case for Christianity against Judaism and paganism and the "Fathers" who dominated the next three centuries is not clear. Usually, the Fathers are credited with developing Christian theology in general and christology in particular considerably beyond what either the New Testament or their predecessors (both the apostolic writers and the apologists) had achieved. In many ways the Fathers continued to do apologetic work. For example, Origen and Augustine, the two towering intellects, both defended Christianity against pagan writers' attacks. But the deeper currents of their work involved thinking through what Christ ought to mean in the light of Hellenistic culture. They were concerned, in other words, with understanding: probing the Christian mysteries more deeply, getting a better appreciation of God's plan of salvation. Most of their motivation in this concern was pastoral: how better to preach, teach, and defend Christian faith. But they were driven as well by the less applied, "purer" desire to satisfy their intellectual curiosity, to enlighten their own minds and hearts.

Irenaeus, bishop of Lyons, who worked at the end of the second century C.E., is the first of the Fathers who flourished before the Council of

Nicaea. He is most famous for his defense of Christianity against the Gnostics, who posed a considerable threat to traditional faith. By and large the Gnostics depreciated the Incarnation of the Word and offered alternative schemes of redemption. Irenaeus did not so much propose Christianity as a superior sort of knowledge (as Clement of Alexandria later chose to do) as reassert the traditional elements of the bishopric, the Scriptures, the sacraments, and the creeds that stressed both the sole divinity of God (strict monotheism) and the absolute centrality of the incarnate Word to God's plan of redemption. Jesus Christ was the only revelation and redemption that Irenaeus would accredit. Irenaeus stressed the full humanity of Christ, developing a doctrine of "recapitulation" according to which Jesus Christ gathered up or summarized all of human evolution or development. Indeed, Irenaeus spoke of Christ as the recapitulation of Adam: a full gathering up of all the human potential that had existed from the creation of the race, in order to return it to God.

Irenaeus strode a middle ground between the Eastern and Western wings of Christianity. More firmly planted in the East was Clement of Alexandria, the first major figure of that most important early Christian theological center. Clement, too, labored at the end of the second century C.E. He was a convert from paganism, well educated in the Greek tradition, and he became the head of the very influential catechetical school developed at Alexandria.

In the early years of the third century Clement composed several works that in effect laid out a Christian gnosis or wisdom. He stressed how the divine Logos functioned in the conversion, moral transformation, and progress in divine truth that God had made available through Jesus Christ. Clement was quite successful in bridging the gaps between pagan culture and Christian faith, so that cultured Greeks no longer had to look down on Christian faith as something only for the illiterate or crude. Plato was Clement's hero among the Greeks, but in some places Clement maintained that most of what the Greeks developed they stole from Moses and the Jews. Nonetheless, Clement thought it possible for the Christian to be a genuine Gnostic (different from the heretics who denied the goodness of material creation, but like them in claiming a knowledge of salvation). Jesus is the source of the light of saving knowledge, but Clement does not lay great stress on Jesus' humanity. It is the Logos that most matters. Finally, we find in Clement some of the skepticism about how deeply human intelligence can penetrate the divine mysteries that later became a full-fledged "negative theology" (one in which what human beings don't or can't know about God is at least as important as what they can know).

Origen (about 185–254 C.E.) succeeded Clement as the leading figure in Alexandria. He had a somewhat troubled church life, often being on the outs with his bishop, and later he worked more in Caesaria than in

Alexandria. He is best known for his voluminous scriptural commentaries, in which he developed the allegorical method to new heights. One of Origen's principal convictions was that Christians came in two categories: the simple, who had to be satisfied with faith in Christ crucified, and the more advanced, who could ascend to the contemplation of the Word that dwells with the Father. In stressing the latter sort of Christianity, Origen both drew upon Greek philosophical convictions (according to which **theoria** was the highest human activity) and inevitably deepened the Alexandrine speculation about the Logos that Clement had initiated.

Some of Origen's speculations have led to the suspicion that he was less than fully orthodox. He has been accused of subordinating the Son to the Father, and so paving the way for the Arian heresy. Some of his writings seem to teach the eternity of creation and the finitude of God, and he is famous for teaching that in the end God will save all creatures from hell, including the devil. Nonetheless, many of Origen's scriptural exegeses were brilliant feats of imagination, and his reflections on the relations between the Logos and the Father prefigured later trinitarian theology.

With Irenaeus, Tertullian (about 160–220 C.E.) was a leading force in the development of Western patristic theology. He was from Carthage, in Africa, and was the first major Christian theologian to write not in Greek but in Latin. Eventually Tertullian became a Montanist, joining a group more ascetical or puritanical than what orthodox Christianity could approve. Even in his catholic (orthodox) works, however, he displays a rigorist temperament, being quite severe in his stress on legal rectitude.

Some of Tertullian's writings are more apologetic than doctrinal, in that one of his early concerns was the defense of Christians against punishment by the Roman authorities (who sometimes considered them at least potentially seditious). In other works directed against those whom he considered heretics, Tertullian argued that the Church, through its official leaders, is the authoritative interpreter of Scripture (and so can pass judgment on deviant, innovative, or otherwise unorthodox explanations of traditional faith). In his more precisely christological writings, such as "On the Flesh of Christ" and "The Resurrection of the Flesh," Tertullian was at pains to oppose the Docetists, who were denying or making light of Jesus' true and full humanity. Despite this support for Christ's full humanity, Tertullian's ascetical writings and treatises on penance greatly downplayed the rights of the flesh. Thus he spoke of marriage as a sort of legitimated debauchery and taught that monogamy means that if one's spouse dies one cannot remarry. However, against the heretic Marcion, Tertullian argued that material creation is good (there is no dualism of good and evil fighting it out to determine the nature of creation), and he buttressed this conviction with references to both the

Incarnation, by which divinity itself took flesh, and the sacramental practices of the Church, which employ material elements to communicate divine grace.

Against those who seemed to teach the Incarnation of the Father, Tertullian made it plain that the unity of God must not lead to this conclusion. The Son of the Father alone became incarnate. Tertullian places the Logos within the eternal aloneness or self-sufficiency of God. The "economy" of creation and salvation stems from God's choice to speak the Word forth, a speaking (*sermo*) that was in effect the generation of the Son. Like many of the other Ante-Nicene fathers, Tertullian seems instinctively to subordinate the Son to the Father. This is not so much a literal denial that the Son and the Father are equal as the effect of stressing the unity or "monarchy" of God and attributing such unity to the prime **hypostasis,** which is the Father. Instinctively, therefore, the Son/Word and the Spirit seemed somewhat derivative. Later orthodox trinitarian theology fought this tendency, but it shows the strong hold that monotheism (both that of the Jewish Scriptures and that of the Hellenistic philosophers who taught the oneness of the ultimate principle) had on early Christian speculation.

These Ante-Nicene fathers, and others that we have no space to discuss, did much of their work under the pressure of what they considered deviant, heretical interpretations of catholic (universal) Christian faith. Much of their work, in other words, was apologetic or **polemical.** This meant that some of the terms of their discussions were set by others: people interpreting the Scriptures in what seemed to them untraditional ways; people putting forward Gnostic schemes that seemed to threaten genuine salvation, or to depreciate the importance of the redemption accomplished in Jesus Christ, or to question the goodness of creation. So began the balancing act that orthodox theology has come to consider a major responsibility. The Ante-Nicene fathers we have treated all felt the burden to balance both past tradition and current culture, both Christ's divinity and Christ's humanity, both the oneness of God and the richness of the trinitarian community, both human sinfulness and divine grace. The measures in which they apportioned these several elements varied, and the balance was never exactly the same from one Father to the next. But running through the orthodox line that led up to the Council of Nicaea was a very strong sense of the need for balance and fullness, and at the basis of this conviction lay the Jesus Christ who was both man and God.

Arius and Athanasius

Despite the general agreement that a twofoldness in Jesus Christ grounded an orthodox attitude of both/and rather than either/or, serious problems arose about the relation of Christ to God the Father. The proposal of Arius of Antioch that Christ as the Logos was like to the Father but not of the same rank, and the arguments of Athanasius of Alexandria countering this view, set much of the agenda for the **ecumenical** Council of Nicaea (325 C.E.) that issued the interpretation of christological faith that became the benchmark for orthodoxy in later generations.

Jaroslav Pelikan, a leading American historian of dogma, has described the center of the Arian position as follows: "No action of God, neither the creation of the world nor the generation of the Logos, could be interpreted in such a way as to support the notion that 'the Father had deprived himself of what he possesses in an ungenerated way within himself, for he is the source of everything.' God was 'the monad and the principle of creation of all things,' and he did not share this with anyone, not even with the Logos."[4]

From this resolute stress on the transcendence of the divine (Father), the Arians moved to deny that one could call Christ divine without sizable qualifications. Two scriptural passages that they regularly employed were Deuteronomy 6:4 ("Hear, O Israel: The Lord our God is one Lord.") and Proverbs 8:22–31, where Wisdom is said to have been created, for the sake of God's other works, before the creation of the earth. Identifying Christ with the divine Wisdom, the Arians said that both as Logos and Son of God Christ was a created being. As one of their more famous phrases put it, "there was a then when he did not exist." Christ therefore became (merely) a unique, most exalted creature—the first and foremost of God's works. In him was solved the problem of the "unendurable absoluteness" of the unoriginated Father, for he could mediate between divinity and the rest of creation. Both cosmologically and soteriologically (in both creation and salvation), Christ was the bridge. He could not be this mediator or bridge, the Arians said, especially for salvation, if he were strictly divine and so immutable, impassible (unable to suffer), and the other things that one must predicate of God. He would not have been able to become human, suffer on the cross, and the like. He could be worshiped, be thanked, and be part of the baptismal formula, but to call the Logos strictly divine was to blaspheme.

In response, Athanasius and the others whom he led in opposing Arius pressed forward a different interpretation of the traditional faith and verbal usage regarding Christ. To their mind the traditional faith forthrightly asserted that Christ was God. Precisely what this had meant was the point of the controversy, since the Arians were quite comfortable using such titles as Son of God. The Council of Nicaea, called to try to silence the preachers and teachers who were presenting the Arian position, stressed that Christ could not be called a creature. The Arians were not mentioned by name, but there could be no doubt that the creed issued at Nicaea was aimed at them.

The key word in the position of those who opposed Arius was *homoousios*, meaning "of the same substance." In applying it to Christ, the Logos incarnate, Nicaea meant to deny any difference between the divineness of the Father and the divineness of the Son (except for their being, respectively, Father or unoriginated originator and Son or originated). The Son was the "only begotten" of the Father, and this begetting was not a creation but an expression of the single divine substance.

There were several background factors at work in this declaration of the *homoousia* of the Logos with the Father, and more than several historical consequences. Prominent among the background factors was the Church's now somewhat lengthy experience of controversy with pagans, which had made Church leaders come to stress that God had created the world from nothingness. To safeguard the purity of God, the (orthodox) Church had realized, one must deny that creation in any way came about from something preexistent or standing alongside God. Creation had to be from nothingness, by the sheer choice of God to diffuse or communicate an existence that God alone independently possessed. A second background factor was the conviction that had arisen that salvation— liberation from sin and entry into divine life—could be accomplished only by God. Putting these two background pressures together, Nicaea fought hard for the strict divinity of the Logos. If the Logos were not on the heavenly side—the strictly divine side—of the divide between the Creator and all creatures, then the Logos, like everything else less than God, would continually be slipping back toward nothingness. Equally, if the Logos were not fully divine, he could not have worked human beings' liberation from sin and their entry into divine life. Athanasius coined the maxim that condensed much of the Eastern orthodox tradition defended at Nicaea: the Logos had become human so that human beings might become divine. The implication was that anything less than a full humanity and full divinity in the Logos incarnate would be neither the faith originally handed down nor the reality necessary for salvation.

Nonetheless, the historical consequence of this Nicene declaration, when taken in concert with the other conciliar definitions that followed it (up to the christological climax at Chalcedon in 451 C.E.), was such a stressing of the divinity of Christ that his humanity was placed somewhat in peril. Although this was not the intent of the orthodox party, that party's reaction against the Arian position that Christ was a creature tended to remove from orthodox piety a full appreciation of how the divine had chosen to make its definitive manifestation or revelation to human beings through the flesh of one of their own kind. A theologian such as Edward Schillebeeckx, laboring to update christology for the late twentieth century, is in many ways still working against these effects of Nicaea. In his rereading of the biblical materials and his interpretation of today's intellectual horizons, Schillebeeckx struggles above all to make the historical Jesus the crux of doctrine and faith.

What has come to be known as the Nicene Creed is actually a profession of faith from later times (perhaps 450 C.E.) that owes a debt not just to the Council of Nicaea but also to the Council of Constantinople (381 c.e.). However, it runs in the tracks of Athanasius and against the Arian christology, and so it is worth quoting at this point as a major statement of orthodox Christian faith: "I believe in one God, the Father Almighty, maker of heaven and earth, and of all things visible and invisible. And in one Lord Jesus Christ, the only-begotten Son of God. Born of the Father before all ages. God from God, Light from Light, true God from true God. Begotten not made, consubstantial with the Father: through whom all things were made. Who for us men and for our salvation came down from heaven. And was incarnate by the Holy Ghost of the Virgin Mary: and was made man. He was crucified also for us under Pontius Pilate, suffered and was buried. He rose again the third day according to the Scriptures; and ascended into heaven: and is seated at the right hand of the Father. And he will come again with glory to judge the living and the dead. And of his kingdom there will be no end. And in the Holy Ghost, the Lord and giver of life: who proceeds from the Father. Who together with the Father and the Son is adored and glorified: who spoke through the prophets. And in one, holy, catholic, and apostolic Church. I acknowledge one baptism for the remission of sins. And I look for the resurrection of the dead. And the life of the world to come. Amen."

Nestorius and Cyril

The declarations of the Council of Nicaea against Arianism did not settle the conflict, and the Council of Constantinople (381 c.e.), which also contributed to the thinking behind the creed we have just cited, was called by the Emperor Theodosius I to try again to bring religious peace to the Eastern wing of the Church. Constantinople reaffirmed the teachings of Nicaea, and it dealt as well with the views, unacceptable to the orthodox, that came to be known as **Apollinarianism.** Apollinaris, bishop of Laodicea, was a friend of Athanasius, whom he had sheltered when Athanasius was forced (by Arian opponents, after the Council of Nicaea) to flee from Alexandria. Apollinaris tried to defend Nicene christology by stressing the unity of divinity and humanity in Christ, Christ's full divinity, and a lack of moral development in Jesus Christ.

This last tenet, which Apollinaris thought a necessary consequence of Christ's divinity (God does not develop), dovetailed with Apollinaris' view that there was no human spirit in Christ. Christ had a body and a soul, but the spirit (the third feature of every human being, according to Apollinaris' **anthropology**) was lacking. Constantinople I (there were subsequent councils, II and III, held in 553 and 680) condemned this position and asserted that Christ's full humanity entailed his having a human spirit. On this point, therefore, the council clarified one of the dangers latent in the Athanasian stress on Christ's divinity. That stress ought not at all to detract from Christ's full humanity.

Between 381 and 451 c.e., when the Council of Chalcedon took place, the major event was controversy over the relation of Christ's two natures. In 431 C.E., at the third ecumenical council (Nicaea and Constantinople I were the first two), held at Ephesus, the position of Nestorius, bishop of Constantinople, was rejected. Nestorius had taken offense at the term **theotokos,** a title of the Virgin Mary. The term, meaning "God-bearer," had become traditional, supported by both eminent orthodox theologians and popular devotion to Mary. Nestorius seemed to fear that the term confused the relation of Christ's divinity and his humanity. To Nestorius' mind, Mary could be the bearer only of Christ's humanity. No human being could give birth to God.

Those who opposed Nestorius chose as their champion Cyril, head of the church at Alexandria. Part of the ensuing controversy between Nestorians and followers of Cyril fed on the rivalry between Constantinople and Alexandria, since both cities were luminaries of the Eastern wing of the Church. In addition, Cyril seems to have loved controversy, and this particular skirmish again pitted Alexandrine theology against Antiochene (Nestorius had been schooled in Antioch). Cyril's position was that the unity of the two natures in Christ made it fitting to speak of Mary's having borne the Logos. The question, then, was the relation between Christ's divine and human natures. After Cyril, and somewhat dependent on the victory of his position that there was in Christ a hypostatic (personal) union of the two natures, came the heretics known as the Monophysites, who held that there was only one genuine nature in Christ, the divine. Nestorianism may be seen as suspecting the dangers of Monophysitism in both the theotokos doctrine and Cyril's notion of the hypostatic union.

At the time of the controversy itself, things were not so clear as the books of history and theology now tend to make them. Terminology was in flux, and we really don't have the requisite sources to say with full certainty precisely what nuances Nestorius and his followers wanted to place. This is frequently the case in doctrinal history, especially with the positions that finally lose the battle. As well, there were many other skirmishes in the stretch of time between Nicaea in 325 and Chalcedon in 451, and many intrusions of the emperor and political factors. Church and State, as we call those entities today, were not separate but mutually interacting. After 313 Christianity was a tolerated religion, and then it came to be favored by the emperors (partly from the conviction that it was the truest faith, partly from the conviction that it offered the best hope for keeping their realm unified and loyal). Thus, even so apparently and utterly religious a matter as christology was thought to be fraught with (secular) political overtones. Consequently, the century and a quarter between Nicaea and Chalcedon was tumultuous and complicated, and our distillation of the christological essence is in many ways quite misleading—something of a cartoon.

Nonetheless, in the light of later history, the upshot of the passage

toward Chalcedon was the spotlighting of the question of unity and duality in Jesus Christ, as the passage toward Nicaea had been the spotlighting of the relation of the Logos (who had taken flesh) to the Father.
We can see in the list of excluded positions that Chalcedon drew up the
complexity of the contemporary christology, and we can see the way in
which the position of Cyril of Alexandria gained the most support. Excluded from approbation as professing the true, orthodox faith (and
so excluded from communion with the one, holy, catholic, apostolic
Church) were (1) "those who deny the title *Theotokos* ('God-bearer') to
the Virgin Mary, thereby implying that the Humanity of Christ is separa-
ble from His Divine Person; and (2) . . . those who confuse the Divine
and Human natures in one, and therefore hold that the Divine nature is
by this confusion passible."[5]

The target of (1) was the Nestorians. The target of (2) was the followers of Eutyches, head of a large monastery in Constantinople and a
fierce opponent of Nestorianism. Chalcedon therefore sought a middle
way, a balanced central point, between the affirmation of two natures in
Christ and the confusion or melding of the two natures. In affirming the
theotokos it was sanctioning a very traditional term and supporting the
inseparable relation or union of the two natures in Christ. In denying
that this union made the divine nature passible or able to suffer, Chalcedon was expressing the quite traditional and Greek notion that divinity would not be divinity if it could suffer, change, be finite, or exhibit any of the other qualities intrinsic to created beings.

More positively, Chalcedon asserted the teachings of several documents, such as the **synodal** letters of Cyril to Nestorius and the Eastern
Christians, and the letter of Pope Leo I (which became known as Leo's
Tome) to Flavian, the patriarch of Constantinople. These letters elaborated the position (considered the pivot of orthodox christology since
Chalcedon) that Christ had one person and two divine natures, or was
one person in two natures. The two natures were held to be united but
not confused. Their union was considered unchangeable, indivisible, and
inseparable. The one person (hypostasis) was that of the Logos. But this
"person" was not our modern Western person (center of a finite consciousness). Consequently, the council did not mean to deny to Jesus
Christ what we today would call a human personality. To do that would
have been to fly in the face of its own teaching—and the teaching of traditional Christian faith—that Jesus Christ was fully human. The question rather was where to place the unity of the God-man, and the answer
from Chalcedon (as supplied more by Cyril and Leo than by any other
theologians) was in the hypostasis or individual reality of the Logos.

In ironic fact, the Eastern and Western theological traditions had different instincts about this central christological matter, which in turn
were compounded by the differences suggested by Greek and Latin terminology. Cyril, writing and thinking in Greek, made relatively little

distinction between *person* and *nature*. Leo, writing and thinking in Latin, made relatively more. This was somewhat parallel to the two schools' differing initial instincts about the relation of unity and trinity in the Godhead itself. There the formula "three persons in one nature," which used the same terms as the Chalcedonian christological formula "one person in two natures," first brought to mind for an Easterner the threefoldness of God. By contrast, a Westerner first thought of oneness.

The Eastern Tradition

Conciliar theology, hammered out in the Eastern part of the early Church, gave Christianity a first set of dogmas: officially defined and promulgated articles of faith. The East has always held these dogmas in great reverence, so much so that the theology of the Eastern Orthodox Church has long been dominated by an effort to preserve continuity with the past—to be fully traditional. After characterizing Byzantine theology in this way, Kallistos Ware, a leading present-day Greek Orthodox theologian, goes on to summarize the main characteristics of Greek theology in the years 325–1453 (from the Council of Chalcedon to the capture of Constantinople by the Turks) under four headings.

First, from 325 to 381, the period of the first two great ecumenical councils, the focus was trinitarian theology. Christologically, therefore, the focus was on the relation of the Logos to the Father (and, to a much lesser extent, on the relation of the Logos to the Spirit). Second, from 431 to 681, the period set off by the third and sixth ecumenical councils, the focus was christological issues proper: the relation of humanity and divinity in Jesus Christ. Third, from 726 to 843, the focus was the iconoclastic controversy: what ought to be the status of the representations (icons) of Jesus, Mary, and the saints? The orthodox defended the use of holy images (ultimately, by the christological argument that the Logos had taken flesh and so sanctioned material representations of sacred things). The iconoclasts ("icon-smashers"), who often had the support of the ruling emperor, claimed that reverencing the icons was idolatry. Fourth, from 858 to 1453 two trends prevailed. Negatively, the Eastern and Western branches of Christendom became increasingly estranged, the major rupture being the mutual **anathemas** of 1054, in which Rome and Constantinople (the Western and Eastern centers of power), declared one another's faiths unacceptable. Christologically, the major point was the **filioque** controversy over whether the Spirit proceeds from the Father alone, as the Nicene Creed suggests, or whether the Spirit proceeds from the Father "and from the Son" (*filioque* in Latin), as Western tradition had come to teach. Positively, these were centuries in which the Eastern theologians developed a profound mystical theology to undergird the life of prayer and monastic piety. Central to this development was an understanding of Christian spiritual growth as deification. The christological implication was a richer appreciation of the communion with God that the saving work of Jesus Christ had made possible.[6]

In dealing with the christological developments of classical Eastern Orthodox theology, Jaroslav Pelikan has stressed the Eastern concern throughout with salvation. It was from their faith that salvation had occurred in Jesus Christ that the Eastern fathers worked out their understanding of what Jesus Christ had to be: "The christological abstractions of the several theories that we have been expounding were all concerned with the salvation of man through the God-man. The theory eventually affirmed as orthodox claimed to be defending salvation by a view of the God-man in which he, being fully divine and fully human and altogether one, had within himself both the universal and the particular."[7]

To cover such traditional understandings of the doctrine of the person of Christ as the *theotokos*, orthodoxy developed the notion of the "communication of properties." This meant that the unity of Christ was such that one could predicate either divine or human properties of the one "person" at the center of the God-man. As human, Christ had a set of human properties (mortality, finitude, passibility, and so on). As divine, Christ had a set of divine properties (immortality, infinity, impassibility, and so on). One could predicate either set of properties of the unified God-man, and so it was legitimate to speak of the Logos as having been born of the Virgin Mary, having suffered on the cross, and so forth. Further clarification would make it plain that such properties as birth and suffering accrued to the Logos in virtue of the Incarnation, and that had there been no Incarnation he would not have come to possess such properties. But faith's insistence on the full humanity and full divinity of Christ, combined with faith's equal insistence on the unity of the personal reality of Jesus Christ, made the doctrine of the communication of properties both necessary and inevitable. The formula of Chalcedon, as we have seen, wanted to safeguard the integrity of the two natures, so that they would not be confused or melded. Nonetheless, the power of Cyril's theology of the unity of Christ sanctioned such further elaborations as the doctrine of the communication of properties.

In the battles after Chalcedon, orthodoxy had to spell out many implications such as the communication of properties. When, for example, some proposed that Christ had only one (divine) action and one will, orthodoxy reacted negatively: the full humanity of Christ demanded that one credit him with a full human action and a full human will. The full divinity of Christ equally demanded that one credit him with a full divine action and a full divine will. The unity of divinity and humanity in Christ argued that these two actions and two wills were perfectly coordinated. But to substitute the divine action and will for a human action and will was to denature Christ, to destroy the intent of the conciliar confessions of his full humanity.

A further problem in such rather speculative battles was the question of Christ's sinlessness. The full humanity could not mean actual sin. The union of Christ's humanity with divinity seemed to render that impossible, as did the traditional confessions of faith that one found as early as such Scriptures as Hebrews (4 : 15: "yet without sin"). Relatedly, Christ could not have been ignorant as ordinary human beings are, since he was the Logos incarnate. This second point, however, posed a more formidable problem, for the Gospels, in their depiction of a fully human Christ, sometimes showed him as ignorant or emotional in ways that the Greek understanding of divinity made impossible for the Logos. Indeed, Luke 2 : 52, summarizing the development of the child Jesus after he was found in the Temple, says, "And Jesus increased in wisdom and in stature, and in favor with God and with man." Precisely what, then, did Jesus' full humanity signify about his limitations, whether intellectual or moral?

The Eastern Orthodox met this question by filling out more implications of the notion of two complete natures in Christ. He must have had two knowledges, for instance, and in the realm of human knowledge one (for example, Luke) could say that Jesus developed or grew as a normal human being would. There was nothing in the notion of human nature itself, however, that implied or demanded sin. Sin was a deficiency, not a positive attribute, and one could think of a sinless but complete human nature. Thus the traditional notion that Jesus Christ was "like us in all things save sin" did not detract from his full humanity.

Relatedly, the biblical portraits of Jesus' emotions—his anger when cleansing the Temple (Mark 11 : 15 – 19), his grief when praying in the garden (Matthew 26 : 36 – 39)—called for a distinction. He had the full range of emotions proper to a human being, except the emotions that are involved in sinful actions (hatred, excessive anger, lust, and so on). Jesus must have had a natural appetite for food and drink. He must have warmed to the affectionate response of friends such as Martha and Mary, just as he condoled with them in their grief at the death of Lazarus, their brother. But the Eastern fathers found no place in Jesus for sexual appetites or desires. To their mind, these also were not intrinsic to human nature.

Augustine and Aquinas

The Eastern developments that we have noted have set the main agenda for christology East and West, in that both East and West have considered the dogmas of the early ecumenical councils privileged expressions of faith that any orthodox, tradition-affirming subsequent theology would have to take as a benchmark and set of guidelines. Nonetheless, the Western fathers and medieval theologians pursued the task of elucidating the faith with their own distinctive accents. They were, for example, inclined to stress morality rather than **ontology,** the soteriological dimensions of Christ's work rather than the divinization so beloved in the East. The two giants of Western theology from the conciliar period to the end of the High Middle Ages (thirteenth century) were Augustine (354–430 C.E.) and Thomas Aquinas (1225–1274 C.E.). Let us therefore study their christologies, remembering that while they were the foremost Western Christian thinkers, many other theologians helped to shape the piety and sense of Christ that arose in the West.

Augustine came to Christian faith from the dualistic religion called Manicheanism, which taught that the two great principles of good and evil constantly battle for supremacy in the world. Conversion to Christ therefore seemed to Augustine a great relief from the sinful bondage in which Manicheanism had held his mind (and from the sinful bondage in which lust had held his body). His understanding of Jesus Christ frequently leapt to a great gratitude for both the illumination that, as the divine Word, Jesus cast over believers' minds, and for the rescue from Satan that Jesus' sufferings on the cross had won. In a sermon for the feast of the Ascension, for example, Augustine spoke as follows of Christ's defeat of death and Satan: "We have our Lord and Savior Jesus Christ hanging on a cross, now enthroned in heaven. He paid the price when he hung upon the cross; he gathers what he purchased when he sits enthroned in heaven. If he had not been put to death, death would not have died. The Devil was overcome by his own trophy, for the Devil rejoiced when, by seducing the first man, he cast him into death. By seducing the first man, he killed him; by killing the last Man, he lost the first from his snare."[8]

In exploring Christ's work of salvation, of course, Augustine had to ponder the implications of Christ's humanity, for it was his solidarity with human beings in humanity that enabled Christ to be the universal savior. Augustine was too much the heir of Platonic speculation on the Logos, however, not to wonder about the connection between Christ's humanity and the divine principle that caused it to be salvific. Note in the following quotation, from another sermon, the implicit "communication of properties" that Augustine puts forth: "From what he has of himself he is the Son of God; from what he has of us he is the Son of man. He has received the lesser part from us; he has given us the greater part. For he also died because he is the Son of man, not because he is the Son of God. Nevertheless the Son of God died, although he died according to the flesh and not according to the Word. . . . Therefore because he died, he died of what he had of us; because we live, we live from what we have of him."[9]

The rhetorical brilliance with which Augustine played out the unity and duality behind the God-man's works set a high standard for later Western christology. At times when Arianism threatened true faith,

Western orthodoxy stressed the divinity of Jesus Christ, making sure that its worship plainly exalted the Word who had become flesh for human beings' sake. When this stress on Jesus' divinity threatened to make him remote from daily religious life, movements arose to refocus piety on his humanity: his infancy with the Virgin, his sufferings on the cross. At the time of Anselm, archbishop of Canterbury (1033–1109), a medieval sense of God's honor and human beings' responsibility combined to fashion an imagery of Christ's repaying a debt that sinful human beings had contracted. Christ's death was then seen as a reparation for the offense against the divine honor that sin always entailed.

For Thomas Aquinas, the most honored of the medieval theologians, theology was a science, and one could think through the connections among the various doctrines systematically. Thus Thomas tended to incorporate his reflections on christology into his whole systematic theology. In the opinion of some historians of doctrine, this led to a less christocentric presentation of faith than what one finds in either Scripture or the patristic period: "The going forth of all things from this God and their return to him, the triune fullness of life who communicates himself and not only created realities, can be taken also as the basic conception of the whole history of salvation. In such a system, a Christology could also be incorporated which would be conceived as absolutely neutral, as soon as Christ is clearly enough considered as he in whom all things proceed from and return to God. But the question is whether in the concrete development of this system Christology does not appear too late in Thomas, as the whole Christian anthropology and the teaching on grace and Christian life have been elaborated previous to the Christology."[10]

The gist of this criticism, then, is that theology had so swollen by the time of Aquinas that its precisely Christian fulcrum was in danger of being undervalued. Could the theologians indeed know anything ultimate about the inner life of God communicated in grace apart from the concrete exemplification of this life in Jesus Christ? Could they properly discourse on the sacraments or on salvation if they were wandering away from the lens that had given vision to both Scripture and earlier theology: the specific life, teaching, death, and resurrection of Jesus Christ?

These are in part methodological questions, of more interest to professional Christian theologians than to ordinary students of christology. But in part they are germane to any historical consideration of what Jesus Christ has meant to orthodox Christian faith, because they show how even within orthodoxy one may give more or less weight to precisely christological issues. In other words, without denying any of the traditional teachings about Jesus, one might not rivet the center of theology to christology. Grace, or the Church, or the sacraments, or Scripture might instead be the actual center of one's faith or theological work. By the canons of today's Christian theologians, this latter option almost always leads to a less vigorous Christian faith than what a christocentric design would produce. We have noted, for instance, the concern of Edward Schillebeeckx to make contemporary what he takes to be the original New Testament reference of all faith to the example or person of the historical Jesus of Nazareth. Somewhat similar is the conviction of Hans Küng, in his large work *On Being a Christian,* that Jesus is the truly distinctive feature in Christianity. It is no accident that both of these scholars were brought up on the theology of Aquinas. While acknowledging a permanent debt to Aquinas' genius, both have found it necessary to try to develop theologies more clearly pivoted on Jesus Christ.[11]

Despite the less than pivotal place of explicit christology in Aquinas' system, however, it was his convictions about the Incarnation that buttressed Aquinas' realism about the natural and human worlds. Thus Josef Pieper has written: "It has been said—and rightly, it seems to me—that Thomas might never have had the courage to defend natural and visible reality, in particular man's corporeality, as an essential part of man, and would never have had the courage to draw the ultimate conclusions from this conviction, had he not thought in terms of the Incarnation of God. The Gospel of John, Thomas says, makes itself so clear on the point that the Logos 'became flesh,' in order to exclude the Manichaean opinion that the body is of evil. One who believes that the Logos of God has, in Christ, united with the bodily nature of man, cannot possibly assume at the same time that the material reality of the world is not good. And how can visible things be evil if the 'medicine of Salvation' deriving from that prototypical Sacrament is offered to man in the same visible things, *per ipsa visibilia,* when the Sacraments are performed!"[12] Thus Pieper would make Aquinas' at-home-ness in the world and sense of freedom to investigate all of reality the effect of his profoundly Christian conviction that in the Incarnation God had once and for all shown the goodness of creation.

The Reformers

After Aquinas theology, along with the Western Church in general, suffered some hard times. The leading Protestant reformers, Martin Luther and John Calvin, came after two and a half centuries of turmoil. In terms of christology, the reformers developed a faith and doctrine more historical and personal than what the **Scholastics** had bequeathed them. Luther especially advanced the equation of faith, grace, and Christ. For him, Paul's teaching that human beings are made right with God only by faith, not at all by works, was the heart of the Christian Gospel. Faith therefore was the single access to the riches of divine grace. Unless one opened one's heart to God's love, neither forgiveness nor divine life could pour in. Christ was the one in whom God had made it possible for human beings to believe and so to receive the grace that would bring them justification. Luther's Christ was much more the figure one finds in the New Testament than what tradition had developed from this initial portrait. For Luther it was only by Scripture (as well as only by faith and grace: Scripture was where one found God's Word of grace) that one gained access to God's saving plan. Inevitably, therefore, Luther and his followers developed a convergence between the Word of God found in Scripture and the Word of God that took flesh in Christ. Christ and Scripture overlapped and interwove. Scripture was the prime witness to Christ and the prime place where the believer might find Christ. Christ was the epitome of Scripture, the one whose story the Old Testament prefigured and the New Testament proclaimed as news almost too good to be believed.

A key word in Luther's christology was *imputation*. This was a notion he got from Paul, especially from Romans 4, where Paul discusses the righteousness that God imputed or "reckoned" to Abraham. The passage has been sufficiently influential in the history of Western christology, especially that of the Protestant churches, to merit quotation: "What then shall we say about Abraham, our forefather according to the flesh? For if Abraham was justified by works, he has something to boast about, but not before God. For what does scripture say? 'Abraham believed God, and it was reckoned to him as righteousness' [Genesis 15:6]. Now to one who works, his wages are not reckoned as a gift but as his due. And to one who does not work but trusts him who justified the ungodly, his faith is reckoned as righteousness. So also David pronounces a blessing upon the man to whom God reckons righteousness apart from works: 'Blessed are those whose iniquities are forgiven, and those whose sins are covered; blessed is the man against whom the Lord will not reckon his sin' [Psalm 32:1-2]. . . . But the words, 'it was reckoned to him' [Abraham] were not written for his sake alone, but for ours also. It will be reckoned to us who believe in him that raised from the dead Jesus our Lord, who was put to death for our trespasses and raised for our justification" (Romans 4:1-8, 23-25).

Martin Luther found in these words the key to the sort of faith he was seeking. Feeling unable to save himself, to accomplish the moral perfection that he desired, Luther saw Paul's words as a lifeline. If he could have sufficient faith, the merits of Christ would become his own. In place of the works or deeds that he could not accomplish, the works of Christ would satisfy to make him righteous before God. Abraham had served Paul as the great father figure of faith. It was not for his deeds but because he believed in God's promises that Abraham became the father of the chosen people. In a parallel manner, Luther thought, it was not by an independent righteousness that one might be able to stand before God, but through faith in the works and person of Jesus Christ.[13]

The second leading spokesman for the Protestant Reformation was

John Calvin. He agreed with Luther that Scripture ought to furnish the believer's whole security, but he elaborated a more systematic version of reformed faith. In the *Institutes*, Calvin's most important work, the design moves from God the Creator and creation to human sinfulness and the work of Christ. Book 2 begins Calvin's treatment of the work of Christ, and Book 3 treats of the ways to appropriate Christ's work. One could say, therefore, that Christ is the center of Calvin's layout of Christian faith.

The first title or function under which Christ appears is that of the mediator who can restore the righteousness that human beings have lost through sin. The Incarnation appears as the means that God chose to accomplish this. Insofar as the divine will was to restore righteousness through a life that could swallow up death, a righteousness that could overcome sin, and a Lord who could conquer the devil, the Incarnation became God's chosen means. Calvin treats passingly of the classical christology and the traditional creedal teaching about the two natures, but his main interest is soteriological. Jesus' function as the mediator of redemption is what holds his fascination. To spell out this mediation, Calvin treats of Jesus' threefold office. Jesus was anointed (made the Christ or "anointed one") to serve as prophet, priest, and king. The Church, which is Christ's Body, shares this threefold office, so one may seriously speak of the prophecy, priesthood, and kingship of Jesus' members.

The effect of all of Christ's work, for Calvin, is the atonement. Jesus Christ has reconciled human beings to the God from whom they had been estranged. By his obedience, Christ's sufferings became the means for overcoming the alienation between God and humankind. By pleasing God, Christ removed the wrath that sin had aroused. In Book 3 Calvin spells out the ways that the grace of Christ can come to Christ's followers. The union necessary for this grace was accomplished from Christ's side by the Word's taking flesh, and then by his coming to dwell with his followers in the Spirit. From the believer's side, the Spirit is the principle of union, grafting members into the Body of Christ. All of this takes place in faith, and without a faith-union with Christ in the Spirit, believers would have no share in the prophecy, priesthood, or kingship of Christ.

Calvin is not merely concerned to lay out these aspects of Christ's saving work in tidy fashion. In parts of the *Institutes* he crosses the line between detached theology and pastoral care, urging believers to imitate the Christ to whom they owe so much. For example, in 3.6.3 he discourses on the example of Christ: "The Scripture deduces its exhortation from the true source when it not only enjoins us to refer our life to God the author of it, to whom it belongs, but, after having taught us that we are degenerated from the original state in which we were created, adds that Christ, by whom we have been reconciled to God, is proposed to us as an example, whose character we should exhibit in our lives. What can be required more efficacious than this one consideration? Indeed, what can be required besides? For if the Lord has adopted us as his sons on this condition—that we exhibit in our life an imitation of Christ, the bond of our adoption—unless we addict and devote ourselves to righteousness, we not only most perfidiously revolt from our Creator but also abjure him as our Saviour."[14]

In their different ways, Luther and Calvin (and the other Protestant reformers) reset the intellectual and emotional terms of the christological discussion. Drawing somewhat on medieval fascination with Christ's sufferings (see, for example, *The Imitation of Christ*), they used biblical texts to tie Christ's sufferings to believers' justification. None of this was new, in the sense of an innovation on the previous tradition. But the mood, tone, and emphasis that the reformers achieved was certainly fresh. The believer was encouraged to feel compunction and celebrate righteousness and refer it all to Christ the Lord. Christ the Lord was the one in whom God had accomplished what sinful human beings by themselves never could have accomplished: regained intimacy with the divine, finding God to be not a condemning judge but a benevolent parent.

The Moderns

Just as the Protestant reformers were the heirs of the medieval Scholastics, bringing forward a new synthesis of Christian faith that inevitably led to new christological emphases, so the many changes in the world that we group together under the heading of "modernity" could not fail to have their impact on faith and christology. The eighteenth-century Enlightenment was probably the most important intellectual movement in the time between the Protestant Reformation and the twentieth century, because just about all the traditional christological tenets received not just criticism but criticism based on a thoroughgoing and new attitude (of depending completely on human reason and not trusting the faith of past ages).

Dennis Duling has summarized under ten headings the claims of Western Christianity that came under assault from the seventeenth century on: (1) Christianity is a revealed religion; (2) revelation is based on Scripture and interpreted in the Church; (3) Scripture and Church teach a Trinitarian God; (4) God created a good world out of nothingness; (5) Adam sinned and all human beings inherited his sin (and so now die); (6) Mary conceived and bore Jesus virginally; (7) Jesus is true God and true man, the mediator between God and the human race, and the antonement for human sins; (8) we can prove the divinity of Jesus through his miracles, above all his Resurrection; (9) Jesus will come again to pass judgment and establish his kingdom; (10) we can trust the Bible for divine revelation.[15]

The new physical sciences and philosophies, all of which took human reason and critical testing as their watchword, soon showed that these assumptions of traditional Christian faith could not be proven beyond a sizable doubt. In a radical shift away from the traditional Christian views of authority and reality that it had lived by for seventeen hundred years, the West pivoted to a new "enlightened" point of view whose consequences we are still living out. Thus Heribert Raab has made historical claims for the eighteenth-century Enlightenment that initially seem farfetched but on reflection probably are defensible: "The Enlightenment denotes the most revolutionary of all movements which the Occident has undergone in the course of history. . . . Man and man's fulfillment are the primary concern of Enlightenment thought. The concern is, if not exclusively, at least more centrally than hitherto, with education, *cultura animi*, humanity, civilization. For this purpose supernatural revelation and grace seemed hardly necessary."[16]

To be sure, most of the West lagged far behind the Enlightenment leaders in accepting or implementing this program. But from the time of Kant, certainly, the most influential outlooks were humanistic rather than Christian, rationalistic rather than determined by faith. In this context, Jesus could no longer be what the classical dogmas had declared him to be. For the moderns who played out the theses of the Enlightenment, Jesus had to be merely human, could not be the Incarnate Word of God. There was no sin of Adam (original sin) requiring atonement. By and large faith had kept people from flexing their intellectual muscles, from moving out to conquer the world of nature and human problems.

So, faith came to seem a relic of a past benighted age, and the Christ of faith became a similar relic. At most one could study the teachings and example of the Jesus of history, perhaps concluding that he had had some remarkable insights and that he had preached an elevated morality. But any point at which he referred to a heavenly father, or spoke of being in conflict with Satan, or promised to return from heaven on clouds of majesty to consummate history, he cast himself outside the rational pale. This was mythological talk, not to be taken seriously (or at least not to be taken literally) by people advanced to the level of critical reflection. Criticism, the talent in which the Enlightenment took most pride, implied that what could not pass muster before the bar of human judgment deserved little support. Any appeal to faith, whether in the name of Jesus himself, who obviously had required faith as the condition for revealing himself or the Father, or in the name of the Church, got one patronized by the intelligentsia.

The application of critical thought to historical studies, and then to the body of Scripture itself, moved the Enlightenment into the bosom of Christian theology. This was a complex and painful process whose last chapters are yet to be written, but it divided the churches into those wanting to open themselves to the best of current scholarship and those fearing that scholarship had become the enemy of saving faith.

Kant, who wanted mainly to set religion within the limits of reason, and Hegel, who worked out a new theory of consciousness that tried to interiorize truth and one's relationship to God, both stayed on the edges of Christian church life. Hegel had the peculiar distinction of greatly shaping both Karl Marx, who mainly turned away from religion, and Sören Kierkegaard, who gave later Protestant theology a new infusion of existential vigor. In his own right, Hegel labored, however differently than past orthodox theologians, to hold together in Jesus Christ both the human and the divine. He did this by stressing the **dialectical** character of thought and the action of divinity. By the marriage of these two, what ordinary consciousness—whether Christian or purely human—cannot comprehend or accomplish can come to be: "How can what, at least in the first instance, Christian consciousness cannot hold together yet *be* held together? Only by divine action. This cannot be the life of Christ, taken by itself: Hegel rejects a liberal Christianity which, confined to the life of Christ, finds divinity at most in his teachings. These latter cannot by themselves compose the Divine and the human, nor can obedience to them redeem man from his fallen condition."[17] The divine Spirit working in Christ and the believer must accomplish the union of divinity and humanity, the work of redemption.

One might say, therefore, that despite the turn of modernity from faith to reason, many traditional motifs continued. Even when opponents were denying many of Christianity's traditional christological beliefs, those beliefs framed the discussion of what human beings might hope, how human nature ought best to be understood. Some historians of science have found parallels in modern physics. Even when scientists pronounced themselves disaffected from the Creator God who gave a Logos or intelligibility to the material world, they continued to work with convictions that in the beginning their predecessors had derived from Christian faith. Thus Stanley Jaki, commenting on the philosophy of Max Planck, one of the founders of modern physics, has written: "Planck did not seem to realize that such words [of trust in the Almighty] were logical only if God was in some mysterious way a personal God, a notion which, even in its vaguest form, was a remnant of Planck's heritage from Christian theism. He never perceived the measure of his debt to that heritage. To the end he waged a spirited crusade on behalf of a world view distinctly metaphysical and ethical, without seeing that it made logical sense only if the world was the product of a rational, personal Creator, a notion maintained by historic Christianity and from which the republic of science received crucial benefit."[18]

The interpretation of what happened to christology in modernity therefore depends somewhat on the observer. Among the common people, things no doubt continued much as they had in medieval and Reformation times: Jesus was the God-man to whom one looked for salvation. Among the intelligentsia rationalism seemed to be winning the day, and what to make of Christ in light of the various new criticisms (philosophical, historical, and later literary) was a great problem. The more that physical science unrolled the map of the universe, the less likely seemed the world view of the Bible or Christian tradition. Gradually, however, people such as Hegel, and then today's historians of ideas, realized that world views change more slowly and with more debts to the past than many moderns themselves thought. The assumption of an intelligible world, for example, owed great historical debts to the Christian views of the Creation and the Incarnation. The assumption of a perfectible human nature had a complicated relationship to the Christian notion of a salvation in principle achieved by Christ. So even when liberal theologians watered christology down to a simply human Jesus who was merely a great teacher or moral exemplar, the actual conduct of the best minds frequently still moved in Christian traces.

Recent Christology

In the nineteenth century, christology was most shaped by the application of new techniques of historical criticism to the Bible. Under analysis, the Bible turned out to be a very human and a very complicated work. If one could discern a variety of different authors and traditions, what was left of the traditional notions of **revelation** and **inspiration?** In what way could the Bible be the privileged Word of God or Christ be the unique bringer of salvation? When one joined these critical questions to the social questions that were preoccupying the industrializing nations, the result was an increased stress on a liberal or ethical Jesus. It was the justice he had preached, the social concern he could inspire, that made Christ beloved in forward-thinking Protestant churches. In the Roman Catholic and Eastern Orthodox churches change was much slower. Indeed, Roman Catholicism largely turned its back on modernist themes, taking the new criticism and secularism as a dangerous trend.

After the First World War, however, liberalism came under serious challenge. Led by the Swiss Calvinist theologian Karl Barth, European Protestant theology took a turn toward neo-orthodoxy. By this term commentators mean a new form of the traditional emphases on God's sovereignty, the depth of human sin, the absolute necessity of faith, Jesus Christ, and the Word of God. Liberalism had implied that human beings could mount up to God and revelation rather easily. For Barth and his followers, the distance between the divine and the human was chasmic, as the tatters in which Europe lay after the war silently showed.

Among the other leading figures of twentieth-century christology, Rudolf Bultmann and Paul Tillich deserve special notice. Bultmann was an outstanding New Testament scholar who looked upon Christ as the one calling human beings to a decision. To Bultmann's mind, most of the

New Testament's presentation of Jesus Christ was cast in mythological terms that modern human beings could not accredit, but a decision for or against Christ and authenticity remained a powerful evangelical challenge. Tillich was more interested in the correlation between religion and culture. For him religion was the soul of culture and Christ was the "new being" in whom humanity could see its richest potentialities. In the United States, the brothers Reinhold and H. Richard Niebuhr adapted neo-orthodox themes for an American audience, producing in the process a powerful analysis of the sinful structures that mottle so much of social life and a keen analysis of the different ways in which Christian faith has interacted with the surrounding culture.

Among Roman Catholics, perhaps the most influential christologist was Karl Rahner, who flourished in the 1960s and 1970s. Rahner had picked up much of the existential mood behind the work of Barth, Bultmann, and Tillich, but he joined this mood not with Calvinist or Lutheran instincts but with a revived interest in Thomas Aquinas. The result was a number of studies in which Rahner challenged the assumption of his fellow Catholic theologians that they knew precisely what *divinity* and *humanity* meant. Since the time of Aquinas, new studies of consciousness had made these terms more problematic.

For Rahner, the divine was much more mysterious than theologians generally seemed to assume. As Aquinas had taught, even in heaven, enjoying the **beatific vision,** human beings would find God mysterious. But to be human is precisely to be oriented toward the divine for the fulfillment of one's constitutive drives of knowing and loving. If, then, God turns out to be mysterious, always fuller than what human beings can grasp, human nature itself is untidy, open-ended, not something we can pin to the examining board like a captured butterfly.

The christological use to which Rahner put these theses was a sacramental view of Jesus Christ. For him, Jesus Christ is the best place to see what divinity is like (in human terms) and what humanity can become. Indeed, what God has done in Jesus Christ—taken a human being into absolutely fulfilling intimacy with the divine—is what God wants to do for all human beings. The communication of grace and divine life that we call the Incarnation is but the fullest version of a universal human vocation. In all times and places, therefore, the divine is present as a mystery of love and light that wants to communicate itself. Christology is the portion of theology that discloses to us what God is up to everywhere.

The recent Protestant theologians have updated the traditional Reformed stress on the Word of God, while the recent Catholic theologians who have been influenced by Karl Rahner have updated the traditional Roman stress on sacramentality. In Eastern Orthodoxy Christ has continued to be the living Lord present above all in the pneumatic divine liturgy. However, in the last decade or so all three major Christian traditions have come under challenge from liberation theology. This is a general movement, rather than the product of a particular church, and it has Latin American, African, Asian, black American, and feminist schools. Common to them all is an insistence that Jesus Christ must mean the liberation of people from personal and social oppressions. Otherwise, the Gospel cannot be good news.

The liberation christologists are in good part a response to Marxist challenges. Karl Marx, following on Hegel, said that Hegel's dialectic was correct but needed to be taken more materially and historically. It was in economics and social structures that history was working out its meaning. The liberation theologians usually reject Marxist atheism, but they accept the challenge to locate the saving energies of God in the actual lives of the poor and suffering masses.

Perhaps the fullest liberation christology that has appeared to date is *Christology at the Crossroads*, by Jon Sobrino. Toward the end of the work Sobrino summarizes his main convictions in several theses. The following provide a sampling of his outlook: "6.2. Jesus was condemned for *blasphemy*, not for heresy. Thus his conception of God was not only different from, but radically opposed to, that held by the established religion of the standing order. a. Jesus unmasked people's domination of others in the name of religion, people's manipulation of the mystery of God through merely human traditions, and the religious hypocrisy that used the mystery of God to avoid the obligations of justice. In that sense the religious leaders were correct in realizing that Jesus was preaching a God opposed to their own. b. Jesus' religious revolution had to do both with his conception of God and with his conception of the place and means that provided access to God."[19]

Summary

In tracing the Jesus of postbiblical theology, we began with the generation after the apostles. The apostolic fathers, so called because they were in direct line with the eyewitnesses of Jesus, mainly wrote pastoral reflections on Jesus. Thus Clement of Rome proposed Jesus as a model of humility to Christians bickering at Corinth. Ignatius of Antioch mentioned the twofold nature of Christ as flesh (human) and spirit (divine), but he did not develop this distinction speculatively. Hermas, mainly concerned with penance and the ethical life, probably thought of Christ in pneumatic terms influenced by the Wisdom literature of the Hebrew Bible. Polycarp of Smyrna offered Christ as a model for his people who had to endure sufferings. The Didache suggests the eucharistic sense of Christ that had arisen by the end of the first century, while the Epistle to Diognetus introduces the theme that Jesus is the great revelation of God and God's ransom for sinful humanity. The Epistle of Barnabas displays the typological exegesis of Scripture, familiar to us from Hebrews, that makes Jesus the fulfillment of Jewish prophecy.

The apologists moved beyond these rather fragmentary and diverse christological beginnings to argue for Christ's superiority to both Jewish and pagan religion. Thus they developed the typological and allegorical interpretations of the apostolic fathers, to show that Jesus and Christianity represented the purest Israelite religion. To the Stoics, who were greatly influencing pagan culture and religion, the apologists argued that Christ the Logos was the expression and fullness of natural Law (God's own Reason). Justin Martyr, perhaps the most important apologist, made Christ the Logos present in all human virtue and reason, even that of supposed atheists. The other leading apologists also were drawn to the concept of the Logos, and this led to spadework on what later became trinitarian theology. Generally speaking, however, early Christian theology did not have a clear sense of the precise relations between Jesus the Logos and the Holy Spirit.

The Ante-Nicene fathers did apologetic work, but they also pitched in with weighty reflections on the meaning of the Logos. Irenaeus of Lyons, fighting against Gnosticism, argued that Jesus Christ was absolutely central to God's plan of redemption, and that in him God had recapitulated all of human evolution. Clement of Alexandria proposed Christian faith as a gnosis superior to that of the pagans, and at the center of his scheme was a knowledge that Christians owed to the divine Logos. Origen, the greatest speculator among the early Greek fathers, wrote brilliant typological exegeses of Scripture in defense of the Logos, but at times he seemed to subordinate the Logos to the Father as though the Logos were finally created. Tertullian, an influential early Latin father, had a rigorist view of faith in which subordinationism of the Son to the Father also seemed a danger. By the end of the Ante-Nicene period, however, faith had developed a sufficient history to have prompted a catholic sense that virtue usually was a matter of both/and rather than either/or.

Arius and Athanasius summarize the complex doctrinal battles that came to central focus at the Council of Nicaea. Arius, from Antioch, essentially made the Logos the first of God's creatures. Athanasius, from Alexandria, countered that this was not traditional faith. Rather, the Logos had to be confessed to be of the same substance as the Father. The problem was to preserve an exalted sense of God's distance from creation without injuring the long-held faith that to work salvation Jesus had to be fully divine.

Nestorius and Cyril, representing the polar positions at the Council of Chalcedon, focused much of their controversy on the *theotokos*. Nestorius objected to this traditional title for the Virgin Mary, arguing that no human being could bear God. Cyril defended the title, arguing that the unity of the two natures in Christ was such that one could predicate of Jesus Christ both human and divine qualities (interchangeably). The council, aided by writings of Cyril and Pope Leo I, worked out the formula that Christ has two natures and one personhood. This somewhat paralleled the orthodox Trinitarian doctrine that God is three persons in one divine nature. In both areas, the word *person* has proved a problem, since theologians quickly realized that in the Trinity it cannot connote a finite center of consciousness, and in christology it cannot deny to Jesus a human personality.

The Eastern Orthodox tradition basically has been content to repeat and try to probe more deeply the doctrine of the first seven ecumenical councils, among which the teachings of Nicaea and Chalcedon bulk the largest. The notion of the "communication of properties" clarified some of the christological disputes, and further clarifications came through spelling out of implications of Jesus' full humanity: a human intelligence, will, soul, freedom, finitude, and the like.

In the West, Augustine and Aquinas paced the way from the fifth to the thirteenth centuries. Augustine used his great rhetorical gifts, Platonic instincts, and sense of having been freed from Manicheanism and sensuality to probe the riches of Christ's death and resurrection for human beings' salvation. Aquinas did not make christology the first or the most central part of his theological synthesis, but much in his realistic and positive view of creation and human reason ultimately depended on his incarnational faith.

The leading Protestant reformers wanted a faith and a christology more resolutely biblical than that of the medieval Scholastics. Luther found his hermeneutical key in Paul's Epistle to the Romans. The idea that human beings are justified by faith, and that (like Abraham) they may have their faith imputed or reckoned to them as righteousness, was for Luther the center of the Gospel. Calvin most stressed that Jesus is the mediator of redemption, and that Jesus' threefold office of prophet, priest, and king continues in his Body the Church.

The moderns, greatly shaped by discoveries in the physical sciences, moved away from traditional faith and relied on human reason. During the Enlightenment, which is probably the decisive modernist movement, autonomous human reason was seen as the only truly moral recourse that responsible human beings had. This attitude meant, at least for the intelligentsia, the demolition of the traditional world view, which relied greatly on revelation. Kant wanted to restrict religion to the limits of reason, while Hegel worked out a dialectical understanding of reason and the divine Spirit that made Christian faith more interior. Nonetheless, even when they were repudiating the old Christian world view, many philosophers and scientists actually assumed the intelligibility of the world, the perfectibility of human nature, and other central tenets that had been greatly shaped by Christian history.

Recent christology, bringing this long evolution of reflection about

Jesus Christ down into our present century, moved from a liberal christology, marked by a stress on the man Jesus and a critical approach to the Bible, to a neo-orthodox reassertion of the distance between God and humanity (and, consequently, of the crucial importance of God's Word). Roman Catholic christology, in the person of a theologian such as Karl Rahner, deepened its appreciation of the mysteriousness of the divine nature and came to think of Jesus in more sacramental terms. More recently, both of these emphases have somewhat given way to liberation christologies, which are insisting that Jesus has to be seen as the one who brings people freedom from the social, economic, and other oppressions that are ruining their lives.

--------------------------- STUDY QUESTIONS ---------------------------

1. What is the "holy vine of David" that the Didache says has been made known through Jesus, God's Son?

2. How can Justin Martyr argue that there is no reason or virtue apart from the Logos that became incarnate in Christ?

3. What was the importance of the humanistic interpretation of Christ inaugurated by Clement of Alexandria?

4. How did the Arians employ Proverbs 8:22–31 in their christology?

5. Explain the christological significance of the *theotokos*.

6. How does the orthodox notion of the communication of properties relate to Cyril's stress on Christ's personhood?

7. What does Augustine have in mind when he speaks of the price that Christ paid when he hung on the cross?

8. How does Luther correlate Abraham and Christ?

9. How did the Enlightenment diametrically oppose traditional christology?

10. How was the Word of God stressed by neo-orthodoxy different from the Jesus of liberal Christianity?

--------------------------- NOTES ---------------------------

[1] 1 Clement 16, in *Early Christian Fathers*, trans. Maxwell Staniforth. Baltimore: Penguin, 1968, pp. 30–31.

[2] G. W. H. Lampe, "Christian Theology in the Patristic Period," in *A History of Christian Doctrine*, ed. Hubert Cunliffe-Jones. Philadelphia: Fortress, 1980, p. 26.

³Didache, 9:1, in *The Faith of the Early Fathers*, vol. 1, ed. William A. Jurgens. Collegeville, MN: Liturgical Press, 1970, p. 3.

⁴Jaroslav Pelikan, *The Christian Tradition: A History of the Development of Doctrine*, vol. 1. Chicago: University of Chicago Press, 1971, pp. 194–195.

⁵*The Oxford Dictionary of the Christian Church*, ed. F. L. Cross. London: Oxford University Press, 1958, p. 259.

⁶See Kallistos Ware, "Christian Theology in the East," in Cunliffe-Jones, ed., *A History of Christian Doctrine*, pp. 183–185.

⁷Jaroslav Pelikan, *The Christian Tradition: A History of the Development of Doctrine*, vol. 2. Chicago: University of Chicago Press, 1974, p. 75.

⁸J. Rogers, R. MacKenzie, and L. Weeks, *Case Studies in Christ and Salvation*. Philadelphia: Westminster, 1977, p. 47.

⁹Ibid., pp. 47–48.

¹⁰Alois Grillmeier, "Christology," in *Sacramentum Mundi*, vol. 3, ed. Karl Rahner et al. New York: Herder and Herder, 1969, pp. 187–188.

¹¹See Hans Küng, *On Being a Christian*. Garden City, NY: Doubleday, 1976.

¹²Josef Pieper, *Guide to Thomas Aquinas*. New York: Mentor-Omega, 1964, p. 116.

¹³See Benjamin Drewery, "Martin Luther," in Cunliffe-Jones, ed., *A History of Christian Doctrine*, pp. 322–330.

¹⁴John Calvin, *On the Christian Faith*, ed. John T. McNeill. Indianapolis: Bobbs-Merrill, 1957, p. 69.

¹⁵See Dennis C. Duling, *Jesus Christ through History*. New York: Harcourt, Brace, Jovanovich, 1979, pp. 134–135.

¹⁶Heribert Raab, "Enlightenment," in *Sacramentum Mundi*, vol. 2, ed. Karl Rahner et al. New York: Herder and Herder, 1968, pp. 230–231.

¹⁷Emil L. Fackenheim, *The Religious Dimension in Hegel's Thought*. Boston: Beacon Press, 1967, p. 141.

¹⁸Stanley L. Jaki, *The Road of Science and the Ways to God*. Chicago: University of Chicago Press, 1978, pp. 179–180.

¹⁹Jon Sobrino, S.J., *Christology at the Crossroads*. Maryknoll, NY: Orbis, 1978, pp. 367–368.

4

Contemporary Christological Issues

Jesus versus the Church

We have spent two chapters considering the historical course of the Christian understanding of Jesus. In this chapter we turn to contemporary concerns, indicating some of the questions that present-day problems—social, natural, and personal—are posing in christology. Unfortunately, we cannot integrate these questions into a neat, wholly logical package. Perhaps they are best considered as somewhat discrete indications of the wholesale renovation that Christian theologians now suggest christology requires, if it is to prove viable in the twenty-first century.

A major issue, shaping many christological reflections both inside the Christian Church and outside, is the relationship between Jesus and the Church. Many more people admire Jesus than admire the Christian Church, and even when we provide for the ways in which such a contrast may be inevitable, a provocative gap remains. So, for example, there has been the rather bitter gibe that "Jesus preached the Kingdom of God and what arrived was the Church." The Church is considered all too human, soiled by legalism and this-worldliness. As a result, many question whether the Church can validly represent Jesus of Nazareth, whether the Christ really does abide in so ragtag an assembly. Most mainstream Christian theologians finally affirm that the Church is providential and inevitable, somehow willed and accepted by God. But many agree with outside critics that it is legitimate, even necessary, to distinguish carefully between the commitments asked by Jesus Christ and the requirements imposed by the churches.

For example, Edward Schillebeeckx, whose volumes on Jesus and the Christ are a milestone in recent christology, has spoken very critically of his own Roman Catholic church's leadership. In the following exchange with Huub Oosterhuis, a leading Dutch religious poet, Schillebeeckx makes it plain that his christological studies have freed him to analyze the Church quite bluntly.

"O. This book containing our conversations may perhaps be bought by people who no longer feel at home in the Church and who have no possibility of criticizing or accusing that power [of the leaders of the Church] that you have mentioned. The only way they may have of protesting it is just to stay away—the silent 'lapsing' that has taken place during the past thirty years or so in the Netherlands and elsewhere. And hardly anyone comes forward now as a candidate for the priesthood! But the bishops are still asking us to pray for new vocations. What do you think ought to be done about this?"

"S. On the one hand, our bishops are making it impossible for people to come forward as priests, but on the other hand we are asked to pray for priests. That is a falsification—a falsification of what prayer really is as well. Thomas Aquinas had a relevant comment to make here. In one text he said: There are certain matters in which man has such control of himself that he may act completely on his own account, even if this goes against a possible prohibition issued by the pope. In such a case, a papal commandment or prohibition must be seen as wrong. It has *ipso facto* no validity or power. Then in another text, Thomas says: It is sometimes necessary to oppose a papal commandment, even at the risk of being excommunicated. Thomas is clearly relativizing the Church's hierarchy! For him, the highest authorities are the gospel and the human conscience. If the system is functioning properly, the Church acts as a mediator between the two."[1]

The implication of this sort of exchange, which one is more apt to meet in Roman Catholic than in Protestant contexts, is that allegiance to Christ and the Gospel is less a matter of obedience to Church authorities than a matter of following one's conscience under the Spirit of Christ. Thus, one may say that much of the agenda of the sixteenth-century Protestant reformers has been accomplished, even in the Roman

Catholic church. Catholics may still feel that Christ has sanctioned a hierarchical leadership in his community, but the liberals among them protest against that hierarchy whenever it seems to be blocking out the Gospel or crushing the individual conscience. Christ then becomes a touchstone for criticizing not just secular society but also the Church. When the Church is not showing the freedom and love that are so prominent in the work of the evangelical Christ, the Church (the whole community of Jesus' followers) is to be called to account.

Generally the tactic in such a calling to account is precisely what we can see in the New Testament studies by reformers such as Elisabeth Schüssler-Fiorenza. For Schüssler-Fiorenza, the original liberation of Jesus, who opened the Kingdom of God especially to society's poor and marginalized people, was curtailed by a patriarchal impulse in the early Church. Out of either a desire to accommodate the Church to the family structures and mores of Hellenistic society, or an imperfect grasp of Jesus' Gospel, early Church leaders clamped down on the egalitarian impulse behind Jesus' evenhanded treatment of men and women, making women second-class citizens.[2]

Analogously, black churchpeople in the slaveholding American colonies and early states witnessed a twisted effort on the part of pious white Christians to evangelize slaves while keeping them in bondage. In fact, some states passed laws making it explicit that for a slave to receive Christian baptism did not give that slave legal emancipation. The awareness behind such laws, of course, was that scriptural passages such as Galatians 3:28 could be interpreted as teaching that after baptism (when one stood "in Christ") distinctions such as Jew and Gentile, male and female, slave and free person fell away. Baptism and Church membership meant a radical newness and a radical equality. But slaveholding Christians tried to have it both ways, missionizing unbaptized blacks while retaining the legal reality that slaves were not full human beings, let alone people freed by Christian baptism.

In cases such as this, the Church emerges as the enemy of Jesus, not so much by necessity as by accident. That is, the gap between Jesus and the Church comes from the failure of churchpeople to live out the standards (the love) of Jesus Christ, not from a more basic claim of the Church to carry on Jesus' work of salvation. Were the Church in the forefront of emancipation and other forms of liberation (as frequently many individual churches or groups of Christians have been), the majority of critics would not want a wedge driven between Jesus and the Church. Indeed, the doctrine that Jesus is identified with the Church as with his Body, or as a vine with its branches, would seem positive and persuasive to most Christian observers. Some few might worry about the ever-present danger of substituting something human (and therefore fallible and liable to sin) for God and God's sole Christ, but many more would

bless God for having raised up such a corps of signally human and helpful followers.

For theologians such as Albert Nolan, writing in a South African
context, the distance between Jesus and many who claim the name
Christian is clear and instructive. Because of this distance, Jesus belongs
to all people, in the measure that they are willing to embrace his demanding message: "Many millions throughout the ages have venerated
the name of Jesus, but few have understood him and fewer still have tried
to put into practice what he wanted to see done. His words have been
twisted and turned to mean everything, anything and nothing. His name
has been used and abused to justify crimes, to frighten children and to
inspire men and women to heroic foolishness. Jesus has been more frequently honored and worshipped for what he did not mean than for what
he did mean. The supreme irony is that some of the things he opposed
most strongly in the world of his time were resurrected, preached and
spread more widely throughout the world—in his name. Jesus cannot be
fully identified with that great religious phenomenon of the Western
world known as Christianity. He was much more than the founder of one
of the world's great religions. He stands above Christianity as the judge
of all it has done in his name. Nor can historical Christianity claim him
as its exclusive possession. Jesus belongs to all men."[3]

Peace

Frequently the impulse to claim Jesus for all people, denying that the
Church or Christians have exclusive rights to the veneration or interpretation of God's Christ, goes hand in hand with the sense that Jesus
has especially to be correlated with the search for peace. Indeed, a number of Christian churches, many of them associated with the left wing or
more radical side of the Protestant Reformation, are frequently referred
to as "peace churches." If not completely pacifist in their doctrine, they
at least have singled out peacemaking as one of Christianity's principal
tasks. The American Friends Service Committee, for example, makes
quite practical the commitment of the Friends, or Quakers, to breaking down walls of hostility and promoting peace in the world's most
troubled areas. At least implicitly, Jesus stands behind such work as a
model man of peace who urged his followers to respond to violence and
hatred with self-sacrificing love.

In the preface to a report on peace prospects in the Middle East, the
American Friends Service Committee bleakly notes that since its founding in 1917 there have been only two years when the committee has not
been called upon to minister to refugees driven from their homes by war.
From this nearly constant experience has come the conviction that until

the roots of war are torn out there will be little lasting peace: "More recently, the committee has gone beyond only providing immediate aid in the wake of war to try to deal with the roots of violence, which lie in injustice and the denial of human rights and the terrible poverty that afflict so many millions at home and around the world. To change these conditions is to build the foundations of peace, which must be the concern of all men and women of goodwill. In these difficult enterprises we have often known disappointment. Our workers have provided food, comforted the homeless, marched for justice, and stood beside the outcast, but they have failed to reach to the hatreds and despair that corrode the soul and alienate the human family across neighborhoods and across nations. But we have also seen miracles, where humanity and caring were reborn and compassion returned, where hatred has given way to forgiveness and where community has been rebuilt. These miracles happened because special individuals dared to live as if change was possible, and it became possible. They were competent people, able to understand difficult problems, able to find places to take hold, and able to discover what tasks needed to be done. But competency wasn't enough, it had to be undergirded with the certain faith that human beings can rise above their baser natures and respond to stimuli other than fear and threat and naked power."[4]

The authors of the report observe rather wryly that none of the parties to the turmoils in the Middle East is likely to be completely happy with their analysis and program for change. Too much suspicion and vested interest prevail for any realistic observer to expect otherwise. But the compassionate tone of the report, and its call to all parties to move to higher moral ground, make it a fine example of how Christ continues to inspire peacemaking efforts almost two thousand years after his own nonviolent death in the cause of showing people a better way to live.

Certainly a key portion of such a better way to live lay in the open community that Jesus wanted to fashion. The Kingdom of God that he preached was an invitation to people of all backgrounds and classes. At its best, the Christian community gathered in memory of Jesus has been catholic: open to all, actively trying to cross whatever lines of separation might harden into military zones. In his little book *Making Peace in the Global Village*, Robert McAfee Brown has suggested the modest way in which the followers of Christ, at their best, have brought out the global dimension of a healthy christology and ecclesiology: "Pointing to the church as a present embodiment of the global village may seem impossibly romantic. But what is being pointed to is not an organizational structure so much as something more fundamental—a network, a remnant that tangibly exists wherever two or three persons find themselves gathered together in the name of Jesus Christ. I have had the good fortune of experiencing the reality of this network a number of times in recent years, in scattered enough places to make me sure that I am not fantasizing. To me it comes clearest in liturgy, as people from extraordinarily diverse and often divisive backgrounds gather around a common table and discover, in their allegiance to the Lord who presides at that table, a unity that does indeed shatter those other realities of diversity and division."[5]

Peacemaking or reconciliation goes to the heart of christology and Church life, many present-day theologians say, since any work to remove injustice is work to tear out the roots of war, and any genuine experiences of community across lines of national, racial, sexual, or other divisions are bound to promote peace. For many, the addition of nuclear arms to the current problems of peacemaking only increases the importance of clarifying this dimension of christology. In a nuclear age, numerous Christians have started to say, Jesus must emerge as a powerful reason to reverse the arms race and overcome the conditions that have brought us to the precipice of horrible destruction.

For example, the 1983 pastoral letter of the American Catholic bishops, entitled "The Challenge of Peace," has a fairly thorough treatment of the centrality of peacemaking in the message of Jesus and the work of the Church. For the bishops, the power of God shown in Jesus' resurrection provides the key to understanding Jesus' gift of peace: "Only in light of this, the fullest demonstration of the power of God's reign, can Jesus' gift of peace—a peace which the world cannot give (Jn. 14:27)—be understood. Jesus gives that peace to his disciples, to those who had witnessed the helplessness of the crucifixion and the power of the resurrection (Jn. 20:19, 20, 26). The peace which he gives to them as he greets them as their risen Lord is the fullness of salvation. It is the reconciliation of the world and God (Rom. 5:1–2; Col. 1:20); the restoration of the unity and harmony of all creation which the Old Testament spoke of with such longing. Because the walls of hostility between God and humankind were broken down in the life and death of the true, perfect servant, union and well-being between God and the world were finally fully possible (Eph. 2:13–22; Gal. 3:28)."[6]

The Poor

Many contemporary analysts of peacemaking underscore the disparity between the standard of living in the Northern nations and the standard of living in the Southern nations. This gap is like a volatile gas, ready to explode into war. As the report of the American Friends Service Committee indicated, one cannot approach the task of peacemaking realistically without setting to work on the economic and social injustices that underlie most situations that are liable to flame into war. It was logical, therefore, that the American Catholic bishops followed their pastoral letter on making peace in a nuclear age with a letter on economic justice. Christologically, they were refusing to separate Christ the Prince of Peace from Christ the prophet insisting on social justice.

In the first draft of their letter, the bishops started to study the connection between Catholic social teaching and the economy of the United States by exploring the biblical foundations of the Christian view of economics. Section 46, which begins the detailing of New Testament foundations, explicitly likens Jesus to the prophets (who figured prominently in the bishops' treatment of Old Testament foundations): "Like the prophets, Jesus takes the side of those who are powerless or on the margin of his society such as the widow (Luke 7:11–17; Mark 12:41–44), the Samaritan (or stranger in the land, Luke 17:11–19), the sinful woman (Luke 7:36–50), and children (Mark 10:13–16). He rejects those religious practices that enable people to escape the obligation to care for their parents (Mark 7:9–13) and criticizes the Pharisees because they have neglected the more important aspects of the law: 'Justice and mercy and faith' (Matthew 22:23). He tells parables which give hope to the poor and the oppressed (Luke 14:7–23; 16:19–31; 18:1–8); and in his description of the final judgment, he says that 'all the nations' will be judged on how they treated him when he was hungry, thirsty, a stranger, naked, sick and imprisoned: 'As you did to one of the least of my brethren, you did it to me.' (Matthew 25:31–46). To turn aside from those on the margins of society, the needy and the powerless, is to turn away from Jesus, who identifies himself with them. Such people present his face to the world."[7]

Although most of the texts cited in this quotation are from the synoptic Gospels, for many liberation theologians the Pauline christological identification of Jesus with his people would leap to mind. The poor, the marginalized, the wretched of the earth somehow coincide with Jesus, somehow are part of his "Body." To neglect them is to neglect him, and to reverence or love him is to serve them. In other words, the second great commandment that Jesus preached, love of neighbor as self, folds into the first great commandment to love God. Insofar as Jesus is the icon of God, the incarnate focus for worship and love of the Father, service of Jesus' people, among whom the poor are especially prominent, will be part and parcel of worshiping God. Thus the influential Roman Catholic theologian Karl Rahner, some years before the United States bishops' pastoral letter on economics, spoke of the unity of love of God and love of neighbor.[8]

Concerning the precisely economic aspects of poverty, some New Testament commentators see in Jesus' speech at the synagogue in Galilee (Luke 14:16–30) a radical call to redistribute wealth. The text speaks of Jesus' having proclaimed "the acceptable year of the Lord." Protestant liberation theologian Robert McAfee Brown suggests that behind this somewhat bland phrase lies political and economic dynamite: "For what does 'the acceptable year of the Lord' mean? It means 'the Jubilee year.' And what does the Jubilee year mean? Leviticus 25 : 1–24 provides a full answer, and it will help us understand why tumult breaks out in the synagogue, and why the authorities in Jerusalem were after Jesus almost as soon as he had eluded the folks in Nazareth. . . . A Jubilee year is a sabbatical year on a grand scale: . . . 1. As with the regular sabbatical year, the soil is to lie fallow. 2. Debts are to be canceled. (The phrase in the Lord's Prayer 'Forgive us our debts as we forgive our debtors' is what the year of Jubilee enjoins.) Everybody gets a fresh start. The Lord's Prayer is a great Jubilee prayer. 3. Slaves are to be freed. The Jubilee injunction 'Proclaim liberty throughout the land to all its inhabitants' (Lev. 25 : 10, . . .) means exactly what it says, and the phrase 'liberty to the captives,' in both Isaiah and Luke, is an echo of the Jubilee command. . . . 4. And, speaking of the economy: Capital is to be redistributed. In Israel's agrarian economy, the Jubilee year provides that land acquired since the previous Jubilee shall revert to its former owners. Whatever inequities have accumulated in the interval will be set right in this fashion; people cannot accumulate inordinate amounts of land at the expense of others. Overriding reason: the land is not theirs but Yahweh's. 'The land shall not be sold in perpetuity,' Yahweh says, 'for the land is mine' (Lev. 25 : 23)."[9]

In this interpretation of Jesus' programmatic speech at the beginning of his public ministry, the Kingdom of God coincides with the Jubilee year. The acceptable time is a return to radical justice, because God has intervened to make a completely new beginning. Liberation christology wants to keep this desire for new beginnings alive. It wants constantly to retrieve the hope that what is now tilted and unjust can be made right— because of Christ's victory. As long as there is dreadful poverty alongside comfortable affluence, Christian analysts such as Brown say, the world will be desperate to hear of a Jubilee year and a Kingdom of new beginnings. A christology that wants to enfranchise the poor, to make the slums as significant as the wealthy suburbs, keeps in mind Jesus' identification with society's most outcast people.

The Asian Theological Conference held in Wennappuwa, Sri Lanka, in January of 1979 was one of the first Asian cooperative ventures in liberation theology. The reflections of Samuel Rayan of India on his choice to make his conference project living in the slums summarize the concrete feelings that a christological option for the poor is likely to entail. When Rayan finds himself reluctant to make the slums his project, he makes an examination of conscience: "I therefore began to ask myself what fear was lurking within me, from what possible inconvenience I was shying away, and what middle-class sensitivity was ruling my motives. In that mood my option could only be the city slums. I had never lived in any. I knew the disgust with which I had seen them and the swiftness with which I had passed them by. I knew there was compassion somewhere in my soul which yearned to be with those discarded people and to lift them out of the filth and the stench. It is the stench I cannot stand, and the filth. I am middle class, bourgeois, clerical. But I guess I care for people. I knew the anger in my heart's depths against whatever was responsible for messing up our world with slums and shacks and hunger and squalor, and women in rags and children with thin limbs and bloated bellies, and men broken under the weight of failure and hopelessness. I let this mood and its memories revive and wander freely over all the hills and valleys of my soul. For me the Asian Theological Conference had already started." [10]

Asian, African, and Latin American christologies now regularly associate following Jesus with trying to help the poor. At least implicitly, their sense that God above all wants justice, simple decency among human beings, makes them search for Christ in the suffering faces of their continents' poorest people. Otherwise, they say, the notion of salvation has little meaning in their lands. Otherwise, Jesus would not be much of a Messiah.

Ecology

On the whole, liberation theologians have been slow to see the links between ecology and the labor to alleviate the suffering of the poor. In this they have not distinguished themselves from the mainstreams of either Protestant or Catholic theology, which have considered ecology marginal to the general thrust for peace and justice. So, for example, the large collection of documents edited by Joseph Gremillion, *The Gospel of Peace and Justice: Catholic Social Teaching Since Pope John*, devotes only two and a half of its more than six hundred pages to environmental issues. [11] Apart from the school called process theology, mainstream Protestant theology has been little better. Indeed, some partisans of third-world peoples have even condemned the few calls that first-world theologians and economists have issued (for a steady-state economy that would honor the limits of nature's carrying capacity) as badly motivated.

For example, C. T. Kurien, director of the Institute for Development Studies in Madras, India, bitterly attacked a proposal for a steady-state economy made at the 1979 World Council of Churches conference "Faith, Science, and the Future" at the Massachusetts Institute of Technology: "May I submit that the 'limits-to-growth' slogan and its antidote, the 'sustainable society,' are both reflections of the anxiety of a pampered minority that its way of life is being threatened." [12] Kurien feared that ecological concerns might impede the economic development on which depend the hopes of the poor in India and other underdeveloped countries. At the end of the 1970s the average per capita monthly expenditure in rural India was about $6.63 per month, $5.00 of which went for food. Obviously the poor of India were not the great consumers whose runaway life-styles were threatening the carrying capacity of the earth. Even when one also considered the disturbing figures on India's population growth, the much greater per capita consumption of raw materials by citizens of the affluent nations put the burden of responsibility back in their court.

It is true enough, first-world Christian theologians might reply, that the industrialized nations have spearheaded the developments that have brought us to the brink of environmental crisis. The pollution of the global atmospheric, water, and land systems is mainly due to Northern and Western technology. But it is not true that one can consider the plight of the world's poor apart from their present share in the degradation of the natural environment. One single case, from the leading Latin American petrochemical center of Cubatao, Brazil, suggests why this is so.

Cubatao has about eighty thousand inhabitants. "Of every 1,000 babies born in Cubatao, 40 are dead at birth and another 40 perish within a week. This is at least eight times the infant mortality level in the United States. . . . Moreover, most of Cubatao's dead infants are manifestly deformed, and a number of infants who survive are either deformed or seriously weakened. In effect, the babies are contaminated in the womb and break down, just as a pollution monitoring machine set up in 1975 broke down in 1977 because of the intensity of contamination to which it was exposed. Before breaking down, however, the machine indicated that residents of Cubatao were showered with 1,200 particulates per cubic meter of air. That is more than twice the amount the World Health Organization has said produces 'excess mortality' after 24 hours."[13]

The first connection between contemporary christology and ecology therefore may lie in the oppression that environmental degradation inflicts especially on the poor. It is largely the poor who must live in the polluted industrial cities and work in the hazardous factories. It is largely the poor who manifest such environmentally related diseases as black and brown lung. The urban slums that lack decent housing, sanitation, air, and water do not hold the rich captive. The erosion and bad land management that contribute to the world's famines do most damage to the children of the world's poor. If liberation christology is going to highlight the identification between Jesus and the world's suffering poor, it will inevitably run into ecological problems.

A second link between christology and ecology lies in the relations between the Logos who took flesh and the natural world that is now under assault. On the whole, as the ecologically sensitive among them have admitted, Christians have been slow to see the connection between the subhuman world and the Christ to whom they sing their hymns, but a little reflection on such important texts as Colossians 1:15–20 might suggest that damage done to creation is damage done to a Christ-centered process. This is a perspective of faith, of course, not something that secular ecologists would immediately find persuasive. Still, christ-ologists are finding ample stimuli in the traditional Christian reflections on the Logos to justify their thinking about environmental problems in terms of what such problems reveal about people's attitudes toward the creative God and the incarnate Word.

"If people lay waste to the earth," a growing number of theologians are saying, "feeling no kinship with subhuman creation and no sense of stewardship for the fate of the planet's ecosystems, they have missed something central to an incarnational faith." For an incarnational faith thinks of the body and the world as its congenial milieu. In contrast to Gnostic tendencies to suspect or despise material creation, the Johan-nine literature of the New Testament went out of its way to stress that the Logos literally had taken flesh. It is not a far step to infer that this stress should lead to an appreciation of the body and the physical world.

True enough, Christians sometimes have read Genesis 1:28 (on human beings' commission to subdue the earth and have dominion over it) as a license to exploit physical creation. Today, however, it is plain that such license runs counter to the reverence for life that most christ-ologists think faith in a good Creator must promote. Less plain, perhaps, but equally fundamental, is the inference that environmental pollution affronts the God who drew near to the world in the Incarnation and made it home. For Pauline theology that world was natural as well as hu-man. All creation, Romans 8:19–22 teaches, has been in labor for re-demption. If redemption is at the heart of christology, ecology should soon come to stand by christology's side. For the world will not seem redeemed so long as it is burned by acid rain, fouled in its water supplies, gouged by land policies that pay it no reverence.

For some conservative theologians, however, nature is more to blame for our ecological problems than industrial developers are. Here we may have a case of blaming the victim and forgetting the connection between Christ and a creation in labor for redemption, but perhaps this charge will get on the agenda of future discussions between theologians and ecologists. On the chance that it might, let us cite Michael Novak's ver-sion: "Nature was raw and cruel to nature long before human beings in-tervened. It may be doubted whether human beings have ever done one-tenth of the polluting to nature that nature has done to itself. There is infinitely more methane gas—poisonous in one respect, and damaging to the environment—generated by the swamps of Florida and other parts of the United States than by all the automobile pollution of all places on this planet. In our superhuman efforts to be nice and to feel guilty, we try to take all the credit for pollution, improperly."[14] Whether christology becomes a help with environmental problems or a hindrance therefore remains to be seen.

Universal Salvation

In the eyes of a growing number of Christian theologians who have studied the non-Christian religions, the same Logos who raises hopes for the redemption of all creation raises hopes for the salvation of all human beings. Although Jesus himself mainly was concerned with his own Jewish people, by the time Pauline theology had developed, christology was reaching out to all people, Gentiles as much as Jews. This missionary interpretation of Jesus Christ no doubt accounted for much of Christianity's early growth. The central conviction of the New Testament is that in Jesus Christ definitive salvation had appeared. If this salvation were applicable to all people, had in principle no restrictive ties to Jewish or Hellenistic culture, Christianity could really be a universal religion.[15]

In fact, Christianity has often hedged the cultural flexibility that universal salvation would seem to imply. Often it has insisted that converts accept Western culture, and it has been slow to appreciate the very complex issues involved in distinguishing what is transculturally essential to its faith and what is a matter of the historical accident that Jesus was a Jew of the first century and that his followers first multiplied in a Hellenistic cultural milieu.

The first set of obstacles to a universalist christology therefore rotates around the question of missionary adaptability. How flexible can the Church be in translating the messiahship, saviorhood, and ethics of Jesus? What Asian, African, and Indian equivalents should it accept? The second set of obstacles, linked with the first, involves estimates of the possibility of salvation within non-Christian cultures. This ultimately is a question of grace, which of course is tied to judgments about the function of Jesus in any person's salvation. For many Christian theologians and missionaries throughout the centuries, not to be an explicit member of the Church and an adherent of Christian faith and practice was to be damned. The ancient phrase of Cyprian, bishop of Carthage in Africa (died 258 C.E), that "outside the Church there is no salvation" could be taken literally or with some latitude. When it was taken literally, those who had not been baptized were in thrall to Satan and bound for hell. In that context, universal salvation could only be potential: any people who heard the Gospel and joined the Church could be saved (through the merits of Jesus Christ). This is the interpretation that continues to rule in many conservative Christian churches today. It entails a rather literal reading of Peter's statement in Acts 4:11–12: "This is the stone which was rejected by you builders, but which has become the head of the corner. And there is salvation in no one else, for there is no other name under heaven given among men by which we must be saved."

A middle-of-the-road position affirms the necessity of Christ for salvation but says that people of goodwill who through no fault of their own never have the chance to be converted to Christianity may still be saved. In this interpretation, goodwill, as shown in a life reverent toward the mystery of God and helpful toward one's neighbor, is a tacit or implicit act of faith. Were such a person to encounter Jesus Christ, the argument runs, he or she surely would embrace Jesus Christ and so be saved. Thus the "good pagan," growing up in Asia or Africa at a time when Christianity had no local presence, could still gain salvation. Such salvation would derive from the death and Resurrection of Christ, but the good pagan would not have to know about the death and Resurrection of Christ. It would be enough to have lived well (ultimately in virtue of grace derived from Jesus Christ) according to the lights of one's own conscience. This middle-of-the-road position therefore holds to the decisive importance of Jesus Christ but does not demand explicit awareness of his actual history. Jesus could, in other words, influence people who had never heard of him.

This in itself is not an unreasonable position, of course. All sorts of things have influenced people without their being aware of them: viruses, nuclear radiation, genes, evolutionary history, and myriads more. Nonetheless, it is hard for such a position to specify precisely how Jesus accomplishes the salvation of those who never hear of him. Unless one pushes hard the notion that the Logos is at the center of evolutionary history, and that what Jesus Christ as the Logos enfleshed has placed in history functions as an exemplary cause (a somewhat old-fashioned notion, going back to Aristotle, according to which most things are made by reference to a pattern or exemplar), one will have little explanation of one's pious hope that Jesus does actually enable good pagans or non-Christians to be saved.

Most orthodox christology nowadays works out some notion of this middle-of-the-road position. So, for example, Karl Rahner's theory of "anonymous Christianity" and Paul Tillich's theory of "implicit Christianity" use the notion that Jesus Christ is the fullest expression of what it means to be human (a form of the argument from exemplary causality) to argue that anyone who achieves human goodness, maturity, or authenticity does so in the lineaments of Jesus Christ. If God is at work in such achievements (here the assumption is that one cannot become authentically human without divine grace), then we can infer that God's work is to the pattern of Jesus Christ, which makes salvation (the healing and elevation of human nature into fulfillment and union with God) completely christocentric.

In recent years, more radical theologians have been troubled by this middle-of-the-road solution. They agree with the notion that authentic humanity (the good pagan) deserves or equates with salvation. (No one strictly deserves salvation, if humanity is sinful and salvation takes people beyond their natural capacities into the very life of God.) They may even agree that Jesus Christ is the exemplar of salvation, the fullest revelation of both divinity and humanity. But they are leery of pushing "good pagans" or adherents of other religious faiths that speak of salvation (Judaism, Islam, Hinduism, Buddhism) into Christian boxes.[16]

For these radical theologians it is quite possible to know about Jesus Christ, reject him (at least verbally and conceptually), and still achieve authenticity/salvation. It may even be possible to know of Jesus and the Christian Church, reject them in the name of atheistic (for example, traditional Marxist) allegiances, and exhibit striking human goodness (worthy of salvation). Jesus then may not be functioning in any straight-forward way as a savior. He may even apparently be part of what people are rejecting as inauthentic, phony, a hindrance to justice or human fulfill-ment. Some more radical christologies therefore want to lessen the abso-luteness of the claims made for Jesus' part in universal salvation. They may prefer to say that, by God's grace and will, Hinduism or Buddhism or even Marxism can be saving on their own, without complicated, para-doxical dependencies on Jesus and the Church (cartwheels to make every person of goodwill an anonymous Christian or implicit member of the Church). This could help ecumenical dialogue, such theologians say, and it could remove the impression many non-Christians receive that Chris-tianity is an elect religion and that it sees all other faiths as second-class.

The question to be asked of this sort of christology, moderate theo-logians say, is whether it does in fact maintain the traditional Chris-tian conviction that salvation definitively appeared in Jesus Christ. If one holds such a conviction, all salvation would seem dependent on Jesus, and therefore one is bound to get into the cartwheels. So, against the most radical christologists who want to bracket questions of Jesus' role in the functioning of non-Christian faiths, the countercharge has arisen that they are untrue to what has long been believed to be at the heart of Christian allegiance. Interestingly, though, neither middle-of-the-roaders nor radicals dispute the universality of salvation. Both take it for granted that people of goodwill and good moral performance, wher-ever found, can win the favor of God. The question is how this favor relates to what God did in the specific history of Jesus of Nazareth, who died on the cross and was raised to what his followers considered Christhood. This question awaits a definitive answer.[17]

Fundamentalism

Perhaps there will never be a definitive answer to the question of how Christ relates to the salvation of non-Christians. On the way to any an-swer at all satisfactory, however, one has to pass through the trials of fundamentalism. For unless these have been mastered successfully, texts such as Acts 4:11–12 will immediately prohibit any cartwheeling to connect Jesus with people who have not explicitly confessed his name.

Actually, fundamentalism is a relatively recent phenomenon. For the writers of the New Testament, the patristic writers, the medievals, and the leading authorities of the Reformation, it was axiomatic that Scrip-ture spoke symbolically. Out of the fullness of their hearts, the biblical authors spoke in images, tropes, allegories, parables, and the rest, trying to give their readers hints of a mystery too full and subtle ever to be captured in literalist prose.

Nowadays, most academic Scripture scholars are well aware of this symbolic character of Scripture, and the new techniques of literary analysis are very sophisticated about the polyvalence (several weightings) of religious texts.[18] On the other hand, some of the most prosperous Christian churches promulgate a literalist view of Scripture, arguing (or simply laying it down) that Scripture is infallible and historically inerrant. Thus James Barr, a respected Protestant student of fundamentalism in particular and of biblical interpretation in general, has written: "Fundamentalism begins when people begin to say that the doctrinal and practical authority of scripture is necessarily tied to its infallibility and in particular its historical inerrancy, when they maintain that its doctrinal and practical authority will stand up *only* if it is without error in its apparently historical remarks. The centre of fundamentalism is the insistence that the control of doctrine and practice by scripture is dependent on something like a general perfection of scripture, and therefore on its historical inerrancy; and this in turn involves the repudiation of the results of modern critical modes of reading the Bible."[19]

From a Roman Catholic viewpoint, the starting conviction of fundamentalism that the Scriptures are the word of God (in a rather narrow and literal sense) renders fundamentalism unacceptable: "Because of its insistence that the scriptures are the word of God, fundamentalism stands in radical opposition to Roman Catholicism, and the historical-critical method of biblical interpretation, the former because of its insistence on 'human' tradition, the latter because it understands the scriptures as works of human literature. The roots of fundamentalism go back to the denominational orthodoxies of the seventeenth century and the revivalist movements of the eighteenth and nineteenth centuries. The conservative evangelicals or fundamentalists of the present era share with their forbears an apologetic mode of theology reflecting an historicist notion of truth as well as an insistence on the 'fundamentals,' especially creation, sin and redemption, the second coming, personal salvation, the Virgin Birth and the divinity of Jesus, and a literalist interpretation of miracles. Their point of view is represented through preachers such as Billy Graham and Hubert Armstrong, as well as through the press, for example *Bibliotheca Sacra,* the *Evangelical Quarterly,* and the publications of the Inter-Varsity Press."[20]

Although fundamentalism therefore is primarily a matter of how one regards the Scriptures, it soon becomes a christological issue. For, first, if the fundamentalists are correct, all that the New Testament says about Jesus is to be taken literally, and much that the Old Testament says prophetically is to be applied to Jesus as its literal fulfillment. In actual fact many texts are interpreted in virtue of positions that fundamentalists already hold. Thus the Old Testament prophecies about the Messiah are read in the light of the infancy narratives of the New Testament and later Christian theology to yield a Virgin Birth. The words of the Johannine Christ are taken to be words literally spoken by Jesus of Nazareth, with the result that Jesus is believed to have explicitly claimed divinity. The hymns of the New Testament Epistles (for example, Philippians 2:5–11) are read with little reference to their symbolic debt to the Old Testament and so make Jesus the earthly form of a preexistent Son existing alongside God the Father as nearly a second God. The miracles attributed to Jesus in the New Testament are taken as eyewitness snapshots, so that Jesus becomes a mover of nature, a doer of physical prodigies.

Christologically, therefore, fundamentalism usually produces a Jesus so divine that his humanity drips away. Come down from heaven, working miracles right and left, he must have known all things, have completely controlled his destiny. How, then, could he have suffered the ambiguities, confusions, and heartbreaks undergone by the rest of humankind? How could he really have been, as Hebrews rather poetically describes him, a high priest able to represent human beings because of what he himself suffered and learned through obedience?

Above all, how could Jesus be a matter of changeable significance, a Lord who interprets contemporary experience, which is distinctive and is not merely a rehash of first-century or nineteenth-century experience? If today people hear God's voice in a parabolic, almost Zen-like Jesus who proposes puzzling sayings and holds out nearly impossible ideals (if we take them literally), must they harden their hearts into a fundamentalist christological mode, insisting that Jesus spoke no Semitic hyperbole, meant every "seventy times seven" and mountain moved by faith to be taken literally?

In contrast to such a fundamentalist christology, the exegetes who see Jesus as a master of metaphor in his own teaching, and as God's metaphor in his overall being, insist that Jesus becomes livelier when one grants him symbolic license to exaggerate, to allude, and to use words and gestures to indicate the divine mystery that no literal speech ever can handle well. The divine is best approached by analogical speech, these interpreters believe, and one gets more Christ, not less, by dealing with Jesus poetically.

Finally, if one pushes to the foundations of these two different interpretational stances, the fundamentalist literal one and the critical poetic one, one comes upon different understandings of the Incarnation. For fundamentalists Jesus is not so mysterious (however much we may fail to grasp his full import): God dwelt within him and directed his life, keeping Jesus marching ahead according to a plan conceived in eternity. For critical christologists, the life of Jesus is utterly mysterious, sacramental, and symbolic through and through. Jesus is as the Johannine writings describe him, a strewer of signs, and only by accepting these signs in faith, moving into them from the heart, can one appreciate the this-worldly, fully incarnational significance of divine grace.

Sexuality

Historically, the doctrine of the Virgin Birth of Jesus, which bulks large in fundamentalist christology, has had ambiguous roots in the New Testament. So, for example, the eminent New Testament scholar Joseph Fitzmyer concludes a brief discussion of the question as follows: "It is good to recall that even in the Gospels which have an infancy narrative and assert the virginal conception of Jesus there are elements of a tradition which either do not reckon with it or have not been integrated into such a belief. For instance, Luke 2:41 speaks of Mary and Joseph as 'his parents' (cf. v. 43), and Mary says to the twelve-year-old Jesus, 'Your father and I have been looking for you' (2:48). This is simply said, with no qualifications such as 'foster father' or 'putative father.' And Matt 13:55 records the query, 'Is not this the carpenter's son?' Cf. John 6.42.

"In sum, one has to recognize that the New Testament data for this question are not unambiguous; they do not necessarily support the claim that this belief was a matter of 'the constant teaching of the Church from the beginning' (M. Schmaus, 'Mariology,' *Sacramentum Mundi* [New York: Herder and Herder, 1968–70], 3. 379). The data rather suggest that this belief became part of the developing christology of the early Church, within New Testament times."[21]

The question of whether or not Jesus had a unique, miraculous conception of course bears on how one understands both his humanity and sexuality in general. Concerning the implications for Jesus' humanity, John L. McKenzie has written: "The humanity of Jesus is just as much an article of faith and just as essential in the Christian teaching about the salvation of man through Christ as the divine sonship of Jesus. Our belief in his mediation is based on his identification with both terms of the saving act. Therefore the church has always rejected heresies which denied the full humanity of Jesus, such as those which proposed that he was an optical illusion, that he was not really born but passed through Mary like a tube, that his suffering and death were merely illusion—to wrap it up in a phrase, that he did not have the full experience of the human condition."[22]

Thus, the tradition that Jesus was born of a virgin has rather shadowy New Testament origins, and much in it seems drawn from the sense that Jesus' dignity as the Son of God demanded a separation from the ordinary rise of a human being through sexual intercourse. That Jesus himself was fully human seems a central assumption of both the New Testament and catholic Christian faith. If it were found that this assertion demanded the rejection of the tradition of the Virgin Birth, the latter would have to go. The second question—the whole view of sexuality that a christology indebted to the Virgin Birth must generate—is complicated by the further fact that the New Testament seems to present Jesus as not having married. That would have been rather unusual in the Jewish culture of Jesus' time, so possibly the authors simply assumed that Jesus was married, but the greater likelihood is that Jesus in fact was not married at the time of his preaching and ministry, presumably because that work was all-absorbing. Does the original christology therefore put brackets around sexuality, making it something suspect?

Yes and no, balanced historical analysis seems to conclude. On the one hand, there are reasons for thinking that the early Christian conceptions of God tended to distance the divinity from sexuality. In Jesus' time, pagan divinities sometimes were deeply embedded in sexuality. Both Jewish and early Christian theology likely wanted to ensure that their notion of divinity would not be infected (as they would have seen it) with ties to the cycles of natural fertility or extrapolations from human sexual coupling. In a word, then, there were early tendencies to think of sexuality as unworthy of holy divinity, and so to keep Jesus at some removal from it. The same tendencies led to traditions in both Judaism and Christianity that kept women from being able to preside at liturgical functions and that counseled male liturgical functionaries to abstain from sexual activity prior to such functions. (Feminist theologians sometimes wonder whether the maleness of the historical Jesus renders him unable to be the savior of women.)

The reasons for answering no to the question of whether the original christology led to putting brackets around sexuality include Jesus' full humanity and his own apparent ease with women, with questions of marriage, with children, and the like. Sexuality does not stand in Jesus' teaching as something singled out for special treatment. Jesus is as willing to mingle with prostitutes as with other legal sinners (such as tax collectors). When Jesus speaks of those who are eunuchs for the sake of the Kingdom of Heaven (Matthew 19 : 12), if indeed the saying goes back to Jesus himself, he does not imply that all ought to take this path. It is a gift, and those to whom it is offered should take it. The prior discussion of marriage in Matthew 19 is stringent or highly idealistic, but it is also straightforward and realistic: marriage is the regular, ordinary human estate; the orientation of men and women to one another goes back to God's creative intent and has as its goal the two becoming one flesh—a merged, shared, common fate and identity.

Thus, for a christology to turn out to be pejorative toward sexuality, many christologists now would say, it must be pushed in that direction by believers who have sharper axes to grind than Jesus had. The example of Jesus' apparently single state and the symbolism of the Virgin Birth that Christianity has long venerated (regardless of its ambiguity in the

New Testament texts), along with the historical phenomena of monasticism and the rule of celibacy for many churches' ministers, do all conspire to put some brackets around sexuality. They do relate to the Christian conviction that sexuality must not be idolized or exempted from the relativity or instrumentality that one should accord all creatures. In this regard, sexuality is no different than money or food. All three are good in themselves but capable of abuse. Lust, greed, and gluttony are three of the many ways in which we can abuse creatures, so chastity, poverty, and abstinence can be salutary spiritual disciplines. But in themselves these and all other creatures are not to be feared or used repressively. In themselves they are wonderful gifts of the provident Creator. To see them as tainted or dangerous is seriously to misread the nature of the Creator.

Christology itself therefore probably gives little solid basis for repressive attitudes toward sexuality, just as the Christian doctrine of creation, properly understood, probably gives little solid basis. To segregate the sexes or cordon off sexuality is no more Christian than forbidding card-playing or the use of alcohol. If Christian groups decide to forbid card-playing or the use of alcohol, they have to argue on other than biblical or christological grounds. Similarly, if groups decide to make sex a bugaboo, they have to argue on other than christological or biblical grounds. Christianity will of course be liable to the charge that it is sexist or repressive whenever it treats women as second-class citizens or seems obsessed with homosexuality, premarital sex, divorce, contraception, or abortion. But that will have little to do with either the example of Jesus or healthy christology.

A final aspect of the relationship between sexuality and current christology is the significance of gender in how people relate to God and Jesus. Speaking for many feminists who find the patriarchalism of the Christian church oppressive and believe that a wholesale reform of Christian symbolism is in order, theologian Sandra Schneiders has written: "As women have become aware of their inferior status and actual oppression in family, society, and Church, they have also become aware that the gender of God, God's presumed masculinity, has functioned as the ultimate religious legitimation of the unjust social structures which victimize women. First, the maleness of Jesus has been used in Christian cultures as a support from divine revelation for the age-old claim that maleness is normative for humanity and that men are superior to women. Most Western languages themselves, in which the generic human is always masculine, testify incessantly to the misconception that humanity is originally and normatively male and that women are a derivative and subordinate, if not actually misbegotten, version of the essentially male species. Male privilege, based on this erroneous assumption of male superiority, is firmly entrenched in virtually every sector of human life.

"Second, the 'fatherhood' of God has been used to justify patriarchy or father-rule, the social system which sacralizes male domination and legitimates virtually all forms of oppression of the weak by the strong . . .

"Third, the masculinity of God and of Jesus has been used, in the practical sphere, to deny the likeness of women to God and to Christ and to exclude them from full participation in the life of the Church. Whether this spiritual degradation takes the relatively mild form of excluding little girls from serving at the altar or the more serious forms of exclusion of women from decision-making positions in the Church and enforcement of their sacramental dependence on men, it has a destructive effect on women's spiritual self-image and perverts their relationships with male Christians and with God."[23] It is not hard to predict that the future viability of christology will greatly depend on the resolution of this most fundamental set of sexual issues. If the mediation of salvation through Jesus seems to entail the continued subordination of women to men, many of the most idealistic women and men will feel bound to distance themselves from the Christian churches.

Prayer

If there is some ambiguity about the support that a healthy view of sexuality may derive from christology, there is virtually no ambiguity about the support that a healthy view of prayer may derive. Insofar as Protestant Christianity recently has increased its interest in prayer and personal spirituality, this aspect of christology has come in for special study in Protestant circles. (Roman Catholicism and Eastern Orthodoxy, which both have a strong monastic tradition, have maintained a steady interest in Jesus as a model of prayer, although the recent activism of Roman Catholic spirituality has provoked a balancing resurgence of this interest.) So, for example, James D. G. Dunn, in his large study of the relationship between Jesus and the Spirit, early on devotes a section to Jesus' prayer.

The conclusion of Dunn's study, after he has dealt with the several textual and traditional problems that afflict the main New Testament **pericopes** concerning Jesus' prayer, is that prayer was very important to Jesus himself, probably constituting his regular response in times of crisis and decision: "Particularly noteworthy is the consistent emphasis in both Mark and Luke that Jesus liked to get away, to be alone (Matt. 14.23; Luke 9.18; cf. Luke 9.28f. with Mark 9.2) in his prayer, either in the desert (Mark 1.35; Luke 5.15), or on a mountain (Mark 6.46; Luke 6.12; 9.28) away from the crowds (Mark 1.35; 6.46; Luke 5.16), sometimes going off very early in the morning (Mark 1.35), sometimes spending much or the whole of the night in lonely prayer (Mark 6.46; 14.32–44; Luke 6.12). Noteworthy also is the fact that each of the three occasions recorded by Mark seems to have been a time of stress and crisis; while Luke portrays

Jesus consistently resorting to prayer on occasions of great moment and decision (Luke 3.21; 6.12; 9.18, 28f.; 22.41–5). It is therefore more than probable that *prayer was Jesus' regular response to situations of crisis and decision.*"[24]

Following the work of Joachim Jeremias on Jesus' use of *Abba* in his dealings with God, Dunn goes on to show that Jesus' prayer probably was the familiar speech of a son with his trusted father. In some ways, therefore, it was only natural for Jesus to pray in moments of crisis. Faced with trying circumstances or hard decisions, he would spontaneously turn to the source, the personal power, on which he based his whole life. Later Christian theology drew on this reaction when it developed the notion that Jesus was the incarnate Son of God. For Christian trinitarian theology, the most basic self-definition of Jesus Christ was his derivation from God as a son from a father. Prayer to the Father therefore was but one of several manifestations of Jesus' intrinsic tie to his parental God, merely expressing in action what Jesus was in being. For Jesus himself, however, it is not clear that things arranged themselves in that way. The humanity of Jesus that predominates in the synoptic accounts of his prayer highlights his dependence on God more than his equality with God as divine person to divine person.

Matthew 6 and Luke 11, which both record the Lord's Prayer, are primary New Testament sources for Jesus' teaching on prayer. In Matthew 6 the accent is on sincerity, as though Jesus wanted to be sure that his disciples avoided the corruptions of prayer that he observed in contemporary Judaism (they would be possible in any time and religious culture): "Beware of practicing your piety before men in order to be seen by them; for then you will have no reward from your Father who is in heaven. . . . And when you pray, you must not be like the hypocrites; for they love to stand and pray in the synagogues and at the street corners, that they may be seen by men. Truly, I say to you, they have received their reward. But when you pray, go into your room and shut the door and pray to your Father who is in secret; and your Father who sees in secret will reward you. And in praying do not heap up empty phrases as the Gentiles do; for they think they will be heard for their many words. Do not be like them, for your Father knows what you need before you ask him" (6 : 1, 5–8).

The key to the prayer of the Matthean Jesus therefore is sincerity in making one's prayer to God alone. Prayer is not primarily something that one does to be seen or even to affirm one's socioreligious bonds with fellow believers. Prayer is primarily an address of the heart to God, the sharer of the most secret and intimate portions of one's life and self. God certainly does not need to be told how things are going. God certainly does not need to be burdened with verbose petitions. The key to Jesus' sense of God's concern lies in 6 : 8: "for your Father knows what you need before you ask him." It is as though prayer is more for the asker than for the one asked, and is significant more as an expression of the creature's neediness (and so as a reorientation of the creature to the true way that things are) than as something that God himself needs or wants.

The instructions in Luke are even more insistent that the disciples should rely on God's concern, should keep knocking on God's door (as a strengthening of their trust that God is primed to help them): "Which of you who has a friend will go to him at midnight and say to him, 'Friend, lend me three loaves; for a friend of mine has arrived on a journey, and I have nothing to set before him'; and he will answer from within, 'Do not bother me; the door is now shut, and my children are with me in bed; I cannot get up and give you anything'? I tell you, though he will not get up and give him anything because he is his friend, yet because of his importunity he will rise and give him whatever he needs. And I tell you, Ask, and it will be given you; seek, and you will find; knock, and it will be opened to you. For every one who asks receives, and he who seeks finds, and to him who knocks it will be opened. What father among you, if his son asks for a fish, will instead of a fish give him a serpent; or if he asks for an egg, will give him a scorpion. If you then, who are evil, know how to give good gifts to your children, how much more will the heavenly Father give the Holy Spirit to those who ask him!" (11:5−13).

Here the key line probably is, "If you then, who are evil, know how to give good gifts to your children, how much more will the Heavenly Father give the Holy Spirit to those who ask him!" Jesus cannot think of God except as beyond the best of what human beings are. Human beings, for all their vice and wickedness, usually are good to their children, usually have a soft spot and desire to help. How much more must God have a soft spot for her creation and desire to help all her children in their needs? That Jesus should instinctively think of the Holy Spirit shows what his own sense of God's best gift likely was. Beyond the particular helps for which people ought to pray lies the substantial fulfillment of all prayer, the presence of God (imagined as a Holy Spirit who comes and goes) that makes all of life seem rightly centered and fulfilling.

Jesus himself lived under the inspiration of the Holy Spirit. Early Christianity thought of him as anointed by the Spirit, the way the prophets and kings of Israel had been anointed (whether spontaneously or ceremonially). The Spirit had led Jesus out into the wilderness, and the Spirit struck Paul as a force groaning in the depths of all who reach out to God and enjoy God's life. The Lukan Jesus therefore pictured prayer to a fatherly God as climaxing in the gift of the Spirit. A christology interested in prayer can hardly overlook the encouragement Jesus seems to have given his disciples to ask God for the full coming of the Spirit.

Once again, this takes us away from a literalist approach to christology or the interpretation of Jesus. Jesus has to be respected as a pneumatic figure, filled with the Spirit and constantly referring to Spirit-given experiences such as successful prayer. This depth-dimension or pneumatic aspect of christology dovetails with the symbolic character of

Jesus' preaching and ministry that we have seen favored by today's literary scholars. Symbols or sacraments are the products of pneumatic or inspired understanding. When one is in the grasp of the Spirit the world is rounder, thicker, richer than otherwise. To approach the texts on Jesus' prayer, or any other portion of christology, with a literalist mind would be to risk missing the Spirit and so denaturing Jesus.

Prophecy

The people upon whom the Spirit of God descended most strikingly in Jesus' tradition were called prophets. In the Hebrew Bible, the prophetic call meant the coming of God's word, which the prophet then had the obligation to preach. Probably the classical description of this prophetic call occurs in Jeremiah 1:4–10: "Now the word of the Lord came to me saying, 'Before I formed you in the womb I knew you, and before you were born I consecrated you; I appointed you a prophet to the nations.' Then I said, 'Ah, Lord God! Behold, I do not know how to speak, for I am only a youth.' But the Lord said to me, 'Do not say, "I am only a youth"; for to all to whom I send you you shall go, and whatever I command you you shall speak. Be not afraid of them, for I am with you to deliver you, says the Lord.' Then the Lord put forth his hand and touched my mouth; and the Lord said to me, 'Behold, I have put my words in your mouth. See, I have set you this day over nations and over kingdoms, to pluck up and to break down, to destroy and to overthrow, to build and to plant.'"

For Jesus, the immediate exemplar of this prophetic tradition was John the Baptist, to whom he went to be baptized. John's message stressed repentance in the face of the coming of the Kingdom of God. Jesus' experience at his baptism is the equivalent of a prophetic call such as Jeremiah's, only the symbolism gives more play to the Spirit of God than to God's word: "In those days Jesus came from Nazareth of Galilee and was baptized by John in the Jordan. And when he came up out of the water, immediately he saw the heavens opened and the Spirit descending upon him like a dove; and a voice came from heaven, 'Thou art my beloved Son; with thee I am well pleased.' The Spirit immediately drove him out into the wilderness" (Mark 1:9–11).

The figure of the heavens opening probably is meant to convey the end of the drought of prophetic activity. After its return from exile in Babylon, Israel experienced no vigorous prophecy. The general feeling was that the Spirit had been quenched, that religious emphasis had now passed from charismatic authorities such as the prophets to the priests and teachers who interpreted the Torah. For the early Jewish Christians who were trying to make sense out of Jesus, his bursting on the scene with a powerful message about the Kingdom of God (like John the Baptist's, but more positive) was a renewal of prophecy. Jesus did not constantly defer to the Law, citing texts and precedents. His authority was immediate and personal, as though he had been directly commissioned by God. Eventually the idea grew that he was the eschatological prophet: the herald of the end-time of fulfillment, the definitive bringer of salvation.

The Spirit drove Jesus into the wilderness—presumably that he might pray. The prophetic mission with which Jesus was charged therefore interwove with his need to commune with his Father. Whether one pictures Jesus' prayer as mainly a matter of petition for help with his crises and difficult decisions, or takes a more contemplative view of it as a delightful communion with God (the treasure of his life), Jesus' prayer probably enabled him to work as a prophet. It was probably a religious activity empowering bold speech, dramatic gestures, and finally the ability to endure rejection and suffering. That, too, fits the prophetic model. Jeremiah and the other famous Israelite prophets communed with God in order to obtain the strength to deliver the message with which God had charged them. Because they were a nuisance to the kings and general populace whom they upbraided, they frequently suffered for their bold preaching. That brought them back to God, bruised, needy, and fully convinced that God alone could give them the strength and solace they required.

To call Jesus a prophet is therefore to imply that he was both intensely active and intensely prayerful. The word and Spirit of God kept him to a rhythm of engagement with people's needs and withdrawal for solitude and renewal. By and large, those who focus on Jesus' prophetic ministry nowadays emphasize its political or social dimensions. For them prophecy is not so much the prediction of what will occur in the future as it is reading the signs of present times in light of God's regular demand for justice.

Rosemary Radford Ruether, for example, in a series of lectures entitled *To Change the World: Christology and Cultural Criticism*, makes the prophecy of Jesus a radical social criticism: "In direct rebuke to these ruling classes of Israel, Jesus defines his prophetic mission as a mission to the 'poor,' both in the sense of those impoverished and crushed by debt in this system, and also those despised and reviled by this system of social status and prestige. He goes to all those who are regarded as having no hope of salvation within present society, and preaches the good news to them. This good news is, socially, far more revolutionary than anything imagined by either the Essenes or the Zealots, much less the Pharisees or Sadducees. It overthrows the whole system of status through wealth, rank, education, and religious observance."[25]

For christologists such as Ruether, the prophetic task for which Jesus had been anointed included social reform as a central aspect. If Jesus was to be the eschatological prophet or definitive Savior, he had to show people how to reorder social relations and make them worthy of both human aspiration and divine justice. Jesus' own message and posture bore out this expectation. The Kingdom of God was precisely the renovated state of affairs that would arrive when God's rule was evident and effective. How much this differed from the notion of an age of the Spirit, when all would be led by the divine Teacher, is hard to say. Probably it differed very little.

Most present-day biblical scholars would agree that the Kingdom of God is depicted as coming in Spirit-given power. It blesses the poor and outcast, as an expression of God's transcendent morality (as far from human morality as the heavens are above the earth). As the herald of the Kingdom, Jesus was the announcer and exemplar of the age of the Spirit, which had come to enable God's paradoxical justice to obtain. So we are back again to the thematic proclamation that Jesus makes in the synagogue at Nazareth at the outset of his ministry: "And he came to Nazareth, where he had been brought up; and he went to the synagogue, as his custom was, on the sabbath day. And he stood up to read; and there was given to him the book of the prophet Isaiah. He opened the book and found the place where it was written, 'The Spirit of the Lord is upon me, because he has anointed me to preach good news to the poor. He has sent me to proclaim release to the captives and the recovering of sight to the blind, to set at liberty those who are oppressed, to proclaim the acceptable year of the Lord.' And he closed the book, and gave it back to the attendant, and sat down; and the eyes of all in the synagogue were fixed on him. And he began to say to them, 'Today this scripture has been fulfilled in your hearing'" (Luke 4:16–21).

Prayer, the Spirit, prophecy, the Kindom of God, the poor—they are all interlocking aspects of the christology of the synoptic Gospels. The Christ we find in Matthew, Mark, and Luke is anointed, messianic, because of the Spirit's coming upon him. This makes him a prophet, a man of prayer, a herald of good news to the most wretched people of his society. One cannot pull at any of these strings without drawing out the others. In today's understanding of Jesus, his prophecy is an ingredient in his Christhood.

Eschatology

The synoptic Gospels make it plain that many of the people regarded Jesus as a prophet. They make it plain, as well, that Jesus' opponents feared this popular perception because it made it harder for them to reject what Jesus was preaching. By the time that Matthew, for instance, brings Jesus to the verge of the Passion, relations between Jesus and the Pharisees have almost completely broken down. Jesus' parables have become more pointed, suggesting that the Kingdom of God will be taken from Israel (as represented by those most diligent about keeping the Law) and given to outsiders: "sinners" and even Gentiles.

Thus, after preaching the bitter parable about the vineyard owner who sends various messengers and finally his own son to the renters, only to have them kill all these emissaries and force him to come down on them with wrath, the Matthean Jesus summarizes the situation: "Jesus said to them, 'Have you never read in the scriptures: "The very stone which the builders rejected has become the head of the corner; this was the Lord's doing, and it is marvelous in our eyes?" [We have seen Peter use this text in Acts 4, making it the springboard to his proclamation that salvation is to be found only in Jesus' name.] Therefore I tell you, the kingdom of God will be taken away from you and given to a nation producing the fruits of it.' When the chief priests and the Pharisees heard his parables, they perceived that he was speaking about them. But when they tried to arrest him, they feared the multitudes, because they held him to be a prophet" (Matthew 21:42–46).

The Q community, present-day exegetes regularly note, was especially impressed by the conflict between Jesus and the representatives of the Jewish establishment. For this community, Jesus was the eschatological prophet, the messenger of the last days, when God would finally come to deliver those who were suffering for the sake of righteousness. Q sees Jesus and his disciples (members of the early Church, who often were at odds with their fellow Jews) in terms of martyrdom. The eschatological prophet consummates the long line of those who have suffered because they had to preach God's Word to a populace (Israel) unwilling to hear it. The eschatological time therefore is tense, almost violent. In the theology of Q, Jesus has come to divide households, to set brother against brother and sister against sister. Allegiance to Jesus often will mean paying a high price in terms of rejection and suffering. Q sets the fate of Jesus and the early Church in the perspective of a long-troubled covenant relationship between God and Israel, looking to the divine judgment as the vindication for both the death of Jesus and the sufferings that his followers must endure.

In his book on the Gospels, *Jesus in History*, Howard Clark Kee has summarized the mood of Q on the matter of "eschatological warning" as follows: "After exposing the discrepancy between the Pharisees' outer show of piety and inner lack of devotion, Jesus attacks directly those who have not only failed to hear God's message through the prophets but also shared in murdering these men sent by God. The two specific murders mentioned in Luke 11:51, those of Abel and Zechariah, are probably intended to encompass the whole span of the history of Israel, from the first murder recorded in the first book of the Hebrew Bible, Genesis, to the last murder in the last book of the canon, 2 Chronicles. That is, the

Q tradition affirms that throughout their history those who have called themselves God's people have consistently rejected God's messengers"[26] (see also Matthew 23 : 34–36).

The Pauline and Johannine eschatologies situate Jesus somewhat differently. Where Q and the Synoptics are greatly impressed by Jesus' death as the last outrage in the warfare between God and the people who keep rejecting his messengers, Paul and John probe the wider historical significance of the Christ-event. (Luke also has a clear theology of history, centered upon Jesus, but it doesn't have quite the tension of the Pauline and Johannine interpretations.) For the early Paul, the end-time that Jesus' death and resurrection inaugurated is soon to arrive. The Parousia of Christ will bring the judgment that all righteous people have long sought. For the later Paul and the Pauline school, the death and Resurrection of Christ have become the axial event of a much broader historical process. The resurrected Christ is the firstborn of a new creation. The life of the Spirit poured out by the crucified and Risen Lord is the essence of the final age.

The Johannine theology, contemporary scholarship suggests, takes the arrival of the final age back to the very beginnings of Jesus' mission. With the Incarnation of the Word the grace that moves the world into the eschatological time is poured out abundantly. When Jesus is raised high on the cross, the Gospel of John sees a victory standard. The "hour" of Jesus' passion, which from a worldly point of view seems to be a time of defeat, is from a heavenly standpoint the crucial moment of glorification. Jesus on the cross draws to himself all who are worthy of salvation. Indeed, the crucified one is the standard of judgment by which eschatological justice is meted out. With the outpouring of the Spirit, history has entered its final phase. Heavenly life has in principle been won, and the disciples of Jesus have all that they need to live in the final age. The Kingdom of God (in synoptic terms) has substantially arrived. People may have to suffer and struggle until the Parousia (when the grace and glory of God will finally predominate beyond any question), but the life, light, and love of God won by Jesus and given abundantly in the Spirit will assure them of victory.

From this New Testament heritage, we now realize, Christianity has received a somewhat complicated theology of history. Salvation both had and had not been accomplished. In principle or substantially, Jesus had accomplished the essentials of salvation. The Christ-event was the definitive prophecy, arrival of divine Wisdom in human form, and martyrdom for the cause of God's Gospel. The death and Resurrection of Jesus were the new Passover, changing history from a period of sin or alienation from God to a new, final phase of divine grace.

On the other hand, the consummation of this Passover and age of grace manifestly was yet to occur. Jesus had not yet returned as the triumphant, parousiac Lord. People still suffered grievously if they tried to preach God's will or live out the divine commandments. So the portraits of Jesus, and the consolations derived from Jesus' death and Resurrection, reflect the need of the Christian communities to buoy their faith that what they suffered was worth it. The various "eschatological discourses" in the synoptic Gospels, where Jesus pictures the end of history in cataclysmic terms, along with the book of Revelation, show the almost punitive strain that early Christian faith developed. In order to hang on, to cling to its faith in times of suffering or persecution, the early Church often allowed itself to anticipate God's harsh judgment on the infidels. Christology therefore became more than an expression of the gracious goodness of God, the revelation and love that God freely had offered the world to make it whole. Christology also became part of the divine justice that would punish the wicked.

Summary

In this chapter we have been concerned with contemporary christological issues, most of them seen from the perspective of those inside the Christian Church. Our first such issue was how Jesus relates to the Church. More people today admire Jesus than admire the Church, and many people want to distinguish quite sharply between Jesus and the assembly of his followers. This frequently leads theologians to set Jesus and the Church over against one another in such a way that Jesus becomes a criterion for judging the faith and love of the Church. Orthodox theologians do not deny the function of the Church in God's chosen plan of salvation, but they usually want to make Jesus more significant than his very fallible horde of followers.

Among the followers are many admirable disciples, however, and some of the Christians working for peace today represent a long-standing Christian effort to make the Church a fellowship of reconciliation. Thus the report of the American Friends Service Committee on prospects for peace in the Middle East harkens back to Jesus, the Prince of Peace. And sometimes the Church does in fact bring about the atmosphere of peace and cooperation that its Prince desired, as Robert McAfee Brown's autobiographical reflections testify. The recent pastoral letter of the American Catholic bishops on peacemaking in a nuclear age is another indication that many Christians now want to close the gap between what christology says should be so and what ecclesiology says has yet to happen.

The relation of Jesus to the world's poor people cannot be separated from his relation to peacemaking, for today world poverty is one of the triggers to fearful violence. Thus the American Catholic bishops have followed their letter on peacemaking with a second letter on economic justice. Thus Robert McAfee Brown has followed his book on making peace in the global village with a book on the unexpectedly good news that Scripture has for the poor. Brown is typical of liberation theologians in making the link between helping the poor and following Christ—something the Asian Theological Conference delegate whom we quoted further suggests. To be true to his Lord and Master, the delegate finally found that he had to make the city slums his conference project.

The link between ecology and peace or ecology and the poor may initially seem harder to find, but on further christological reflection it should not be. Although Christian theologians have neglected ecological problems, and some champions of the world's poor have feared that such ecological proposals as a steady-state economy would deprive the poor of a chance to gain economic prosperity, the reality of such polluted places as Cubatao, Brazil, shows that those who suffer most from ecological devastation are the poor. Christologically, the tradition of the centrality of the Logos to creation suggests that today one cannot adequately reflect on either Christ or ecology without attending to the hopes, needs, and rights of a creation in labor for Christ's redemption. However, it remains to be seen what christologists will make of ecology, for some theologians want to downplay human destruction of the environment and so minimize the christological significance of pollution.

Future christology may well have to think in terms of a universal salvation that embraces nature as well as all human beings. Today, however, most discussions of the relation between Christ and global salvation focus on human beings outside the Christian fold. In principle, Christianity has always opened salvation to all people if they would embrace Christ, but in practice this conviction has had broader or narrower interpretations. When salvation was conceived as not occurring outside the Church, or not occurring without the confession of Jesus' name, people not baptized were often pictured as going to hell. Missionaries often drew motivation from this picture, but frequently they preached European culture as much as the Gospel (and so constrained the universality of salvation considerably).

Middle-of-the-road theologians usually have broadened the narrow literalism of conservatives, arguing that all people of goodwill and good moral performance virtually embrace Christ. If people follow their consciences, they may receive salvation (ultimately due to Christ) without entering the Church. More radical christologists now think that this plays games with the actual situation of pious non-Christians or good people opposed to Christianity. For these people human authenticity can be saving on its own, with little explicit connection to Christianity. This problem awaits a definitive solution that would both retain the centrality of Christ and not misinterpret the actual experience of non-Christians.

Fundamentalism is a related christological issue nowadays, because fundamentalists insist on the infallibility and inerrancy of the scriptural text (which often seems to narrow the extent of salvation). This raises many serious hermeneutical issues, and it tends to set fundamentalists at odds with most Roman Catholics and academic scriptural scholars. For the latter, Christ must be interpreted by reference to tradition as well as Scripture, and the human aspects of Scripture suggest a quite nuanced, symbolically sensitive interpretation of most christological texts.

One of the christological texts bearing most directly on the question of the relation between Jesus and sexuality is the story of the Virgin Birth. Fundamentalists tend to take this literally, thus raising questions about the humanity of Jesus: was Jesus normal, really the same as other members of our race? The Virgin Birth, coupled with Jesus' own unmarried status, raises further questions about sexuality in itself. Is sexual activity something that must be kept apart from divinity, as though it would taint God or God's holy messenger? Sometimes the Christian tradition and de facto christology have given this impression, but neither the teaching of Jesus nor what christology necessarily entails forces one to this conclusion. Jesus speaks of sexuality quite straightforwardly, and christology can make sexuality as ordinary as food and money: a creature to be neither feared nor abused. Finally, future christology will be asked to show how the maleness of Jesus and his Father are not tools of women's subordination to men.

Another contemporary christological issue is Jesus' prayer, which the testimony of representative current scholarship makes central to Jesus' own religious life. Thus James Dunn has found Jesus praying at the decisive junctures of his life, and such representative New Testament chapters as Matthew 6 and Luke 11 show Jesus counseling his followers to pray to God in great confidence. The best gift to pray for, Jesus suggests, is the Holy Spirit, so studying Jesus' prayer becomes another stimulus towards conceiving christology as a pneumatic, Spirit-oriented reflection.

One could draw similar conclusions from studying Jesus' prophecy. The Spirit that descended upon Jesus at his baptism and led him throughout his life cast him in the outline of a prophet, and the people regularly considered him as such. Jesus fits much of the profile of Jeremiah and the other biblical prophets, inasmuch as his life swung back and forth between intense prayer and intense action that challenged the current religious mores. Many christologists today tend to discuss Jesus' prophecy in a political context, often coming to conclusions similar to Rosemary Radford Ruether's that Jesus was a radical social iconoclast.

On the question of conceiving Jesus as the eschatological prophet, and the relationship between christology and eschatology, we studied the convictions of the Q community of the New Testament that Jesus was the last and most decisive in a long line of prophets rejected by their

people. This led Q to think of Christian discipleship in terms of martyrdom and to stretch out to God's judgment for its vindication. The apocalyptic sections of the Synoptics go along with this thinking, and both
they and the book of Revelation often have a punitive tone: the enemies
of Christianity will soon pay for their sins. The eschatologies of Pauline
and Johannine theology are more peaceful, seeing either the passover of
Christ or Jesus' Incarnation and being raised on the cross as the decisive
beginning of the new age or end-time.

STUDY QUESTIONS

1. Why does Albert Nolan say that Christ stands above Christianity?
2. What is the significance for peacemaking of Robert McAfee Brown's
    experiences of the Christian Church as a present embodiment of
    the global village?
3. In what sense might one say that the poor present the face of Jesus
    to the world?
4. How might the redemption worked by Christ apply to such eco-
    logically troubled places as Cubatao?
5. How might people who never confess the name of Jesus Christ par-
    take of salvation?
6. What aspects of a fundamentalist approach to christology might
    one consider admirable?
7. Does the doctrine of the Virgin Birth incline christology to depreci-
    ate sexuality?
8. Why do the New Testament texts have Jesus so strongly counseling
    his followers to persist in placing their petitions before God?
9. What sort of a prophetic vocation does Jesus' speech in the syna-
    gogue at Nazareth outline?
10. What is the relation between martyrdom and the eschatological
    prophecy of Jesus?

NOTES

[1] Edward Schillebeeckx, *God Is New Each Moment*. New York: Seabury,
1983, pp. 80–81.

[2] See Elisabeth Schüssler-Fiorenza, *In Memory of Her*. New York: Crossroad,
1983.

[3] Albert Nolan, *Jesus before Christianity*. Maryknoll, NY: Orbis, 1978, p. 3.

[4] The American Friends Service Committee, *A Compassionate Peace*. New York: Hill & Wang, 1982, p. vi.

[5] Robert McAfee Brown, *Making Peace in the Global Village*. Philadelphia: Westminster, 1981, pp. 106–107.

[6] U.S. Catholic Bishops, "The Challenge of Peace," no. 51, in *Catholics and Nuclear War*, ed. Philip J. Murnion. New York: Crossroad, 1983, p. 267.

[7] U.S. Catholic Bishops, "Pastoral Letter on Social Teachings and the U.S. Economy [First Draft]," no. 46, in *The National Catholic Reporter*, November 23, 1984, p. 14.

[8] See Karl Rahner, "Reflections on the Unity of the Love of Neighbor and the Love of God," in *Theological Investigations*, vol. 6. Baltimore: Helicon, 1969, pp. 231–249.

[9] Robert McAfee Brown, *Unexpected News: Reading the Bible with Third World Eyes*. Philadelphia: Westminster, 1984, pp. 95–96.

[10] Samuel Rayan, "Reflections on a Live-In Experience: Slumdwellers," in *Asia's Struggle for Full Humanity*, ed. Virginia Fabella. Maryknoll, NY: Orbis, 1980, p. 51.

[11] See Joseph Gremillion, *The Gospel of Peace and Justice*. Maryknoll, NY: Orbis, 1976.

[12] C. T. Kurien, "A Third World Perspective," in *Faith and Science in an Unjust World*, vol. 1, ed. Roger Shinn. Philadelphia: Fortress, 1980, p. 221.

[13] John Carmody, *Ecology and Religion*. Ramsey, NJ: Paulist, 1983, pp. 3–4.

[14] Michael Novak, "Seven Theological Facets," in *Capitalism and Socialism: A Theological Inquiry*, ed. Michael Novak. Washington, DC: American Enterprise Institute for Public Policy Research, 1979, pp. 118–119.

[15] See Richard G. Cote, *Universal Grace*. Maryknoll, NY: Orbis, 1977.

[16] See Paul F. Knitter, *No Other Name?* Maryknoll, NY: Orbis, 1985.

[17] See Gerald H. Anderson and Thomas F. Stransky, eds., *Christ's Lordship and Religious Pluralism*. Maryknoll, NY: Orbis, 1981; and Donald G. Dawe and John B. Carman, eds., *Christian Faith in a Religiously Plural World*. Maryknoll, NY: Orbis, 1978.

[18] See, for example, Norman K. Gottwald, *The Hebrew Bible*. Philadelphia: Fortress, 1985.

[19] James Barr, *The Scope and Authority of the Bible*. Philadelphia: Westminster, 1980, pp. 65–66.

[20] Raymond F. Collins, "Fundamentalism," in *The Westminster Dictionary of Christian Theology*, ed. A. Richardson and J. Bowden. Philadelphia: Westminster, 1983, p. 223.

[21] Joseph A. Fitzmyer, S.J., *A Christological Catechism*. New York: Paulist, 1982, p. 70.

[22] John L. McKenzie, *The New Testament without Illusions*. Chicago: Thomas More, 1980, pp. 112–113.

[23] Sandra M. Schneiders, *Women and the Word*. New York: Paulist, 1986, pp. 5–6.

[24] James D. G. Dunn, *Jesus and the Spirit.* Philadelphia: Westminster, 1975, pp. 20–21.

[25] Rosemary Radford Ruether, *To Change the World.* New York: Crossroad, 1981, pp. 16–17.

[26] Howard Clark Kee, *Jesus in History,* 2d ed. New York: Harcourt, Brace, Jovanovich, 1977, pp. 94–95.

5

Jesus Compared with Other Religious Leaders

Moses

In the present chapter we leave the line of christological study that we have been pursuing, from the New Testament to current questions. Here our inquiry, rather than being relatively historical, will be comparative: How does Jesus compare with other great religious leaders who have shaped world history? Not only is this question raised increasingly in present-day studies of Jesus and in present-day dialogue among the major religions; it also holds considerable promise of placing Jesus in a new context and so of bringing new perspectives from which to estimate his person and work.

Moses, who lived about 1300 B.C.E., is Judaism's great lawgiver and teacher. If Abraham is considered the father of faith, Moses is considered the friend of God who mediated the covenant that made the Jews God's people. By leading the people out of Egypt, Moses became the great liberator whom the people recalled at each Passover celebration of the Exodus.

Exodus 2:11–15 suggests an initial insight into Moses' character: "One day, when Moses had grown up, he went out to his people and looked on their burdens; and he saw an Egyptian beating a Hebrew, one of his people. He looked this way and that, and seeing no one he killed the Egyptian and hid him in the sand. When he went out the next day, behold, two Hebrews were struggling together; and he said to the man that did the wrong, 'Why do you strike your fellow?' He answered, 'Who made you a prince and judge over us? Do you mean to kill me as you killed the Egyptian?' Then Moses was afraid, and thought, 'Surely the thing is known.' When Pharaoh heard of it, he sought to kill Moses."

Here we have a man with a keen sense of justice who prefers to identify with his own beleaguered people rather than to trade on an assumed Egyptian identity (as the child of Pharaoh's daughter). He is willing to use the violent means of a somewhat violent time to secure justice. But his people reject much of his leadership, questioning by what right he presumes to give them directives. The later stories of Moses' leadership in the desert, after the Exodus, are replete with grumblings against him. He may be God's chosen head, but that does not assure him an easy rule. What sustains Moses, then, is not the wholehearted support of his people but his intimacy with God. From the revelation at the burning bush (Exodus 3:14), the holy God shows Moses special favor. It is to Moses that God gives the commandments and ordinances that are to rule the life of the covenanted people. It is Moses who dwells with God in the cloud that denotes God's glory.

Moses, indeed, becomes known as the man to whom God used to speak as friend. This intimacy reaches a climax in Exodus 33:17–23, where Moses experiences all that a human being can of the divine glory: "And the Lord said to Moses, 'This very thing that you have spoken I will do; for you have found favor in my sight, and I know you by name.' Moses said, 'I pray thee, show me thy glory.' And he said, 'I will make all my goodness pass before you, and will proclaim before you my name "The Lord"; and I will be gracious to whom I will be gracious, and will show mercy on whom I will show mercy. But,' he said, 'you cannot see my face; for man shall not see me and live.' And the Lord said, 'Behold, there is a place by me where you shall stand upon the rock; and while my glory passes by I will put you in a cleft of the rock, and I will cover you with my hand until I have passed by; then I will take away my hand, and you shall see my back; but my face shall not be seen.'"

In commenting on the God that Moses mediated, the historian of religions Mircea Eliade stresses a peculiar blend of "otherness" and concern for ethical propriety: "But the 'negative characteristics' [for example, Yahweh's "wrath"] belong to Yahweh's original structure. What is involved is a new, and the most impressive, expression of the deity as absolutely different from his creation, the 'utterly other' (the *ganz andere* of Rudolph Otto). The coexistence of these contradictory attributes, the irrationality of some of his acts, distinguish Yahweh from an ideal of perfection on the human scale. From this point of view, Yahweh resembles certain divinities of Hinduism, Siva, for example, or Kali-Durga. But there is a difference, and a substantial one: these Indian divinities take their place beyond morality, and since their mode of being constitutes a paradigmatic model, their worshipers do not hesitate to imitate them. Yahweh, on the contrary, accords the greatest importance to ethical principles and practical morality: at least five commandments of the Decalogue refer to them."[1]

Eliade considers Moses the prime intermediary of the revelation of the Israelite God. However, we know relatively little about the historical personage Moses himself: "All that can be said concerning the person known by that name is that he was distinguished by his repeated and dramatic encounters with Yahweh. The revelation of which Moses was the intermediary made him at once an ecstatic and oracular prophet and a 'magician'—the model of the Levite priests and the supremely charismatic leader who succeeded in transforming a group of clans into the nucleus of a nation, the people of Israel."[2]

When we move to compare Moses and Jesus, we have first to confess that the historical sources on which any comparison can be based are fragmentary. We have already seen the complicated situation regarding historical sources for the career and personality of Jesus. In the case of Moses the records are even older and more legendary. Moses, indeed, is substantially more a mythic figure, revered for his idealized functions, than the historical Jesus. Nonetheless, the historical relationship between Jews and Christians made it inevitable that Jesus' first followers would compare him to Moses. Indeed, one might say that for the early Christians Jesus was the new Moses, mediator of a better covenant with God. The Gospel of Matthew, for example, plays out this theme.

The best historical conjecture, however, is that the two men shared a singular familiarity with God. For Moses, the **theophanies** recorded in Exodus suggest a more awesome experience of the Creator of the world and liberator of Israel. For Jesus, the intimacy of a child with its fully-trusted parent predominated. Relatedly, the religion of Jesus had become more interior and less prone to violence than that of Moses. In thirteen hundred years or so of covenant experience, the Jews had made considerable spiritual progress or refinement. Jesus was the heir of the prophets, as well as of Moses. His time could be better aware of the ambiguities in a covenant law that had descended to minute particulars. The sacrifices so important to the religion of Exodus had ceded to the justice that the classical prophets had demanded. The magical aura of the cult had come to mean less than mercy and kindness. Even the notion of a promised land or a free people had been transmuted, so that Jesus could speak of a Kingdom of God not of this world, a resurrection into a realm beyond space and time.

What links Jesus and Moses, however, despite these signs of evolution between their eras, is their initial passion for justice. Moses saw the sufferings of his people and groaned that they might be delivered from Egypt. Jesus' heart went out to suffering people of every stripe, so much so that he began his career with the words of the prophet (Isaiah 61: 1–2): "The Spirit of the Lord is upon me, because he has anointed me to preach good news to the poor. He has sent me to proclaim release to the captives and recovering of sight to the blind, to set at liberty those who are oppressed, to proclaim the acceptable year of the Lord" (Luke 4: 18–19). Jesus and Moses therefore are quite alike in their initial response to suffering. Where they definitively part company is in Christians' divinization of Jesus. The Jews never proclaimed Moses to be divine, but within a generation after Jesus' death and resurrection, Jesus was worshiped as the strictly divine Son.

Buddha

About five hundred years before Christ, in northern India, an ascetic and yogi known as the "Enlightened One" (Buddha), went about preaching a "middle way" (between austerity and indulgence) that could give people release from their sufferings. The Buddha was the heir of Indian spirituality, and he had experienced release from the snares of desire and **karma** through a meditative insight that he expressed in terms of the Four Noble Truths. These truths were that all life is suffering, that the cause of suffering is desire, that if one stops desire (or craving) one can stop suffering, and that the way to stop desire is to follow the Eightfold Path of right understanding, right thought, right speech, right action, right livelihood, right effort, right mindfulness, and right concentration.

Later Buddhist interpretation has made the Enlightened One a heavenly figure, or even a manifestation of ultimate reality, thereby downplaying his human biography. The early sources, however, show a teacher beset with numerous trials: "When the Buddha was seventy-two years of age (in 486 B.C.), his jealous cousin, Devadatta, demanded that he turn over the direction of the community to him. Met with refusal, Devadatta attempted to have him killed, first by hired assassins, then by having him crushed by a falling rock or a dangerous elephant. Devadatta had instituted a schism with a group of monks by preaching a more radical asceticism; but Sariputra and Maudgalayana were able to call back those who had gone astray, and, according to several sources, Devadatta was precipitated alive into Hell. The Blessed One's last years were darkened by disastrous events, among them the ruin of his clan, the Sakyas, and the death of Sariputra and Maudgalayana."[3]

Because the Buddha and Jesus came from such different traditions, it is their contrasts that initially are striking. Even taken simply as human

beings, as religious teachers who made no claim to being divine, they
viewed the world quite differently. For Jesus, the God of the fathers Abraham, Isaac, and Jacob was the unquestioned treasure of life. For the Buddha, there was no God, only a mass of gods whose power was dubious.
Where Jesus saw the human condition as troubled mainly by sin, the
Buddha saw the human condition as troubled mainly by ignorance.
Where the first instinct of Jesus was to reorient the individual through
love of God and love of neighbor, the first instinct of the Buddha was to
get his hearers to meditate on the Four Noble Truths. Jesus expected God
to intervene in human affairs. The Buddha thought that each individual
held the key to his or her own fate. Jesus had no notion of karma or
transmigration. For the Buddha, karma and transmigration were given,
completely assumed.

As a result, the two great religious leaders pictured the world very
differently. Jesus lived out of an intense union with a personal God. The
Buddha had found peace through complete detachment. Jesus expected
to consummate his union with his Father and bring about the Kingdom
of Heaven, while the Buddha's goal was **nirvana,** a state of complete
fulfillment that one could not capture in worldly terms. Jesus showed
special concern for the outcasts of his society. To his mind God had a
preferential love for the poor and abused. The Buddha seems to have considered all people bound in ignorance to be equally wretched. This-
worldly riches meant little compared to the freedom and ultimate peace
that the cessation of desire would bring.

In fact, perhaps the capital difference between the two sages is their
divergence about desire. Jesus urged a love of God with whole mind,
heart, soul, and strength, and a hunger and thirst for justice, that almost
seem erotic. However purified of baser motivations, his ideals are passionate and emotion-laden. The Buddha moves in a cool, detached atmosphere, nothing seeming to disturb his equanimity. To him all material
and historical things are passing, hardly worth taking into account. He
wants to help people improve their situations, remove the thorns that
are giving them pain, but he sees the casting out of craving as the huge
first step in any such therapeutic program.

Despite these quite different outlooks, however, the Buddha and
Jesus come closer together when one begins to probe their innermost religious experiences. These obviously are quite conjectural, granted the
time differences between ourselves and both leaders, but it seems safe to
say that Jesus was centered in a parental God, whom he trusted utterly,
while the Buddha was centered in a freedom from any attachments, a
blessed peace. Both leaders therefore came to deal with the world and
with other people confidently. Both were at home in nature and society
alike. Once the Buddha had solved his life's problem (how to conquer
death, disease, and old age), he spent forty years or so effectively teaching
the **dharma.** Jesus died much younger than the Buddha, but he too was

an effective (if a more fiery) preacher and teacher. But can great religious figures come to a solution of life's problems that makes them at home in the world without discovering something quite similar? Is it not likely that the similarity of their human constitutions, and the similarity of the natural and social worlds in which they dwelt, would have inclined them to rest close to the same center? Let us hypothesize that the answers to these questions should be affirmative and see where that takes us.

Jesus was certainly a mystic, and current scholars sometimes make this a central part of his problem with the Judaism of his time: "The fact seems to be that Jesus was so out of phase with certain patterns of Jewish contemporary teaching that the age immediately after him could not find room for the novelty he comprised. Had he confined himself to wonder-working, perhaps it could have. It probably was not the way his teaching was developed by the gospel writers or their antecedents that made the difference, not even the claim that he was the messiah or in some sense divine. His mystical union with God, uncommon in Jewish piety in that age, coupled with his lack of veneration for the oral law, would have sufficed to render him unacceptable to the teachers of his time. His followers did not walk in **halakah,** the path of observance that came to be the mark of true Jews."[4]

The Buddha was also a mystic, and while the Hindu orthodoxy that he rejected was not so strict as the Jewish orthodoxy that Jesus rejected, the Buddha's mysticism made him a problem to the priestly Hindus called Brahmans. Interpretations of the Buddha's enlightenment experience vary, but it is highly possible that his insight into the relation between rebirth and desire was the key. He progressed from remembering his own previous lives, to perceiving the karmic state of living beings everywhere, to realizing directly the link between desire and bondage to karma and rebirth.[5]

Perhaps, then, the Buddha's direct perception of reality in terms of karmic bondage and the key to release (stopping craving) gave him a confidence about reality parallel to the confidence that Jesus derived from his faith in his heavenly Father. The Father took away the fearsome aspects of reality, overbalancing the hatred and evil. Similarly, because the Buddha knew the key to all suffering, felt he had undercut the imperfect human condition itself (and so had come to the verge of a nirvana that would bring being, bliss, and awareness), he could pass through the world unafraid. Wanting nothing, needing virtually nothing, he could give himself over to teaching and healing others. The Buddha felt akin to the light at the center of reality, to the illumination necessary for anything to exist. Jesus felt himself to be the Son of God, and before long his followers were calling him God's Word. Surely the two leaders were similarly mystical.

Confucius

If the Buddha has been a paramount teacher in India, Confucius has been the paramount teacher in East Asia. Indeed, Confucian ethics remained a formative power even during Chinese and Japanese eras when Buddhism predominated. Confucius, like the Buddha, lived about five hundred years before Jesus. The main records we have, the collection of sayings known as the *Analects* and the sayings of a later disciple named Mencius, depict a rather proper master whose honor was his greatest treasure. Confucius considered himself not an innovator but a renovator of the traditions of the heroes of old. The "way" that he taught was the time-honored wisdom that descended from the golden age when men (classical China was a patriarchy) were full of humaneness and followed carefully the rituals designed to keep society harmonious.

These two concepts, humaneness (*jen*) and ritual propriety (*li*), summarize central parts of Confucius' teaching. Humaneness was a rare virtue that showed humanity at its best. It connoted love, benevolence, the absence of any untoward dispositions or emotions. Were people humane at heart, they would not break out in the wars and strifes that dominated Confucius' day. Were Confucius able to tutor a prince in humaneness and ritual, people might hope to live in a state where justice and culture would flourish.

Li connoted all of the ritual, formal and informal, by which people smoothed social interactions and expressed their relationships to nature and to the ancestors. For Confucius, the way to prosperity had to pass through a knowledge of social etiquette and a disciplined practice. The official rites of the state, which from time immemorial had been looked upon as necessary for prosperity, carried a sacral aura. The daily interactions among family members, friends, colleagues, and the like all were the better for being regulated by a keen sense of form and place. Thus the Confucian world view was quite hierarchical. Men predominated over women, the aged predominated over the young, rulers predominated over ordinary people, and so on. If individual households were well-regulated by the proper submission of women to men and children to parents, the entire state would be in good order.

Herbert Fingarette has made a good case for the profundity of the Confucian understanding of human beings' ritual interactions.[6] In contrast to our Western tendency to depreciate outer forms in the name of interior sincerity or motivation, Confucius instinctively appreciated how greatly we are molded by the ways that we greet one another, work together, pay our respects, venerate the powers sacred in our society, and so on. The result of this appreciation is a high standard of human refinement, what Confucius called the "gentleman," who seldom gives any offense and consistently is gracious.

Much more could be said about Confucius, of course, but we have noted enough to stimulate some reflections on the differences and likenesses to Jesus. First, there is nothing in the world view of Confucius that approximates to the Father of Jesus. Confucius honors the way of the ancients, and he sometimes speaks of humaneness as a mystical or heavenly quality, but Confucian ethics are quite thoroughly this-worldly. Indeed, at many points we see Confucius in effect teaching his disciples that virtue is its own reward. One does not keep to the way of a gentleman for any reason other than its intrinsic rightness or the integrity that it brings. We hear autobiographic echoes of Confucius' own progress along the path toward such an integrity in *Analects* 2:4: "The Master said, At fifteen I set my heart upon learning. At thirty, I had planted my feet firm upon the ground. At forty, I no longer suffered from perplexities. At fifty, I knew what were the biddings of Heaven. At sixty, I heard them with docile ear. At seventy, I could follow the dictates of my own heart; for what I desired no longer overstepped the boundaries of right."[7] The "Heaven" in this quotation is susceptible of religious interpretation, but it is far from the personal, parental God that motivated Jesus.

Second, Confucius, like the Buddha, tends to see the great problems of humanity as residing in ignorance rather than sin. The Confucian program calls for education and discipline, not a renovation of heart called conversion. To be sure, if education and discipline take hold deeply enough, they amount to a conversion. But Confucius does not have the prophetic tradition that Jesus has, the long line of predecessors who called for a reform of human beings' deepest loves and inclinations. He does not have a vocabulary of faith, hope, and love, to name the different modalities by which one may reach out to the mysterious God or express the inward reach of the divine Spirit. There is no discussion of revelation, marvelous signs of the divine power, resurrection, or the Kingdom of God. The entire Confucian orbit is more sober, sapiential, this-worldly than what we find in the Gospels.

Of course, one finds sapiential strains in the Gospels and Epistles, employments of Wisdom motifs from the Hebrew Bible. Before long Christian theology makes Jesus the divine Logos who has inspired any wisdom or virtue that has ever arisen. But the first instinct of the earliest Christian writers is to see Jesus as the prophetic figure whose paradoxical victory by suffering and dying completely overturned ordinary human expectations. To Confucius' mind Jesus' defeat would have been a very unseemly humiliation, so deep a challenge to propriety and integrity that the Master would have needed great time and study to appropriate it.

The great contrast between Jesus and Confucius therefore comes down to their respective senses of what is possible in human life. Confucius thought that it was possible for human beings to live by ethical virtue, decency, and truthfulness—no mean achievement. What might lie beyond the grave was hard to say—so hard that the proper business of gentlemen was this-worldly wisdom, not supernatural speculations. Jesus, on the other hand, defined reality from the perspective of an intense personal relationship with a Fatherly Creator of the world. For Jesus all things were possible, because reality was what the Father chose to have happen, not what nature or human convention said was likely to occur. This is not to say that Jesus disregarded the laws of statistical probability and constantly wondered whether the sun would rise the next day. It is to say, however, that Jesus presents a more poetic, imaginative, unstable or unconventional personal profile than Confucius. He is a powerful seer pictured in late youth or early middle age, when his great energy is completely engaged with the fight against what oppresses people (sin or Satan). Confucius is the voice of longer experience, and perhaps more straitened imagination, heard when it has gone beyond disillusionment with human weakness, can no longer be surprised by human vice, and now is mainly interested in meditating on the cosmic ways that could heal human community.

Perhaps this last notion affords us a link between Jesus and Confucius that may lessen their otherwise stark contrasts. If we are willing to take Confucius' rather vague references to the "way" of Heaven as a possible outreach to a divinity cast in impersonal form, we may suspect that his confidence in the rightness of this way, and in its healing powers, brings him close to Jesus' faith in his heavenly Father.

Ultimately, of course, both final references are mysterious. Confucius gives no indication of wanting to restrict the significance of Heaven or the ancients' way to a code in the delimiting, simply legal sense. The ritual that Confucius encourages is meant to inculcate the dispositions of humaneness, as well as to integrate the individual and the group into the cosmic scheme of things. The emotion that occasionally turns up when Confucius is recalling the beauty of the ritual, or a favorite melody, suggests that something much more holistic than legal propriety is involved. So when the Master says that he could hear the way in the morning and in the evening die content (*Analects* 4:8), we get the feeling that the way was for him a meat and drink much like the will of Jesus' Father. For both great teachers, the main thing was to be connected to the ultimate, holy source of all order and justice.

Lao-tzu

Lao-tzu is the second great master in Chinese history. He is more legendary than Confucius (current scholarly estimates place the author of the *Lao-tzu* or *Tao Te Ching* about two hundred years after Confucius) and more mystical. Like Confucius, he was greatly interested in the principles of statecraft: how to bring the people peace and prosperity. Unlike

Confucius, he taught that the best government was the government least intrusive. For Lao-tzu human beings are at their best when social life is unadorned, when rituals and conventions are few. The closer people can stay to nature and nature's Way, the better off they will be. In the golden ages of the past, people lived simply, with little fuss and practically no legislation. The current spate of laws and customs represents a decline from the earlier vigor, a distancing of humankind from the Way that alone can make it prosper.

For Lao-tzu the Way of nature is beyond human grasp, but it is better evidenced by the female than by the male, by the valley than by the mountain. Most of what people take for power and achievement actually amounts to very little. It is the ugly, gnarled tree that survives the woodsman's axe. It is the emptiness, the space, that makes a house useful, not the furniture or clutter. The best way for rulers to guide a state is by **wu-wei:** active passivity, creative not-doing. That is how water wears away stone, how an infant gets a whole household to revolve around its needs. Good government is like frying fish: the less one stirs and interferes, the better the result.

Commentators dispute over the blend of mysticism and politics in the *Lao-tzu.* Part of the work's perennial appeal, in fact, is its ambiguity, which allows many different interpretations. It seems likely that the author engaged in some sort of meditational practice, for his ponderings of the ultimate character of the Way take us to the edge of human imagination. So, for example, the very first chapter posits a crucial distinction between the aspects of the Way that we can name and the aspects that are too basic or primordial to be caught by human terms: "The Way that can be told is not an Unvarying Way; the names that can be named are not unvarying names. It was from the Nameless that Heaven and Earth sprang; the named is but the mother that rears the ten thousand creatures, each after its kind. Truly, 'Only he that rids himself forever of desire can see the Secret Essences'; he that has never rid himself of desire can see only the outcomes. These two things issued from the same mould, but nevertheless are different in name. This 'same mould' we can but call the Mystery, or rather the 'Darker than any Mystery,' the doorway whence issued all secret essences."[8]

Few scholars would be so rash as to claim certainty for any interpretation of this famous passage, but it strikes the comparative religionist as the kind of speech that "negative theology" generates in many traditions. Negative theology is especially impressed by the difference between the ultimate reality and normal, workaday realities. The difference between God and creatures, for example, is such that only a thin analogy allows us to say that God is good or true in the way we normally employ those words. The ultimate reality, not bounded in the way that things of space and time are bounded, exists in a way that we can only glimpse. Everything that we say about this ultimate reality therefore is quite provisional. We always do well to speak about God or the Way (Tao) humbly, in full awareness that we are trying to empty the ocean with a teaspoon.

The *Tao Te Ching* has many other themes and symbols that any full study of Lao-tzu would have to investigate, but already we can sense the vast differences in mood and outlook that separate it from the New Testament. Where Lao-tzu looks to nature for inspiration, Jesus looks to his heavenly Father. Where Lao-tzu has little use for laws and conventions, Jesus takes a quite nuanced position regarding Torah. Lao-tzu expects little of human beings, so mired are they in artificiality, so forgetful of the "uncarved block" (their raw potentiality) that is their greatest riches. Jesus thinks of human beings as children of a heavenly Father, heirs of the Kingdom of Heaven. For Lao-tzu the problem is human folly and amnesia. People don't have the intimacy with nature, the sense of nature's Way, that is their most basic birthright. For Jesus the problem is human sin: people not doing the good they should do, people enacting the evil they know they should not do. This moral weakness makes no sense, presents a problem deeper than simple ignorance. Only if people gain a new love, set their hearts on better treasures, will they be able to break the cycles of injustice and hurting that now hold them captive.

Like Confucius, Lao-tzu thinks little of an afterlife or a realm we could call heaven. The Chinese ideal was longevity, in the sense of a ripe old age. It was important to reverence one's ancestors, who for some time after death retained a shadowy, ghostly existence, and sometimes **Taoist** imagination took over Buddhist speculation about heavenly realms to create a vivid series of places of bliss and places of punishment. But the *Tao Te Ching* itself is rather sober and this-worldly. If one would stay apart from the foolish crowd, let one's spirit breathe and come into harmony with the Way, one could gain peace and happiness. Anything more external or material was fragile indeed—subject to a dozen whims of unstable rulers or fellow citizens.

The sense of the Spirit that ruled Jesus therefore is quite lacking in Lao-tzu. Nothing of a personal God capable of making the world from nothingness or saving the world from its disorders enters into Lao-tzu's political calculus to provide redemption or rescue. The best wisdom that one can muster is a shrewd sense of how arbitrary human calculations are, how much less than inevitable or certain. Jesus shares some of this outlook, in that he places little trust in popular opinion, but one gets the sense that for Jesus such human unreliability is a somewhat accidental defect. Were people to keep faith with their heavenly Father they could see things aright. No matter how humble their circumstances, how deep their material poverty, openness to the Spirit could make them wise.

Lao-tzu seems to take human perverseness or stupidity as a given. Among the majority, he implies, one will always find foolish judgments, opinions that are untested and won't stand up. The best thing one could do for the state at large, therefore, would be to drop almost all of the laws and regulations. Then people might return to the simple living that preceded this lawless age. The making of laws is a straight formula for making criminals. The more regulations one has, the more the mentality of the lawyer flourishes, to the great detriment of all.

We see, therefore, how little we ought to take for granted Jesus' sense of a revealed religion. The Torah that Jesus mainly accepted (for all that he wanted to simplify it to a wholehearted love of God and neighbor) was a guide thought to come from the Maker of the World. Lao-tzu knew of no Maker of the World. For him the world always had been, and the most that the world gave out was a sense of the Way that gave it direction, the path that could bring human beings into harmony with nature and with one another. No line of prophets mediated the Law of a personal Creator God. No holy writings gathered up words or directives thought to come from the Lord of Heaven and Earth. Lao-tzu's people had no treasury of memories that promised them a future deliverance. No Exodus or giving of the Law on Mount Sinai gave concrete form to their hopes for liberation from present sufferings, for the arrival of a reign that would be worthy of human aspirations toward justice.

The wisdom of Lao-tzu was a wisdom of survival. Granted the bent nature of humanity en masse, how might one best survive? The wisdom of Jesus was more medicinal: How may we straighten human nature? What force may prove more powerful than human malice and death? The ultimate symbol on which Jesus' system came to hang was the Cross and Resurrection. The ultimate symbol to which followers of Lao-tzu could point was the silent, relentless Way. No matter how bad human affairs became, nature always insinuated the Way, the reality that was always greater than human folly.

Zoroaster

Confucius, Lao-tzu, and the Buddha all strike the comparativist as sapiential rather than prophetic figures. That is, they seem more interested in a wisdom that would explain the foundations of the cosmos and the political order than in visions of justice or reform that would set human affairs straight. This is not a hard-and-fast distinction, of course. Seldom do we find religious leaders who do not mix the prophetic and the sapiential. But the general emphasis in the East has been on wisdom, while prophecy has played a more significant role in the West.

Zoroaster is a prophetic figure more like Moses and Jesus than like the Buddha, Confucius, and Lao-tzu. The history of Zoroaster and his movement is rather shadowy, but the current working hypothesis is that he flourished in ancient Persia (Iran) about six hundred years before

Jesus. He was a firebrand, preaching a strict morality that drew on a **dualistic** view of the world. On the one side were the powers of evil led by the evil spirit Angra Mainyu. On the other side were the stronger powers of good led by Ahura Mazda ("Wise Lord"). Zoroaster spoke of numerous intermediary powers, most of them apparently extrapolated from his awareness of his own powers of thought ("truth," "light"). Zoroastrians were to worship Ahura Mazda through a fire sacrifice (symbolizing the purity of the Wise Lord). They were to marry, procreate, till the fields, and help livestock flourish, as contributions to the victory of the forces of goodness and life over the forces of evil and death.

A final judgment would settle this cosmic battle, and at death the individual would pass across a famous bridge: "From the creation through the present age to the final judgment and the reordering of the universe, the events of this world are seen as a contest between the powers of good and evil. It is incumbent on the faithful to choose the right, not only so that individually they may achieve the reward of the righteous beyond death, but so that good may triumph in the world. Upon death, according to Zoroastrian belief, the soul of the deceased crosses a bridge, the Chinvat Bridge ('Bridge of the Separator'), which widens to permit easy passage of the righteous but shrinks to a knife-edge for the wicked so that they fall into the abyss of torment below."[9]

Zoroaster himself, on the evidence of hymns that he left, seems to have meditated and prayed with a great awareness of the relationship between his own mental life and the ultimate domain of the Wise Lord and Evil Spirit. That is, he seems to have reverenced the Wise Lord and the other good spirits as either present in his own good thoughts or as similar in spiritual nature to such thoughts. Thus we find prayers such as the following: "As the holy one I recognized thee, O Wise Lord, when he came to me as Good Mind. To his question: 'To whom wilt thou address thy worship?' I made reply: 'To thy fire! While I offer up my veneration to it, I will think of the Right to the utmost of my power'. . . . As the holy one I recognized thee, O Wise Lord, when he came to me as Good Mind, when first I was instructed in your words. Suffering among men will be caused to me by my zeal to carry out that which you tell me is the greatest good."[10]

Zoroastrian religion therefore involves trying to think of the Right to the utmost of one's power. For the prophet himself, it also involved a commission: he was to preach to others the words of revelation that the Wise Lord had given him. This would bring him suffering, for presumably the people to whom he was preaching would not want to change their untruthful ways. And so it was: as best we can conjecture, Zoroaster frequently had to flee for his life, and he spent most of his career struggling to gain a positive hearing. Eventually his ethical scheme and his main deity Ahura Mazda became the approved religion of the Iranian rulers, and Zoroastrianism has continued to evolve down to the present era, where it is represented by the Parsis in India and has an overall world population of perhaps 275,000.

Zoroaster is similar to Jesus in being a prophet but different in being the prophet of quite a different God. Both men demanded a strict morality, but Zoroaster spoke more of truth or honesty, while Jesus spoke more of kindness and love. Jesus did not share Zoroaster's dualism, for there was no question of parity between Satan and his Father. Jesus did share Zoroaster's sense of a coming judgment (the Jewish eschatology that Jesus inherited probably was considerably influenced by Zoroastrian ideas), but he did not preach a fire sacrifice or depict the believer's battle in terms of a cosmic struggle between forces of fertility and of death. Zoroaster was opposed to asceticism (although fiercely insistent on honesty), while Jesus largely accepted the restraints of the Jewish Law. (Jesus did, however, gain a reputation as a drinker and party-goer. See Matthew 11:19.) There was nothing in Zoroaster's teaching, as we can reconstruct it, that approximated Jesus' central notion of the Kingdom of God.

Relatedly, Jesus depended on an intimate child-parent relationship with his God, and on an overwhelming sense of God's grace. Zoroaster's relationship with his Wise Lord appears considerably more formal and submissive. For while Jesus certainly is presented as completely obedient to his heavenly Father, his prayer is that of a child wholly confident that it will be heard. Indeed, as we have seen, Jesus tells his followers to bother God with their prayers, in the assurance that if they ask for bread they will not receive a stone. And he seems to see more clearly than Zoroaster the personal crux of social evils: the unwillingness of most people to be generous and nonjudgmental, to be like the Father who makes his rain to fall on just and unjust alike.

Thus one does not find in Zoroaster the sense that his sufferings are part of the redemptive process itself. Where Jesus is presented as going to his passion and death as a sacrifice for sins, Zoroaster is presented as the good man who is willing to endure the consequences of his commission to preach the truth or revelation of the Wise Lord. We hear of no resurrection ratifying Zoroaster's mission, and there is not the sense that in Zoroaster God made a new creation, completely overturning the old order of death and destructiveness. Rather, the accent throughout the Zoroastrian prayers is on a blazing desire to live in the ethical light, to do what is right and just. This is a very significant achievement, of course, and Zoroaster's interiorization of the inspirations of the Wise Lord is a noteworthy chapter in the story of the "axial age" (around 500 B.C.E.), when the significance of personal conscience was dawning. But we are left wondering how this fierce ethical instinct was actually enfleshed, let alone how it might have mellowed to go gently with human weaknesses and sins.

Finally, one does not find a strong motif of healing in the Zoroastrian materials, as one does in the materials about Jesus. No doubt Zoroaster thought that living in the light of the Wise Lord was already a significant healing of the incursions that the Evil Spirit was making, but the New Testament portraits of Jesus giving sight to the blind and making the lame walk suggest that for him healing was more physical and closer to the essence of his work. Because of Jesus' power to heal, as well as the power of his teaching, his followers came to see his very arrival as the dawn of salvation. The Kingdom of God that Jesus proclaimed was credible because people had never seen such power go out from a prophet, had never heard words so full of "eternal life."

In other words, salvation bulks larger in Jesus' profile than it does in Zoroaster's, let alone in the profiles of Confucius and Lao-tzu. (The Buddha is a more complicated case, since the quotient of healing, especially of spiritual ills, is higher in the records of the Buddha.) Jesus was quickly interpreted as God's anointed one because he had brought the health or healing that his people associated with the presence of God. In him God was making whole what had become fractured, was buying back what had become lost. Zoroaster was like Jesus in fighting against the powers of evil that could swell up to Satanic force, but we find little indication that his followers looked upon him as a great savior, let alone that they began to acclaim him as divine. Thus there is worship of Jesus but not of Zoroaster.

Muhammad

There is no worship of Muhammad, since the central creed of Islam is that there is no God but God. Yet there is great veneration of Muhammad, because the remainder of the central Islamic creed is that Muhammad is the prophet of God—the seal or consummating moment in the long line of God's messengers that includes Abraham and Jesus. Muhammad lived about five and a half centuries after Jesus, and with Moses and Jesus he stands as a great shaper of Western religious history. Today his followers are second only to Christians in numerical strength, and at the height of the Muslim empires their sway extended from Gibraltar to Delhi.

Muhammad grew up in a polytheistic climate, a world populated with many angels and demons. When he was about forty he felt the need for solitude, so he took himself to a cave outside Mecca. There he began to receive visions of the angel Gabriel, who helped to communicate to him the messages of the sole God Allah. The Qur'an is the record of the revelations that Muhammad received over the twenty-two years or so between the beginning of his prophetic call and his death in 632 C.E. The most beloved of the **surahs** in the Qur'an, which now serves Muslims somewhat the way that the Our Father serves Christians, is the very first: "In the Name of God, the merciful Lord of Mercy. Praise be to God, the Lord of all being, the merciful Lord of Mercy, Master of the day of judgment. You alone we serve and to you alone we come for aid. Guide us in the straight path, the path of those whom you have blessed, not of those against whom there is displeasure, nor of those who go astray."[11]

This surah summarizes much of Muslim piety, and we may presume that Muslims believe that it represents the heart of Muhammad's message and personality. All holy acts begin in the name of God, the merciful Lord of Mercy, because God is the sole Creator, responsible for all that exists. For Islam the central sin is idolatry: setting anything alongside God. That is why Islam could never worship Muhammad, a mere man, and why the sovereignty of God is enforced both positively and negatively. Positively, Allah is the tremendous power suggested by nature, the imperious will suggested by the greatest human rulers. Negatively, to place anything in competition with Allah is to insult the holy force responsible for the world and to pollute one's inmost soul. Above all, the human being is a creature, one designed to "submit" (the central idea behind the words *Muslim* and *Islam*). Not to confess the sole divinity of Allah is to denature one's being and try to tilt reality.

That Allah is merciful, when he might easily condemn, is the core of Muhammad's good news. The Prophet has a wondrous revelation to proclaim, because Allah is slow to anger and quick to forgive, like the Israelites' Yahweh. Muhammad's main criticism of Jews and Christians, whom he considered religious siblings ("people of the Book") because of their monotheism and prophecy, was that they had not kept their sense of Allah sufficiently exalted. Through their teaching that God had taken to himself a Son, Christians were especially deficient in faith. Jews erred principally by failing to accept Muhammad as the seal of the prophets.

Muhammad's preaching stresses the mercy of Allah, who is as near to the believer as the pulse at one's throat, but it also announces a coming judgment. All idolaters and wicked people will be brought to trial and swift punishment, for the sole God is just and true. On judgment day the good will gain the reward of "the Garden," a place flowing with lovely streams and populated with buxom **hur.** The wicked will be cast into "the Fire," where they shall pay the full price for their transgressions. The wise person therefore resolves to serve the true God alone and make only Allah his or her source of aid. That is the straight path, announced by God's chosen prophet. (Spelled out, it includes the "five pillars" that summarize Muslim religious obligations: (1) to confess Allah and Muhammad, (2) to pray five times a day, (3) to fast during the lunar month of Ramadan, (4) to give alms, and (5) to go to Mecca at least once during one's life on pilgrimage.) Not to follow this path, when one has had the great grace of having it proclaimed, is to wander into perdition and court Allah's fierce displeasure.

Compared to Jesus, Muhammad is both more judgmental and more worldly. Both prophets announce a time of crisis, but Muhammad's announcement has more political and military consequences. For Jesus the hour was ripe with the Kingdom of God, a regime that would set right all relations between God and human beings. Jesus himself was manifesting the dawn of this new era, and Christians believed that at Jesus' Parousia the Kingdom would be established forever. Muhammad saw his message as demanding acceptance politically as well as religiously. From his day, Islam has been reluctant to separate the religious and the secular spheres. To be a Muslim has meant to grant Allah full sovereignty in one's life and to bow low to the Prophet (or the **caliphs** who succeeded him at the head of the "House of Islam") in affairs of state as well as ecclesiastical matters. In fact, Muhammad gained considerable prowess as a warrior, winning back the Mecca from which he had been forced to flee and beginning the campaigns that soon after his death sent Islamic armies forth on a far-reaching tide of conquest. So where Jesus' sense of battle (against Satan or the Jewish religious establishment) was mainly spiritual, Muhammad took on foes with the sword as well as the word.

A second difference between Muhammad and Jesus lay in their understanding of human beings' basic problem. They agreed that most human disorder sprang from insufficient submission to God. However, where Muhammad wanted people to be slaves of Allah, bowing their backs and touching their foreheads to the ground five times each day at prayer, Jesus wanted people to deal with God as a completely trusted Father, as one who could not fail to hear their prayers. Jesus did have a place for God the judge, and Muhammad could speak tenderly of God's beauty and mercy, but the initial picture in each man's mind was instructively different. To Muhammad, Allah was the Lord, the sovereign creator and ruler of the worlds. To Jesus, God was first of all "Abba," the Father who never left him, whose Spirit always was nigh. Jesus thought that human beings ran afoul of God and one another because of their sinfulness, which boiled down to a refusal to open their hearts wide and to love. The Father was too good for human beings to accredit, more demanding in his goodness and holiness than lazy and weak creatures could accept.

Muhammad thought that human beings were weak and forgetful. He seems not to have been influenced by the Adamic myth that spoke of a primal disaster setting all human beings on the outs with God. For him human beings' waywardness did not present the mystery of iniquity, the ways in which sin is utterly irrational and thus beyond human understanding. To Muhammad the main requisites were quite plain: submit your mind, your heart, your body to the will of the sole God (who has spelled out his desires in his revelations to me). To Jesus the drama was more murky: how could people reject the goodness for which their hearts had been made, the messenger who came to them only for healing and love?

Islam does not speak of a saving death and resurrection by which God intervened to turn the human condition around. The salvation that streams from the Qur'an is the healing possible when one rightly hears the divine revelation. Similarly, Islam does not speak of the divinization of the believer, the share in God's own love-life that Christianity associates with grace. Quite enough is the reward of the Garden and the sense of being pleasing to God. There is no way that God could cross the chasm separating creatures and Creator to communicate a share in the divine life. Muslim mystics occasionally spoke of union with God, but if they went on very long in this vein they ran into trouble with the guardians of Muslim orthodoxy. Thus al-Hallaj, one of the most famous Muslim mystics, was slain because he spoke of becoming one with divinity. Jesus probably would have been slain as well.

Socrates

Socrates, who lived about four and a half centuries before Jesus, often is placed in counterpoint with Jesus as the "good pagan" contrasted with the reputed Son of God. Our picture of Socrates mainly comes from Plato, whom he obviously impressed very much. For Plato, Socrates was the wisest man in Athens (mainly because he knew what he did not know), and perhaps the most pious man as well. Socrates consistently followed the voice of his **daimon** or inner spirit, refusing to do anything that this call of conscience forbade. Thus when the council of Athenian elders put Socrates to death on the charge of impiety, Plato saw revealed a great depth of human depravity. Apparently his beloved city could not tolerate a man who wanted only to show it its follies and pretentiousness. Apparently, pursuing the truth—trying to learn what things really were in themselves—was more than the average city father could bear.

The image of Socrates that has come down to later Western history stresses his fidelity to conscience. He was willing to die rather than abdicate his hard-won beliefs, and he comported himself in the face of death with consummate dignity, since he was convinced that preserving the integrity of one's soul was much more important than saving one's poor body (which was soon to die anyway). The full portrait of Socrates that Plato paints is richer than this sketch (from the *Apology*), telling us that Socrates considered his main province the doings of the god Eros. In matters of love of beauty and truth, Socrates felt that he should cede to no one. The Platonic dialogues also portray Socrates as a dialectical gadfly, ceaselessly trying to talk through a problem and expose his interlocutors' inconsistencies. He fiercely opposed the **Sophists,** who would sell out the truth for rhetorical advantage. And he was a great patriot, serving his city-state as a soldier and being convinced that his work of trying to raise the ethical standards of the general citizenry was a great civil service.

In the *Phaedo*, which purports to be the record of a conversation with Socrates the day before he accepted the state's punishment and drank the draught of hemlock, Plato gives us a description of the life of philosophy that Socrates exemplified. The description makes it plain that for Socrates philosophy was nothing merely doctrinal but rather the education of an immortal soul for a blessed afterlife: "A philosopher's soul will take the view which I have described. It will not first expect to be set free by philosophy, and then allow pleasure and pain to reduce it once more to bondage, thus taking upon itself an endless task, like Penelope when she undid her own weaving. No, this soul secures immunity from its desires by following reason and abiding always in her company, and by contemplating the true and divine and unconjecturable, and drawing inspiration from it, because such a soul believes that this is the right way to live while life endures, and that after death it reaches a place which is kindred and similar to its own nature, and there is rid forever of human ills. After such a training, my dear Simmias and Cebes, the soul can have no grounds for fearing that on its separation from the body it will be blown away and scattered by the winds, and so disappear into thin air, and cease to exist altogether."[12]

The similarities and differences between Jesus and Socrates have long fascinated students of Western culture. Insofar as Christian religion and Greek philosophy (along with Jewish religion and Roman law) have been at the wellsprings of Western civilization, the influence of these two paradigmatic figures could hardly be overestimated. Both made their deep impressions in good measure, of course, because they paid a high price for their ideals. Socrates went to his death, ripe in years but nonetheless before his natural time, because he would not desist from irritating people who found his revelations of their ignorance humiliating. Indeed, he would not flee from prison, when he well might have, because he counted himself a great supporter of the city-state, and fleeing would have violated his implicit contract to honor what the city-state prescribed in his case.

But the deepest cause of Socrates' willingness to seal his teaching with the witness of his death was the conviction expressed in the passage we have quoted. By his fidelity to the life of philosophy he could hope to have prepared a soul worthy to enjoy a blissful afterlife. No earthly existence in the flesh could compare with this spiritual life to which he could look forward, so not even the natural revulsion of the spirit at the prospect of being separated from the body was to be taken overly seriously. Thus the *Apology* concludes; "Now it is time that we were going, I to die and you to live, but which of us has the happier prospect is unknown to anyone but God."[13] We may be quite sure that Socrates was confident that in God's knowledge he would fare very well.

Jesus is not presented as so calm in the face of death. At his "agony in the garden" (Matthew 26 : 36–46), his soul was sorrowful unto death. This did not keep him from going forward with his mission, any more than earlier presentiments of his final suffering had, but it did cast a pall over his final days. Similarly, the death that Jesus died on the cross had little of the detachment and dignity with which Plato surrounds the demise of Socrates. Jesus dies as a common criminal, broken in body and perhaps feeling abandoned in spirit. His disciples have fled. The only followers who remain loyal are the band of women standing by the cross. According to the Jewish law, Jesus dies accursed (a judgment that stimulated Paul to rethink Jewish law completely and find it wanting).

Christian interpreters of Jesus, for all the influence of the Resurrection and a horizon of victory, had to contend with an almost grisly paradox. Not thinking of the human being as an immortal soul residing only passingly in a mortal body, they had to accept the breaking of their leader, his ruin in historical terms. The Resurrection was God's nearly unthinkable act of raising Jesus to the divine sphere where such ruin became glorious. It was the reaction of the Father to the fidelity of his beloved Son, and it made the death of Christ the means for radically renewing all humankind. In Pauline terms, the death of Christ was the defeat of Satan and death. Christ "became sin" for the sake of humankind, suffering in all innocence the punishment merited by all those who had ever closed themselves to God. This moved his death, and his overall meaning, onto a plane completely different from that of Socrates. It made Jesus the Messiah and God-man who had ushered in a new creation.

Apart from their different views of the soul and the different sorts of death they underwent, Socrates and Jesus also differ in their views of God. Socrates accepts the polytheism of his Athenian culture, however much his own spiritual refinement may lead him to collectivize the notion of the divine. But the divine is not his intimate parent, and it is not necessary for the forgiveness of sins or the salvation of a humanity ruined apart from it. The human vocation, according to Plato, is to become as much like God as possible, and Christian theologians drew on this classical notion when they worked out their ideas of divinization. Socrates, in his lofty ethical achievements, is a godlike figure, and Greek culture would have had little difficulty in granting him some sort of more-than-human status. But Socrates himself wants little of this. His stress, rather, is on the grandeur that comes from cultivating the soul, from helping it develop the immortal potential within it.

Jesus thinks in less ontological terms. For him the prophetic call to love God and do justice to one's neighbor is the paramount voice to heed. As well, Jesus is concerned to heal suffering humanity. Socrates, by contrast, is interested only in the sort of healing that good teaching can bring about. Those who persist in their ignorance and folly have only themselves to blame. In the Socratic outlook, no mystery of sin tilts the entire board; Satan is not the ultimate counterplayer, intent on human beings' destruction. Thus, no Kingdom of God is dawning, no time of crisis is announced. Socrates is concerned to give a good example and to be true to his own principles. He is concerned to show that death is not the greatest enemy. Jesus wants only a complete love.

Krishna

Krishna is the most popular of the Hindu gods, and probably he is the god who is treated most closely to the way that many Christians treat Jesus. In devotional Hinduism (**bhakti**), which is the most popular strain of the Hindu tradition (philosophical Hinduism, yoga, and **tantra** by comparison are minority strains), Krishna is the most beloved god, around whose figure a rich mythology has arisen: "In the *Mahabhrata* and later *Puranas*, especially the *Bhagavata Purana*, Krishna is the son of Vasudeva, and hence called Vasudeva, a wonderful and mischievous child, a youth amorous of the Gopis (milkmaids), a hero, warrior, and king. Finally he dies by being shot inadvertently in the foot and returns to heaven. None of this comes in the *Bhagavad-Gita*, where he is the divine instructor of Arjuna and supreme Deity with little reference to Vishnu [whose **avatar** he is considered to be in many other legends]."[14]

In most of devotional Hinduism, Krishna is the object of a warm, even an erotic, love. He represents divinity as playful, beautiful, and concerned about human beings. People can lay before Krishna their troubles and their hopes. Often he functions as the human face of a deity with whom they passionately desire mystical union. Little in the traditions about Krishna makes him a historical figure by the standards of current historiography. Unlike Jesus, he was not a "real" human being born of ordinary parents such as Mary and Joseph. But for many Hindus this sort of reality is much less important than the spiritual reality that Krishna has as the beloved partner of their prayers and imaginative life. Where a god such as Shiva appears almost fierce in his holiness, as an ascetic who holds the powers of destruction (considered necessary for the ongoing pulsation of creation and destruction by which the Hindu universe runs), Krishna is gracious and approachable. He is the best-known form of Vishnu, who in turn is the member of the Hindu "trinity" (Brahma-Vishnu-Shiva) most concerned with creativity, and he gives creativity or ultimate reality a very winning countenance.

Still, Hinduism also has endowed Krishna with the splendors or powers of divinity proper, and seldom more dramatically than in the *Bhagavad-Gita*, its most influential work. Thus in 11:9—13 the Gita has Krishna (whom it here calls Vishnu) grant Arjuna, the human figure whom Krishna has been counseling, a vision of Vishnu's true, unveiled reality: "With these words, Visnu, the great Lord of mystic power, gave Arjuna the vision of his highest, absolute form—his form with many mouths and eyes, appearing in many miraculous ways, with many divine ornaments and divine, unsheathed weapons. He wore garlands and robes and ointments of divine fragrance. He was a wholly wonderful god, infinite, facing in every direction. If the light of a thousand suns should effulge all at once, it would resemble the radiance of that god of overpowering reality. Then and there, Arjuna saw the entire world unified, yet divided manifold, embodied in the God of gods." [15] This is the passage that J. Robert Oppenheimer, the American father of the atomic bomb, had flash through his mind when he saw the first atomic device exploded.

Krishna, then, can denote the fullest powers of divinity, the blinding light by which the universe hangs together. The key to his popularity in Hinduism, however, probably lies less in this famous theophany than in the ultimate revelations of the final chapter of the Gita (18:64–65), where the god promises Arjuna (that is, all potential devotees) that he truly loves him. In the full spectrum of Hindu theology, such love is extraordinary. It puts a very personal cast on what generally is an impersonal ultimate. In yoga, for instance, the general advice is to distance oneself from all emotion, so as to experience in oneself the pure spirituality that is the presence of divinity (conceived as the ultimate stuff of all things). But the bhakti or devotional love that Krishna has sponsored contradicts this yogic wisdom, saying that emotional warmth (which requires no special education, training, caste, or sexual dispositions) can take one to the highest union with ultimately reality.

Jesus often has functioned in Christian spirituality as the object of an intense devotional love. The Roman Catholic devotion to the Sacred Heart of Jesus, for example, expressly encourages what a comparativist might call a Christian bhakti. The Johannine literature of the New Testament is explicit in making love the best analogue for the Christian God, and in saying that there is no greater love than laying down one's life for one's friends as Jesus did. The Pauline hymn to charity (1 Corinthians 13) pitches in with similar convictions. The typical Hindu's love of Krishna may be more romantic than the typical pious Christian's love of Jesus, but even this judgment would demand some qualifications. If one scraped a bit below the psychological surface, the Christian mystics' theme of spiritual marriage might come into greater prominence.

The main differences between Krishna and Jesus therefore relate not so much to the love they have elicited from their followers as to their own historical identities. As noted, Krishna is a figure of myth rather than actual history. Moreover, the stories about him are considerably less tragic than the stories about Jesus. No crucifixion calls into question the rightness of the plan that Krishna centers. No resurrection symbolizes a very mysterious, paradoxical divine action to remake human nature. Krishna sponsors a love that could spill over into helpful attitudes towards one's neighbors, but he does not preach a call to conversion, social justice, the Kingdom of God, and the other items on Jesus' quite prophetic agenda. Various demons try to trouble the child Krishna, but usually he crushes them easily. He is not a figure pursued by a Satan who will dog him to a Calvary, who will turn the leaders of the religious establishment against him.

Relatedly, Krishna is not the challenge to Hindu orthodoxy that Jesus was to Jewish orthodoxy. To be sure, Hindu "orthodoxy" is much harder to define. The Hindu way has been to reach out and embrace almost any new development, casting few anathemas or excommunications. When the religion of the priests, which was centered on sacrifice, came under assault from various sides (the Upanishads and the rise of Buddhism both may be seen as attacks on **Brahmanism**), this more inclusive reaction determined that later movements, such as the various waves of Hindu devotionalism, would not be considered heretical. So Krishna has not, through Hindu history, forced the typical Indian to choose in the way that Jesus has forced both Jews and Gentiles. The *Bhagavad-Gita*, for instance, allows one to worship Krishna through devotional love, but it also lays out several other legitimate spiritual paths (**margas**). The Christian notion that Jesus is the way, the truth, and the life has frequently carried an exclusive sense (the only way, truth, and life), but this has seldom held true for Krishna.

Finally, various differences between the world view that Jesus inherited and the traditional Hindu world view conspire to give almost all of the ordinary person's reactions to Jesus and Krishna a different resonance. When Jesus spoke of God and the Kingdom of Heaven, Jewish monotheism made it plain that he had in mind the unique Creator of the world whose fuller reign would automatically mean greater human prosperity. When Jesus spoke of death he meant a once-and-for-all happening, the consummation of a unique human life.

Traditional Hinduism has parceled divinity out among many different gods, usually noncompetitively. Thus Krishna could exist alongside Shiva for centuries. Moreover, none of the Hindu gods was the Creator of the world in the Jewish or Christian sense. The Hindu world might come into being and pass out of being through the agency of a god such as Vishnu, but this was not the creation from nothingness that Western theology has taught. Indeed, ultimate reality frequently was depicted as beyond the realm of the gods: an ineffable **moksha** ("release") on a quite different plane. Relatedly, the cycles of rebirth through which the person had to go prior to a complete liberation (into moksha) made death and birth quite different than they were for Jesus. Overall, then, Krishna and Jesus have been quite diverse saviors.

Marx

Karl Marx (1818–1883) is unlikely to have thought of himself as a fit candidate for comparison with Jesus. Nonetheless, the large portion of the world map that today derives much of its "faith" or ultimate sense of reality from Marx justifies our probing the question of his likeness to and his difference from the Christ. Marx was born of Jewish parents who had converted to Lutheranism early in his childhood. By the time he had received his university degree, he was a passionate atheist, which put him on the outs with the authorities of Prussian society: "As an undergraduate Marx had identified himself with the left wing of the young Hegelians and was known as a militant atheist whose creed was (and remained): 'Criticism of religion is the foundation of all criticism.' This reputation made an academic career impossible under the Prussian government."[16]

Marx therefore made his career, such as it was, through journalism and forays into the international labor movement. Essentially he was supported by his friend Friedrich Engels, and he devoted much of his time to the research that went into the writing of his massive *Das Kapital.* Although he did have considerable influence during his lifetime— for example, through the *Communist Manifesto,* which he and Engels wrote in 1848, and through his dominance of the First International (meeting of working people in 1864)—his main impact has come since his death, through the adaptation of his ideas to such socialist regimes as Leninist Russia and Maoist China. He probably functions today mainly as the exemplary visionary who first stressed the crucial importance of labor, economics, the materialistic side of history, and the like.

For some contemporary Christian liberation theologians, who are trying to develop a christology centered on Jesus' power to emancipate human beings from all of the forces that threaten to crush them, including oppressive economic regimes, Marx is a spirit kindred to Jesus insofar as Marx condemned the worship of mammon that afflicted the European society of his day. So, for example, José Miranda has written a detailed study of Marx's writings that shows him explicitly developing the New Testament theme of anti-idolatry (calling capitalism's worship of profit an idolatry). In quite dubious language, Marx accuses the whole of his society of having taken over the worst traits of Judaism (the stereotype of Jewish preoccupation with money). Still, Miranda sees this charge as a properly Christian concern for the bad effects of mammon: "First, Marx says that society as a whole has turned Jewish. He is not attacking the Jews but capitalist society as a whole. Second, the Judaism in question here consists in the worship of the god Mammon, and Marx says so explicitly. Third, Marx uses the popular image of the Jew—without verifying how true and objective it is—to confront those who hold that image and tell them: you are precisely that! Fourth, and most important, the objection to Marx's argument on the grounds of its anti-Semitism is merely a way of closing one's ears to the real message of this work and all Marx's later economic writings, i.e., that the capitalist system is essentially the institutionalization of the idolatrous worship of Mammon."[17]

For our comparison, a point of special interest is Marx's dependence on certain biblical themes first broached by the Israelite prophets and then furthered by Jesus. In effect Marx made his own the biblical view that one could not serve God and mammon. He also appropriated the related biblical view that injustice toward one's neighbor was a prime form of irreligion. Thus, in another work, Miranda has tried to show the kinship of Marx and the biblical prophets, insofar as both were fiercely insistent on social justice and held out strong hopes for a better future human order.[18] Miranda points out that on occasion Marx would quote Revelation 13:17, which speaks of buying and selling under the mark of the beast. The idea is that Marx deeply associated himself with the biblical demand for justice and with the biblical concern for the power and the proper delimitation of mammon (money and this-worldly prosperity of all sorts).

Now, obviously enough, a simple comparison of Jesus and Marx that finds them in sympathy regarding the limited goodness (and the great potential evil) of money is far indeed from establishing their comparable stature as world-religious leaders. The whole precisely theological dimension of Jesus' life, which was so thoroughly rooted in the love of his heavenly Father, has little explicit analogue in the life of Marx. Few followers have made great claims for Marx's personal sanctity (although he did endure significant poverty and family tragedy), and virtually nothing in Marx's own world view made a place for the transcendent, more-than-historical dimensions of Jesus' Kingdom of God.

Moreover, Marx offers nothing approaching Jesus' radical solution to the problem of sin and evil through self-sacrificing love (although sacrifice on behalf of the working masses plays a large role in Marxist thought). The determinedly materialistic character of Marx's beliefs, even when one shows that for him "matter" included many things that other systems would call spiritual, means that he sees the world quite differently from Jesus of Nazareth. Marx's followers never called him divine or a savior, in the sense that Christians have used those words of Jesus. Prayer and asceticism such as what Jesus exhibited fall outside the Marxist scheme. The willingness of Lenin and other supposed disciples of Marx to use the most brutal violence to try to achieve their ends completely distances Marxist pragmatism from the nonviolence and gentleness of Jesus, who preferred to go to his death rather than resort to military means. (How much the brutality of Soviet or other Marxist regimes should be laid at Marx's door is quite debatable.) On many points, therefore, Marx is a very truncated religious leader, and Marxism is a very grim "religious" (all-absorbing) entity.

Still, we should not gloss over the fact that even now the vision of social justice laid out in Marx's own writings continues to inspire some of the most idealistic people of our planet. In huge portions of the earth (almost the entire Southern Hemisphere, for instance), poverty and injustice are so pervasive that the Marxist call for a radical overthrow of systems of capitalistic domination wins widespread accord.

So, for instance, one reads in Alan Paton's wonderful novel *Ah, but Your Land Is Beautiful* of the appeal that Marxist or socialist thought had among the best people of South Africa in the 1950s.[19] In that situation many "Communists" found themselves allied with Christians in opposing the bastardization of Christianity being put forth by the proponents of apartheid. True enough, the Communists were often dubious allies, not above using current conflicts for their own ends more than for the actual removal of apartheid. But the general point is valid: unless one can see in Marxist idealism a kinship to the prophetic idealism of Jesus Christ, one has read neither Marx nor the New Testament whole. Jesus did make love of neighbor as self his second great commandment. He does in Matthew 25 make treatment of one's neighbor the crux of how one would be judged. He might, therefore, be called a Marxist.

Gandhi

Mohandas Gandhi (1869–1948), the little man who brought India freedom from British rule by the power of truth (**satyagraha**), probably is the recent saint most compared to Jesus. Because of his manifest spirituality and nonviolence, Gandhi struck the pragmatic West as a force of a quite novel order. The British didn't know how to handle a man who simply pointed out to them their consistent brutality and inhumanity (which mocked their own ideals). The great tragedy of Gandhi's life was that he could not completely convince his own Indian people to throw religious hatred and violence out of their hearts. Thus he died a martyr to the enmities between Hindus and Muslims, just as forty-six years later Indira Gandhi, the daughter of his successor Jawaharlal Nehru (but no blood relative of Mohandas) died as a victim of the enmities between Hindus and Sikhs. Nonetheless, despite the failure of Gandhi's dream of a unified and tolerant India, the Mahatma ("Great-soul") continues to influence the world's conscience, insisting to all that truth and love are the only forces capable of making a world worthy of either human potential or the goodness of God.

Gandhi grew up as an observant Hindu, influenced by the pious example of his mother. He was forced into a traumatic marriage in his early teens, studied law in England, and found his political vocation only while laboring in South Africa on behalf of the "colored" minority. In India he became famous for his combination of shrewd political assessments and dramatic spirituality. He tried to form cadres of followers who would endure physical violence without striking back and to negotiate settlements between workers and factory owners, Indians and British, or

Hindus and Muslims by asking all parties to consider one another's interests. Among the key notions in Gandhi's spiritual inventory were satyagraha, nonviolence (**ahimsa**), and detachment (**karmayoga**). He believed in a God who coincided with Truth, and he drew rather eclectically from various religious traditions, especially the Hindu and the Christian.

So, for example, he once lectured to a group of economists gathered in Allahabad on the views of wealth that Jesus espoused (notice some of the affinities to Marx): "'It is easier for a camel to go through the eye of a needle than for a rich man to enter the kingdom of God!' Here you have an eternal rule of life stated in the noblest words the English language is capable of producing. But the disciples nodded unbelief as we do even to this day. . . . And Jesus said: 'Verily I say unto you there is no man that has left house or brethren or sisters, or father or mother, or wife or children or lands for my sake and the Gospels, but he shall receive one hundred fold. . . .' I hold that economic progress . . . is antagonistic to real progress. Hence the ancient ideal has been the limitation of activities promoting wealth. This does not put an end to all material ambition. We should still have, as we have always had, in our midst people who make the pursuit of wealth their aim in life. But we have always recognized that it is a fall from the ideal. It is a beautiful thing to know that the wealthiest among us have often felt that to have remained voluntarily poor would have been a higher state for them. . . . I have heard many of our countrymen say that we will gain American wealth but avoid its methods. I venture to suggest that such an attempt if it were made is foredoomed to failure. We cannot be 'wise, temperate, and furious' in a moment."[20]

It should be noted that in offering such an idealistic view of material possessions Gandhi was not only seconding Jesus but also drawing on his native Hindu spirituality. For while traditional Hinduism has always taught the legitimacy of wealth (**artha**), it has also always subordinated wealth to such higher goods as duty (social responsibility: **dharma**) and spiritual fulfillment (**moksha**). Christianity has thought quite similarly, in that it has affirmed the goodness of creation (and so partially blessed food and drink, material prosperity and celebration) but at the same time taught that union with God and sacrificial love of neighbor are higher goods.

One juncture at which Gandhi criticized Jesus, and again made plain the different assumptions that he as an Indian possessed, concerned compassion for subhuman creation. Thus, in his autobiography Gandhi reports that he somewhat nonplussed a Christian family with whom he used to discuss religious matters by making the following observations: "Once we began to compare the life of Jesus with that of Buddha. 'Look at Gautama's compassion!' said I. 'It was not confined to mankind, it was extended to all living beings. Does not one's heart overflow with love to think of the lamb joyously perched on his shoulders? One fails to notice this love for all living beings in the life of Jesus.'"[21] Christians are not used to hearing their Lord accused of any shortcomings, and so Gandhi found that he was no longer welcome in that Christian household.

Since his death, Gandhi has come in for considerable criticism, as one might expect from a very critical time. Psychologists have had a field day with his family life, poring over the malign effects of his child-marriage, his rather imperious treatment of his wife (he decided, apparently unilaterally, that they would no longer have sexual relations, since he wanted to muster the powers of celibacy to the cause of satyagraha), and his less than fully successful fatherhood. Most political commentators continue to judge that his policies were naive, and most economists can make no sense out of his reservations about technology. So the spinning wheel, which Gandhi made into a symbol of a work purified of materialistic and ambitious taint, seems to many observers a quaint but ridiculous bit of idealism. They may grant that it also symbolized Gandhi's desire to make Indians self-reliant (the British textile industry in India was a good epitome of the foreign control and exploitation that Gandhi wanted to throw off), but at core they see it as a useless stand against progress.

In the same vein, many analysts don't know what to make of Gandhian nonviolence, arguing that in a world where Hitlers and Stalins come to power it gives aid to Satanic enemies. Gandhi was fortunate, they say, to have had the British for his adversaries, because they still had consciences to which his satyagraha could appeal. The families of those whom the British massacred might dispute this, but the point has some validity. Like Jesus, Gandhi ultimately appealed to God, teaching that one cannot define *victory* in worldly terms and that there are things for which one must be willing to die.

Their deaths for heroic causes of course seal the likeness of Gandhi and Jesus, although Gandhi was not executed as a criminal and did not die in disgrace. While some followers no doubt have considered the Mahatma an avatar of a divine force, on the whole he has not been divinized. Hinduism seldom speaks of a redemptive process in which a hero such as Gandhi could play a salvific role. It does speak of various heavens and a completely fulfilling afterlife (moksha), but only in the context of reincarnation, karma, and the endless cycles of a world that has always existed. Thus, the differences in world view through which the teachings of Jesus and Gandhi have resonated are considerable. Gandhi himself could not consider Jesus divine in any exclusive sense. His instinct was to regard Jesus as an avatar of a divinity that could manifest itself in many different forms, as the needs of given ages required.

Despite the many differences in the status they must accord Jesus and the status they can accord Gandhi, many Christians consider Gandhi a great saint and exemplar of Christian ideals. Thus Monika Hellwig recently has written: "The Christian response to political situations of oppression in the West can never be the same after the experience of Gandhi, for he has personified the divine Compassion in our times to an extraordinary degree that echoed the life and ministry of Jesus in unmistakable terms. . . . This is perhaps the clearest sign that Christ is risen and is among us, for the incarnate Compassion of God is most appropriately and powerfully expressed in non-violent action for justice and peace in the world."[22]

Summary

Our task in this chapter has been to illumine Jesus further by comparing him with other great religious leaders. We began with Moses, the founder of Judaism, who is remembered for his intimacy with God, his reception of the covenant law, and his leading his people out of slavery in Egypt. Insofar as the rather fragmentary sources allow us to judge, he is like Jesus in having a keen sense of justice. He is unlike Jesus in not having been considered divine, in not having an intimate child-parent relation with God, and in not entailing the Kingdom of God and resurrection from the dead.

The Buddha stands out as probably the most eminent figure in Indian religious history. He won enlightenment by realizing the Four Noble Truths, and later his followers gave him supernatural, heavenly attributes. A cluster of differences from Jesus come from the Indian assumptions of karma and transmigration. Also, the Buddha did not pray to a personal and parental God as Jesus did. He conceived of the human problem as a matter of ignorance rather than sin, and he did not die a premature, criminal death as the victim of human malice. The salvation that the Buddha offers is therefore in the order of wisdom, rather than the order of redemptive death and resurrection. Still, both leaders were high mystics, and both were great healers.

Confucius, the paramount teacher of China, stressed humaneness and ritual. His way came down from the ancients and it led to a hierarchical structuring of society. Confucius taught that virtuous leaders could bring the people peace and prosperity. His own conviction was that personal integrity was the noblest achievement. Were people to know the ancient ways and walk them, they could achieve noble humanity. Confucius therefore is considerably more humanistic than Jesus. No fatherly God dominates his life, no sin and heaven extend the boundaries of commonsensical perceptions of reality. Confucius does not speak of a self-sacrificing love that would take one to the cross, and he has no place for a resurrection and final judgment. But his sense of attunement with the Way may hint at a mystical dimension in which he and Jesus were much alike.

Lao-tzu, the second Chinese master, thought that the best government was the least intrusive. He was impressed by nature's nonviolent ways of proceeding and by the potency of characteristics that people depreciated (ugliness, which helps things survive; emptiness, which makes a house useful). His sense of the Tao at the foundations of reality was quite mystical and ineffable. Like Jesus, he depended relatively little on human opinion. Unlike Jesus, he saw no human capacity for divinization, heavenly afterlife, resurrection, and redemption. He doesn't speak of revelation or a personal God. His religious kinship to Jesus would have to be teased out of his deep appreciation of the primacy of the Tao.

Zoroaster is like Jesus in being a prophet. His dualism, however, somewhat distances him from Jesus. Zoroaster had an exalted sense of the deity that he called Ahura Mazda, and he thought that husbanding the fertility of the world would help the Wise Lord to defeat the Evil Spirit. There is no intimate dealing with God as Jesus dealt with his Father. Zoroaster has not delineated the heart of human social problems as did Jesus' doctrine of sin. He is not a healer as Jesus was. Mainly, he impresses the reader as a spirit burning for light and truth, zealous for the reign of the Wise Lord, whom he aptly worships through a fire sacrifice.

Muhammad, the chief prophet of Islam, is quite like Jesus in feeling commissioned to deliver a message of utmost significance. His God Allah is the sole deity, as Jesus thought of his Father, but Allah is a more lordly God. Thus the first instinct of Muhammad's followers has been to bow low in prayer, while the example of Jesus has counseled Christians to pray to God "Our Father." Allah is a merciful God, but he will exact a strict judgment. Muhammad's prophecy was more political and military than that of Jesus, and his leadership was quite secular as well as religious. Muhammad made less of sin than Jesus did, and also less of healing. He honored Jesus as a great prophet, but his followers have thought Muhammad himself to be the seal or consummation of divine revelation. Muhammad did not die in disgrace or as the savior of sinful humanity, and he was not resurrected as God's firstborn from the dead. No orthodox Muslim could ever call Muhammad divine. Thus the likenesses and the differences between Jesus and Muhammad are extraordinarily plain.

Socrates often is contrasted with Jesus as the "good pagan" to the Son of God. As portrayed by Plato, Socrates died in great integrity for his beliefs, calm in the conviction that he could expect his immortal soul to prosper afterwards. Jesus, by contrast, died as a common criminal, broken and in disgrace. Socrates has seldom been considered divine. Any salvation that he offered has sprung from his wisdom—which was mainly to know that he didn't know a great many things. The theological dimensions of sin and grace are rather foreign to Socrates, whose principal concern is to combat ignorance. He is rather vague about ultimate justice, heaven, and the like. He shows great nobility, but not the paradox and mystery of Jesus of Nazareth.

Krishna, the most beloved Hindu god, is a mythological rather than a historical figure, and so immediately is quite different from Jesus. Nonetheless, the combination of his lovableness and his divine grandeur makes him somewhat comparable to the incarnate Logos. In the Indian world view, Krishna has not been a savior from sin or the exemplar of resurrection, as Jesus has been for Christians. No Kingdom of God or fierce demand for social justice has been part and parcel of Krishna's glad tidings. It is the love he has inspired that makes Krishna most akin to Jesus, for he, too, has been an enfleshment of the compassion of God.

Karl Marx, a thoroughly human figure, bears some likeness to Jesus insofar as he passionately sought social justice and the alleviation of the sufferings of the poor. Although reputedly atheistic, Marx seems to have borrowed considerably from the New Testament's attacks on mammon and frequently to have written as though he shared many Christian convictions. The evils done by Marxist regimes stand in great contrast to Jesus' ideals (as do a great many things done by supposedly Christian regimes), but how much Marx should be held responsible for the abuses of Soviet or Chinese leaders is debatable. Few people claim any divinity for Marx, or any saviorhood in a Christian sense. His kinship with Jesus therefore is his passion for social justice.

Mohandas Gandhi, finally, is a good candidate for comparison with Jesus. His compassion, nonviolence, and spiritual depth make him the most respected spiritual leader of recent times. He spent himself for Indian liberation and tried mightily to lessen hatreds in the world. His satyagraha was a profound spirituality. Gandhi drew considerable inspiration from Jesus, especially concerning the dangers of riches. His Hindu outlook made him wish that Jesus had shown more compassion toward subhuman creation, and it kept him from thinking that Jesus was uniquely divine. So the strictly theological claims that Christians make for Jesus place him on a different plane than Gandhi. Still, the compassion that Gandhi manifested seems to some Christian theologians a great sign of the presence of the Risen Christ.

STUDY QUESTIONS
---

1. How does the intimacy of Moses with God compare with that of Jesus?

2. Compare the Buddha's Second Noble Truth with Jesus' two great commandments.

3. Compare Confucius' views of ritual with Jesus' views of the Jewish Law.

4. How is Lao-tzu's *wu-wei* different from Jesus' faith?

5. What are the main differences between the God of Zoroaster and the God of Jesus?

6. Is Islam bound to find the Christian doctrine of God idolatrous?

7. How would Jesus likely have evaluated Socrates' convictions about the immortality of the soul?

8. Could one say that devotion to Krishna often has been virtually the same, psychologically, as devotion to Jesus?

9. To what extent ought followers of Karl Marx and followers of Jesus Christ to be able to agree about social justice?

10. Develop the ecological critique of traditional christology that is implicit in Gandhi's comparison of Jesus and the Buddha.

--------------------------------- NOTES ---------------------------------

[1] Mircea Eliade, *A History of Religious Ideas*, vol. 1. Chicago: University of Chicago Press, 1978, pp. 181–182.

[2] Ibid., p. 183.

[3] Mircea Eliade, *A History of Religious Ideas*, vol. 2. Chicago: University of Chicago Press, 1982, pp. 79–80.

[4] Gerard Sloyan, *Jesus in Focus*. Mystic, CT: Twenty-Third Publications, 1983, p. 46.

[5] See Richard H. Robinson and Willard L. Johnson, *The Buddhist Religion*, 3d ed. Belmont, CA: Wadsworth, 1982, pp. 11–15.

[6] See Herbert Fingarette, *Confucius: The Secular as Sacred*. New York: Harper & Row, 1972.

[7] Arthur Waley, trans., *The Analects of Confucius*. New York: Vintage Books, n.d. (originally 1938), p. 88 (Book 2, Section 4).

[8] Arthur Waley, trans., *The Way and Its Power*. New York: Grove Press, 1958, p. 141 (ch. 1).

[9] W. G. Oxtoby, "Zoroastrians," in *Abingdon Dictionary of Living Religions*, ed. Keith Crim. Nashville: Abingdon, 1981, p. 828.

[10] Jacques Duchesne-Guillemin, *The Hymns of Zarathustra*. Boston: Beacon Press, 1963, p. 137 (Yasna 43 : 9, 11).

[11] Kenneth Cragg and Marston Speight, *Islam from Within*. Belmont, CA: Wadsworth, 1980, p. 11 (Surah 1).

[12] *Phaedo*, 84a–b, in *Plato: Collected Dialogues*, ed. E. Hamilton and H. Cairns. Princeton, NJ: Princeton University Press/Bollingen, 1961, p. 67.

[13] *Apology*, 42a, in *Plato: Collected Dialogues*, p. 26.

[14] Geoffrey Parrinder, *A Dictionary of Non-Christian Religions*. Philadelphia: Westminster, 1971, p. 156.

15 Kees Bolle, trans., *The Bhagavad-Gita.* Berkeley: University of California Press, 1979, p. 127 (11:9–13).

16 Neil McInnes, "Marx, Karl," in *The Encyclopedia of Philosophy,* vol. 5, ed. Paul Edwards. New York: Macmillan, 1967, p. 172.

17 José Miranda, *Marx against the Marxists.* Maryknoll, NY: Orbis, 1980, p. 222.

18 See José Miranda, *Marx and the Bible.* Maryknoll, NY: Orbis, 1974.

19 Alan Paton, *Ah, But Your Land Is Beautiful.* New York: Charles Scribner's Sons, 1982.

20 Erik H. Erikson, *Gandhi's Truth.* New York: W. W. Norton, 1969, p. 281.

21 Mohandas K. Gandhi, *An Autobiography: The Story of My Experiments with Truth.* Boston: Beacon Press, 1957, p. 160.

22 Monika K. Hellwig, *Jesus: The Compassion of God.* Wilmington, DE: Michael Glazier, 1983, p. 155.

6

Conclusion

The Sources Revisited

The sources of this book have lain in the New Testament, the history of
Christian doctrine, contemporary christological discussion, and comparative religious studies. From the outset we sought a broadly gauged
approach to Jesus, something that would do justice to the full range of
data that bear on how we should understand him today. To be sure, the
very breadth of the sources has occasioned much selection. The best response to this simple fact is the modesty we shall consider in the next
section. Here, though, we can recall that the world-historical significance of Christ offers some justification for our broad gauge. If we are
even to suggest the meaning that Christ has had, we have to solicit representative opinions from the broad spectrum of those he has influenced.

In a narrower sense, the source that we wish now to revisit is the
primary materials: essentially, the New Testament texts. For all their
historical complexity and theological variety, the New Testament texts
remain our best, indeed our only, close-up portraits of Jesus of Nazareth,
whom his followers have believed was the Christ. James D. G. Dunn,
whose work on Jesus and the Spirit we used in Chapter 4, has also studied the unity and diversity of the New Testament sources about Jesus.

On the precise matter of christology or interpretation of Jesus' messiah-ship (or basic identity), Dunn finds great diversity somehow held to-gether by a strong unifying conviction: "What many Christians both past and present have regarded as orthodox christology may be repre-sented (not altogether unfairly) as a curious amalgam of different ele-ments taken from different parts of first-century Christianity—personal pre-existence from John, virgin birth from Matthew, the miracle-worker from the so-called 'divine man' christology prevalent among some Hel-lenistic Christians, his death as atonement from Paul, the character of his resurrection from Luke, his present role from Hebrews, and the hope of his parousia from the earlier decades. Well might a recent writer entitle his essay, 'One Jesus, many Christs?'—though it would be more accurate to speak of 'one Jesus, many christologies.' Within this diversity, how-ever, a unifying element is regularly discernible: namely, *the affirmation of the identity of the man Jesus with the risen Lord*, the conviction that the heavenly reality known in kerygma and scripture, in community, worship and religious experience generally is one and the same Jesus of whom the Jesus-tradition speaks."[1]

Dunn goes on to detail some of the various formulations of this unity. For Paul, the Risen Christ is the same as the crucified Jesus. For Mark, the Gospel concerns the Son of God but also the Son of man. Luke calls the Jesus of his narratives "Lord." Matthew conveys the sense that the same Jesus of Nazareth whose teaching he interprets is a heavenly presence one can find in Christian worship. The theology of priest-hood in Hebrews depends on the linkage between the earthly Jesus and the exalted heavenly high priest who now intercedes before the divine throne. First Peter urges patience in suffering by referring to the heav-enly glory that came to Jesus because of how he endured his earthly trials. Revelation thinks of Jesus Christ as the heavenly lamb who was slain on earth. And, most of all, the Johannine theology makes the earthly Jesus he who existed before Abraham.

With such a richness in its primary documents, christology could hardly fail to become a varied and complex enterprise. The many differ-ent nuances in the early Church's memory of Jesus—his prayer, proph-ecy, healing, miracles, teaching, parables, suffering, martyrdom, wis-dom, guidance by the Spirit, and more—all begged development. The central phenomenon of his death and Resurrection, or his earthly and more-than-earthly dimensions, solicited constant meditation.

Moreover, the Church that was trying to remember and preserve what Jesus had been and done was at the same time worshiping with con-stant reference to the Risen Lord. The Spirit that moved the most charis-matic of early Christians was the Spirit poured out on the Church at Pentecost by the Ascended Christ. The bread broken and wine shared at the Christian Eucharist was a memorial of Jesus' last meal with his followers, an anticipation of the messianic banquet that Jesus had promised would come in the Kingdom of God, a remembrance of Jesus' death for the sake of sinful humanity, and an experience of communion with the Risen Lord who dwelt wherever two or three gathered in his name.

Inevitably, therefore, christology developed as a hybrid, dualistic, synthetic point of view. Consistently it had to swing back and forth between then and now, between likeness to ordinary human beings and special status, between bondage to a particular speech or world view and heavenly freedom to move where the Spirit wished. Jesus, as the Johannine christology again most clearly showed, was the exact fusion of time and eternity, heaven and earth, God's gracious offer of revelation and humanity's sinful preference for darkness. In many ways the classical dogmatic christology of Chalcedon merely formalized the sense of twofoldness yet unity that lay in the rich New Testament sources. Abstracting from the great variety of details, Chalcedon found a formula that summarized the basic tension: a human side, a divine side, and the unity of the two in the inmost reality of Jesus the Christ.

In his development of the late distinguished New Testament scholar Norman Perrin's lectures on the teaching of Jesus, David Abernathy has a chapter on the relationship between the first century and the twentieth century that shows how the twofoldness yet unity of Jesus the Christ is also a product of Christian reflection today. In other words, the pattern one can see at a distance in the reflections of the New Testament or the reflections of fourth-century Chalcedon remains imbedded in Christian faith or life today: "Our concern is always with the Lord present with us in our experience, with the Lord proclaimed to us by the church. In technical language, this is the Christ of the **kerygma.** *Kerygma* is the Greek word for "preaching" or "proclamation," and we speak of the Christ of the *kerygma* to mean Christ proclaimed by the church as the crucified, risen, and redeeming Lord. It also means the Christ of Christian experience—the Christ who confronts us in the Eucharist or Lord's Supper, the Christ who confronted Paul on the Damascus road, and the Christ who has challenged great figures in the church since the first century. . . . Contrasted with the Christ of the *kerygma* is the historical Jesus, the Jesus we come to know through historical research. . . . From a faith perspective, the words of the historical Jesus must be confirmed in a personal experience of the Christ of the *kerygma.*"[2]

The sources of christology, whether Christians stress the New Testament documents or contemporary kerygmatic experience, always force us to deal with two sides of one man's significance. There are the data on the historical Jesus, the man from Nazareth who said such and such and died under Pontius Pilate. There are the data on Jesus' Resurrection, his influence on later church life, and the exceptional (heavenly) qualities he manifested even before his death. So christology is forever guided by a difference amidst unity.

Modesty

We have alluded to the modesty incumbent on those who would propose a broadly gauged study of Jesus. In each of the areas we have surveyed, we have had to select, interpret, and hope that our presentation was not too distorting. For certainly there is no single Muslim, Jewish, or Indian contrast to Jesus. Certainly there is no monolithic feminist, black, fundamentalist, or peacemakers' christology. Were one to consult a dozen patristic, medieval, Reformation, or modern historians, one would surely come away with at least half a dozen different christological interpretations. Were one to sit at the feet of a dozen ecological, political, or literary analysts of Jesus' significance, one surely would come away with several dozen angles into Jesus' contemporary meaning. Moving outside the New Testament therefore necessitates considerable modesty. The matter of Jesus Christ is extremely diverse and contested, and any presentation claiming full certitude or comprehensiveness or fidelity to the sources surely is bogus.

Much the same need for modesty sounds when one consults the primary christological sources, the New Testament texts themselves. There is no single interpretation of Mark, Luke, Paul, or John. Specialists in all areas of the New Testament offer the student dozens of different christological nuances. The memories of the early Christian communities were so rich, and their needs so diverse, that the very matrix of christology is pluralistic. The unfailing connection between the Jesus of history and the Christ of faith is a precious point of stability, but as soon as one tries to develop that connection, to read out what it implies, the opinions again begin to diverge.

As Patrick Henry's helpful volume on new directions in New Testament study makes plain, the tension between diversity and unity has been with the Christian community, and so with the worlds of both faith and culture, for a very long time: "Even a quick reading of Paul's letters makes it clear that not all Christians in the apostolic age were agreed on all major points of belief and practice. The arguments were fierce, and the amount of apostolic authority persons possessed usually amounted to the sum of apostolic authority that others were willing to grant to them. The book of Acts is a portrayal of the first Christian generation from a later vantage point, and in Acts we can see already the picture of a harmonious 'golden age' of the earliest church well on the way to formation. But the New Testament itself shows us Christians who were at sharp odds over the very fundamentals of the faith. . . ."[3]

If the state of the sources counsels modesty about one's representations and interpretations, all the more does the character of the main actor. The New Testament is a classic, a piece of literature that never goes out of style, because its central figure seems an inexhaustible source of stimuli to reflection.

The Jesus who lives on the pages of the New Testament cannot be separated from the Christ worshiped in the Christian community, but even apart from confessional faith, even taken simply as a literary figure, he is matter for a hundred, a thousand, who knows how many monographs. By the second century, when the New Testament canon was in the process of formation, Jesus had already achieved classical status. Even then, he already was the norm more than the one to be investigated and judged, was the criterion more than the one to be criticized. To be sure, this was because most readers of the New Testament and most contributors to the canonical processes and debates believed that Jesus was the Christ and Son of God. They had given him their allegiance and made him their pearl of great price, so he was bound to be Lord of their inquiries. But these people were not completely credulous. They of course had needs they were asking Jesus to fill, but these needs did not deprive them of their reason. Something they considered objective, real, able to survive all sorts of intellectual and psychological assaults stood there on the pages of the New Testament and called them to come up to the measure of its holiness, to plunge down to the depths of its wisdom.

Discussing the Christian instance of the general phenomenon of religious classics, theologian David Tracy has rightly begun with the event and person of Jesus Christ. Jesus Christ is for Christians the most pressing instance of the disclosure of a reality they cannot but name truth. (Of the **classic** in general Tracy has said, "My thesis is that what we mean in naming certain texts, events, images, rituals, symbols and persons 'classics' is that here we recognize nothing less than the disclosure of a reality we cannot but name truth.")[4] Christology, then, may be taken as the result of the Christian focus on Jesus as such a disclosure: "For the Christian community from the New Testament communities to the present there is one single expression from God proclaimed to be, manifested and represented in a myriad of symbols, images, genres, concepts, doctrines as God's own self-manifestation and thereby—only thereby— as beyond all relative adequacy: the decisive event named Jesus Christ. For the Christian the present experience of the spirit of the Risen Lord who is the crucified Jesus of Nazareth *is* the Christian religious classic event."[5]

Insiders to Christianity, accepting some version of such an estimate of Jesus, will find themselves hushed to modesty by the realization that the study of Jesus means approaching God's decisive self-manifestation. In the presence of such an event, all mortal flesh should keep silent, all merely academic investigation seems to miss the point if not to blaspheme. Christianity owes its existence to the Christ-event. It exists only as many emanations from the single center of the Christ-event. Jesus is therefore classical for Christians in the sense that age after age he measures their holiness and humanity. Christology is faith seeking an understanding of this measurement, faith trying to appreciate just how and why Jesus should be canonical.

Humanistic approaches to Jesus may share some of this Christian conviction, or they may find their proper modesty on other grounds. Even apart from a confessional stance toward Jesus, one may find him admirable, singular, a man worthy of awesome respect.[6] Humanistic approaches to Jesus may also be modest in dealing with his classical status because they wish to respect the mystery at the core of so significant a phenomenon as Christianity. This would be parallel to the wish to respect the mystery of Allah at the core of Islam or the mystery of Brahman at the core of Hinduism. One is humble out of courtesy, but also because one senses that believers see things one must respect.

The Appeal of Jesus

What believers see christologically may be explained in terms of granting Jesus the status of a classic, but few ordinary Christians would use such a term. Unless one is a theologian, used to reflecting on the bigger picture into which Jesus fits or the ground-level makeup of reality that Jesus illumines, christology tends to be simpler, more mythic, and more personal. It is the man Jesus—his kindness, holiness, ability to heal life, ability to express how people ought to relate to one another—that solicits most people's faith. It is the way Jesus depicts God and makes life hopeful that moves most converts.

This is so even in the case of rather cynical converts, people who are surprised to find themselves in the Christian camp because they have long realized how much hokum parades under the banner of religion. Malcolm Muggeridge, a crusty cynic turned evangelical, reports such a surprising changeover in the following terms. It was the very tawdriness of the shrines in Bethlehem commemorating Jesus' birth, juxtaposed with the light shining on the faces of the pious people who went there on pilgrimage, that moved Muggeridge to take Christian faith seriously: "Everything in the crypt—the garish hangings which covered the stone walls, the tawdry crucifixes and pictures and hanging lamps—was conducive to such a mood [of thinking of Bethlehem as a religious Disneyland]. . . . None the less, as I observed, each face as it came into view was in some degree transfigured by the experience of being in what purported to be the actual scene of Jesus's birth. This, they all seemed to be saying, was where it happened; here he came into the world! here we shall find him! The boredom, the idle curiosity, the vagrant thinking all disappeared. Once more in that place glory shone around. . . ."[7]

If people can find in the reality or legend of Jesus the sense that the great thing—God's becoming available in human form—really happened, that the salvation so desperately sought actually occurred and remains possible, then any question of Jesus' "appeal" is almost beside the point. Jesus has received or had projected onto him the most central hopes of the human spirit. He has the appeal of a winsome human being, yes, but the grandeur and splendor of God almost cancel that out by their blinding light. The people whom Muggeridge found moving him to take faith seriously remind us of the crowds of Jesus' own day, whom Jesus did not fully trust. The hearts of the people whom Muggeridge observed were imperfect, impure, filled with confused amalgams of selfish desire and a genuine wish to go beyond themselves to full generosity. The reports they would make of Jesus' appeal would not be fraudulent or without significance as clues to the christological mystery, but one backs away and wonders how closely the historical Jesus of Nazareth resembles the figure they had in mind when visiting Bethlehem.

Perhaps closer to the historical Jesus is the man described by Lucas Grollenberg. This Jesus is an heir of the prophets who takes wholeheartedly the teaching of prophets such as Hosea that God is an ardent lover of humankind: "The faith of Hosea and so many after him, in a God who loves his people and will never write them off, determines the words and actions and indeed the whole personality of Jesus. Jesus' utter assurance seems to come from this sense of being loved by God. He even addressed God as Abba, which is quite extraordinary. Jewish children used the word as an affectionate way of addressing their fathers, rather as English children say 'daddy'. . . .

"Jesus himself wanted to communicate to his fellow men his perfect trust in the God who loved him. When God began to rule supreme, when his 'kingdom' became reality, love was to be the sphere of human relationships."[8]

In this interpretation, the allure or appeal of Jesus is his projected sense of having found the center of reality and fallen in love with it. For Grollenberg, Jesus lived in utter trust that the Creator of the world, the Master of the Universe, cared for him in the way that a loving parent cares for a vulnerable child. This did not make Jesus childish or presumptuous. It made him whole, free, able to go without the defenses and self-concerns that keep ordinary people from seeing the world as a beautiful gift or relating to their neighbors as needy yet lovely fellow creatures. For Grollenberg the center of the christological mystery is the trust that Jesus reposed in his Abba. That wholehearted reliance explains Jesus' sense of the Kingdom of God and what is possible for human beings. It explains his conviction that nothing can separate people from God, not even their sins. In the parables of the lost sheep and the lost coin, Jesus depicts God as restless until the smallest member of his family is home safe and sound. In the parable of the prodigal son Jesus says that God always takes the initiative and seeks people out, even those who have turned their backs on him and played the ingrate.

Much of the appeal of Jesus therefore has lain in his ability to touch wounded hearts. People down on themselves, feeling they were no good or had no future, could hear in his preaching a gentle counsel never to lose heart. Jesus did not tell them that they were not really so bad or that they hadn't made themselves morally ugly. They wouldn't have believed that and Jesus didn't try to make them. His tack rather was to tell them that God didn't much care about moral beauty or ugliness, that God's love was predicated on something far more intrinsic and profound. For Jesus, God loves each creature as only its parent loves a child or its maker loves a product. God finally is moved to search people out and to heal people's wounds because that is God's own makeup: utter goodness, never-failing creativity and love. All of that probably would have moved many people, and probably did move many in Jesus' audiences, but the finishing touch, the final seal, was Jesus' dying for his trust in the goodness of God and being vindicated by the Resurrection. For most of his admirers the Cross showed the reaches of his faith and the Resurrection showed how God rewarded him.

Personal Choices

Academic studies of Jesus usually falter when it comes to the Resurrection. That event almost by definition falls outside the domain of ordinary historical studies, so most scholars content themselves with reporting what the New Testament sources say and making vague references to the possible symbolic meaning of such texts. Fundamentalist works on Jesus embrace the Resurrection accounts literally, often wondering why they don't convince all readers that Jesus is the sole Lord worthy of religious dedication. Somewhere in the middle, critical Christian theologians labor to let the Resurrection be the great force it has been in the development of Christian faith without denying its problematic and symbolic dimensions.

If the Resurrection summarizes the personal problems that Jesus presents to students of his person and life, it does not exhaust such problems. Jesus presented himself as the herald of the Kingdom of God, of the time when humanity could see how life ought to be lived. He exhibited an extraordinary confidence that God was a parent full of care and worthy of unlimited trust. He died faithful to his doctrine of loving even one's enemies. And the Resurrection, along with the other early experiences that formed the Christian community's conviction that he was the Christ, clamors to be read as a claim that Jesus' heralding of the Kingdom, trust in his Abba, and fidelity to love were proved correct, received a marvelous ratification.

It will not quite do, therefore, to leave Jesus as just another salesman in the supermarket of religious or moral teachings. His reality includes his challenge to his hearers to repent and believe in his good news, just as the reality of Muhammad includes Muhammad's challenge to his hearers to accept the revelations of Allah and submit (become a Muslim). Not all hearers of either prophet, of course, have accepted his message.

But all personally engaged hearers have considered accepting it, have weighed the possibility. More often than not those who have not accepted it have suspected from the outset that they would not. They have had their own different religious or moral allegiances, and they have suspected that whatever respect they came to accord Jesus or Muhammad would not cause them to throw over such prior allegiances. But the more serious the hearing they have given, the more willing they have been to perform the imaginative exercises necessary to make Christian or Muslim faith an actual possibility, a live option. Thereby, even when they have remained non-Christians or non-Muslims, they have encountered Jesus or Muhammad as someone quite real and forceful.

One sees glimpses of this effect of serious, personally engaged study (although not the full-blown entity) at the conclusion of such an apparently impartial, straightforward historical account of Jesus as Humphrey Carpenter's little work *Jesus:* "It is because of the simplicity of his teaching that Jesus has, despite all the confusions and perversions of his message over the years, continued to have a powerful influence on the human mind. He was not a philosopher; he did not construct any complete system of ethics; nor did he speak in moral abstractions which can be straightforwardly detached from the context of his religious beliefs. But in the manner of his teaching, his refusal to compromise when faced with any moral dilemma, his emphasis on the universality and totality, the unlimitedness of moral demands on men, there is a force which crosses all religious barriers and appeals to us whether or not we subscribe to his religious beliefs."[9]

What is left out of this conclusion, however, is the question of what to do with either Jesus' forcefulness or his charismatic appeal. Rightly enough, the author does not try to persuade his readers to accept or reject Jesus as the center of their lives or even as their Lord and Savior. He is not writing a confessional work designed to try to bring people into the Christian fold. On the other hand, there is a "one may take it or leave it" air about the conclusion suggesting that the Jesus his readers have studied is after all a matter of less than crucial significance. Life will go on, whether or not one makes Jesus something or someone personally riveting, something or someone who changes one's pathway.

We, too, are not writing a work calculated to try to persuade people to adopt Christianity. But it seems to us derelict to pass over the crucial significance that Jesus himself seems to have accorded his message, or to suggest that Jesus himself thought life would go on virtually unchanged regardless of whether or not one embraced his Gospel. If the pages of the New Testament tell us anything about Jesus, it is that his preaching was fired with the conviction that the hour of crucial decision had come. True enough, Jesus was not such a zealot that he wanted to destroy those who would not hear him or those who heard him and turned away. One finds in the New Testament portraits no solid basis for fanaticism such as that of the Spanish Inquisition, the Christian persecutors of Jews, or today's terrorist Muslims. Jesus could be tolerant, patient, respectful of people's consciences without diluting the force of his kerygma or denying that the **kairos** or crucial hour of decision had come. The moral teaching that Carpenter praises was not the heart of Jesus' mission. The heart of Jesus' mission was the revelation of God, the absolutely decisive offer of divine life.

Insofar as the Parousia has not occurred and life has gone on regardless of people's decisions about Jesus, the decisiveness of Jesus does of course seem diluted. Christians have had to work out ways of explaining Jesus' significance for every human life, ways that could make their Master the judge or standard even of people who had never heard of him or people who had turned their backs on him. This does not mean, however, that the most profitable study of Jesus no longer has to contend with personal choices about what he will be "for me." It does not mean that he, any more than Muhammad or the Buddha, can be done full justice while held at arm's length, while refused entry to the chambers where one makes the decisions that forge a self.

Emilie Griffin's account of her conversion to Christian faith, *Turning*, does a fine job of portraying the stages that may follow if one admits Jesus into one's inner chambers. Moved by a longing for a more meaningful life, Griffin became attracted to Jesus, started to admire the New Testament texts, and then realized that Jesus made remarkable claims to speak in God's name, claims that she could not in good conscience ignore. But how was she to decide whether Jesus truly was the privileged emissary of God rather than just a good man hopelessly deluded? Eventually Griffin realized that only she herself could decide: "I began to see that I would never have through scholarship and study any more hard evidence than I already had in hand. When I came to this fork in the road, I felt that I had come as far as reason and logic could take me. I was beginning to understand for the first time what is meant by an act of faith: a leap, not without trust, not without a framework of reason and thought, but a risk-taking jump into a realm beyond logic and reason. . . ."[10] Our job does not include prompting any particular leap. It does include pointing out how leaping may relate to studying.

Social Implications

Jesus therefore confronts the engaged student with at least the possibility of challenges, of calls to ponder his teaching personally and take it to heart, that may prove momentous. He confronts groups—which at the truly religious level are only individuals trying to form communities—with parallel possibilities. For there are significant social implications in the teaching of Jesus, and people who take Jesus' teaching or person seriously are bound to be different as citizens, members of the labor force, parents, and celebrants than they would have been apart from such seriousness. What, then, are the social implications of christology that we should most ponder?

Mary Douglas, a distinguished British anthropologist, has recently criticized the academic scholars of religion for being so shaped by their personal intellectual and religious preferences that they failed to read the signs of the conservative times that were coming: "Events have taken religious studies by surprise. This set of university institutions devoted to understanding religion without the constraints of the divinity school has generally included religious change in its subject matter. No one, however, foresaw the recent revivals of traditional religious forms. According to an extensive literature, religious change in modern times happens in only two ways—the falling off of worship in traditional Christian churches, and the appearance of new cults, not expected to endure. No one credited the traditional religions with enough vitality to inspire large-scale political revolt."[11] In christology, the typical academic assumption would have been that Jesus would become more passé. He would continue to be a heroic figure, perhaps, but as technology moved more people away from a traditional (mythic) religious consciousness, he would increasingly be relegated to a past era of human history, would increasingly be considered irrelevant to present problems. In fact this has not happened, as Douglas' references to resurgences of traditional Christian faith indicate. Along with the resurgence of traditional Islam, several species of Christian faith have again come to flame, and most of them realize full well that the center of Christian faith is christology.

Nonetheless, the christological implications of such social changes may be less surprising and more troubling than Douglas indicates. The changes by and large represent efforts to minimize the confusions that modern life has caused and to give people clearer directions about how to live. Often the conservative religious movements call for a strict, clearly outlined ethical code, especially in sexual matters, and for a militant attack on enemies who at least temporarily personify evil. Thus one finds Muslims fighting other Muslims, or Jews, or Communists as though such foes were incarnate devils. One finds conservative Christians describing Communists and abortionists as minions of Satan. The Latin American Catholic bishops mainly fall outside this pattern in that their politics are quite progressive, but even they draw psychological strength from targeting the capitalist North as a major source of their problems.

The question for a contemporary christology is, What sort of political regime does Jesus imply? Are there, in fact, social, economic, and political entailments to confessing Jesus to be Lord, or even to admitting that one admires Jesus' New Testament personality? This is not a simple question, and certainly there is no consensus among students of Jesus about how to answer any of its parts. Almost all commentators hold that Jesus' message does have radical social consequences, but how such consequences translate into modern political or economic terms is very difficult to determine.

For example, Jesus clearly preached that God has a special concern for the poor. The Sermon on the Mount (Matthew 5–7), with its famous set of beatitudes, implies that the Kingdom of God will mean a blessing for people presently on the social margins. Does this therefore imply a government and economics pivoted on helping the poor or giving the socially marginal preferential treatment? Most christologists probably would say yes, but some would emphatically say no. There would be much agreement that Jesus' teachings (rooted in the teachings of the Israelite prophets on social justice) and his notion of loving one's neighbor as oneself ought to lead to charitable works to help the poor. But what a given government ought to do would remain unclear—all the more so if the government were pluralistic and thus responsible for representing many non-Christians.

It would be hard to justify christologically governmental policies that worsened the plight of the poor, just as it would be hard to justify policies that hastened the day of nuclear war; but determining whether tight money policies, or capitalistic incentives, or a policy of deterrence does in fact help or hurt the poor, does lessen or increase the chances for war, is seldom easy. Much is in the eye of the beholder or the reading lens of the particular politician. Jesus tends either to fade into the background, as one who may be quoted but is allowed little practical influence, or his teachings are very dubiously invoked in support of particular governmental policies.

It seems safer, therefore, to say that christology does not immediately imply any particular social program, but that a christology taken seriously always offers grounds for sharp criticism of specific social policies. If any policies are systematically hurting given groups of people— the poor, the handicapped, women, racial minorities, or even the wealthy (as persons, not necessarily as the wealthy)—christology suspects such policies are deeply flawed. If any policies depend on thoroughgoing selfishness, a regular resort to violence, or a practical denial that there is anything more to life than temporal prosperity (that is, says there is no God, judgment, heaven, or hell), they are prime candidates for christological criticism. Why? Because they conflict so dramatically with what Jesus preached and how Jesus lived.

Summary

We began by revisiting the christological sources we have used. Broadly, these sources were the accounts in the New Testament, notions from the history of Christianity, contemporary christological issues, and comparative religious studies. More narrowly, the prime christological sources are always the New Testament texts. As James Dunn has shown, these texts show a complex unity amidst diversity. There is no single New Testament christology, but all of the authors' christologies radiate from a central identification of the man Jesus with the Risen Lord. This diversity-yet-unity is reflected in the classical christological definition of Chalcedon, and David Abernathy has suggested that it remains structural for contemporary christological experience.

In describing the modesty that should mark any survey of christology, we drew from the breadth and complexity of our sources the conclusion that dogmatism or unqualified assertion must be resisted. Indeed, we noted Patrick Henry's opinion that diversity has been with the Christian Church and its theological interpretations of human life since the earliest days. Jesus himself is another strong counsel to modesty. Approached with any sense, he soon becomes a "classic," and thus more a judge than a person adequately categorized by any human scrutiny.

The appeal of Jesus relates to his classical status, but few ordinary believers would express their feelings for Jesus in such terms. Rather, most ordinary folk are like the pilgrims Malcolm Muggeridge described, a mixture of genuine reverence or hope and gawking credulity. Lucas Grollenberg may have captured the heart of Jesus' original appeal in describing him as a man completely trusting in God. From such trust Jesus derived both a remarkable freedom and the ability to heal hearts wounded by self-disgust.

Any discussion of either Jesus' perennial appeal or his original charisma soon raises questions about the personal implications of christological study. The Resurrection summarizes many of the extraordinary claims that Christians make for Jesus, but other aspects of his message and person similarly challenge the student to make a personal assessment. Parallel challenges from Muhammad or the Buddha show that Jesus is not unique in this matter, but neither is he just another moral teacher whom one may take or leave. As Emilie Griffin's account of conversion shows, there comes a time when the truly serious student of Jesus has to decide from among the options of faith, rejection, and agnosticism.

The social implications of christology are similarly freighted, although it is hard to derive specific policies or programs from even an admiring study of Jesus. Mary Douglas has suggested how modernistic biases have kept academic scholars of religion from anticipating the resurgence of traditional religion, including traditional Christianity. In many cases this resurgence has been linked with social programs expressing a quite conservative personal or communal morality. One probably can say that Jesus, by contrast, lays out a liberal to radical social program that would pivot on serving the poor and marginal people, but it remains impossible to determine precisely what economic, social, military, or other policies this christological inclination should produce.

STUDY QUESTIONS

1. What are Dunn's summaries of the New Testament authors' views of the identity of the man Jesus and the Risen Lord?

2. Why should the classical status of Jesus lead to modesty in one's study, and what are the dangers in granting Jesus classical status?

3. Evaluate the thesis that Jesus' complete trust in God led to a very appealing freedom and compassion.

4. Explain the sentence, "Our job as authors does include pointing out how leaping may relate to studying."

5. What social programs do you find entailed in Jesus' Sermon on the Mount?

NOTES

[1] James D. G. Dunn, *Unity and Diversity in the New Testament.* Philadelphia: Westminster, 1977, pp. 226–227.

[2] David Abernathy, *Understanding the Teaching of Jesus.* New York: Seabury, 1983, p. 172.

[3] Patrick Henry, *New Directions in New Testament Study.* Philadelphia: Westminster, 1979, p. 151.

[4] David Tracy, *The Analogical Imagination.* New York: Crossroad, 1981, p. 108.

[5] Ibid., p. 248.

[6] See, for example, the appreciative study by the Jewish scholar Geza Vermes, *Jesus the Jew.* London: Collins, 1973, and the similar study by the Marxist scholar Milan Machovec, *A Marxist Looks at Jesus.* Philadelphia: Fortress, 1976.

[7] Malcolm Muggeridge, *Jesus: The Man Who Lives.* New York: Harper & Row, 1975.

[8] Lucas Grollenberg, *Jesus.* Philadelphia: Westminster, 1978, p. 106.

[9] Humphrey Carpenter, *Jesus.* New York: Oxford University Press, 1980, pp. 94–95.

[10] Emilie Griffin, *Turning.* Garden City, NY: Doubleday, 1980, pp. 82, 87.

[11] Mary Douglas, "The Effects of Modernization on Religious Change," in *Religion and America: Spirituality in a Secular Age,* ed. Mary Douglas and Steven M. Tipton. Boston: Beacon Press, 1983, p. 25.

Appendix: The Apocryphal New Testament

In 1945, at Nag Hammâdi in Upper Egypt, thirteen papyrus volumes were discovered that have shed considerable light on early christology. These volumes, written in Coptic, contain forty-five different works and seem to have been part of an ancient Gnostic library perhaps associated with the monastery at nearby Chenoboskion. The Coptic texts probably are fourth-century C.E. translations of earlier Greek manuscripts, some of which may have originated as early as the end of the first century C.E. Work on the finds from Nag Hammâdi has stimulated a reconsideration of the oral traditions upon which the canonical Gospels drew, and nowadays there is greater appreciation of the diversity of early Christian materials (most of which did not make it into the canonical New Testament) than was true two generations ago.

The apocryphal ("hidden") or noncanonical works that scholars now study to broaden their sense of early christology come in several different languages and genres (the collection found at Nag Hammâdi is a rich resource, but apocryphal works from other sources are also significant). The bulk of the **Apocrypha** derives from the second to the ninth centuries C.E., and such diverse languages as Greek, Latin, Syriac, Coptic, Arabic, Slavonic, and Anglo-Saxon are involved. The works say more about Christian piety than they reveal about the historical Jesus, and it is significant that they fall into such different literary genres as gospels, acts, epistles, and apocalypses.[1]

The apocryphal Gospels include works attributed to the apostles James, Thomas, Peter, and Philip, along with works attributed to such other New Testament luminaries as Nicodemus and Mary. Other Gospels are designated as being of the Nazoreans, Ebionites, Hebrews, and Egyptians. In general these writings supply details about the infancy, youth, and postresurrectional periods of Jesus' life, apparently in an effort to satisfy the hunger of popular piety. They say little about the death of Jesus, and frequently the incidents they report are miraculous or fabulous.

The most important of the apocryphal Gospels is the Gospel of Thomas, which consists of 114 sayings attributed to Jesus. This Gospel was discovered at Nag Hammâdi, and it resembles Q, the source that scholars have hypothesized was used in the formation of both Matthew and Luke. Harold W. Attridge has said of the Gospel of Thomas: "Many of the sayings, parables, proverbs, and brief dialogues in the Gospel parallel sayings attributed to Jesus in the synoptic gospels, but appear for the most part to be independent of the canonical versions. The parables, for example, lack the allegorical features found in the Synoptics, features that are generally recognized to be secondary accretions. Thus *The Gospel of Thomas* provides an important resource for the investigation of the earliest forms of the sayings of Jesus."[2]

The theology of Thomas displays Gnostic convictions and themes, including a claim to be bringing forward secret knowledge that guarantees immortality. This knowledge includes awareness of the essential self and a world of light in which the essential self preexisted and to which it is destined to return. Thomas distinguishes sharply between flesh and spirit, depreciating the former and exalting the latter, and it considers the world to be a realm of fallenness and disorder, in which ordinary human beings stagger like drunken people. Properly seen, the body is a wretched, poverty-ridden thing and the world is a corpse. Thus disciples are urged to detach themselves ("fast") from the world and to discipline the flesh. Thereby they will transcend the divisions and dualities that give so much pain and will attain a unitary state in which there is no tension between inner and outer or between male and female.

A good example of the style and content of the Gospel of Thomas is Saying 22, one of the most famous: "Jesus saw infants being suckled. He said to his disciples, 'These infants being suckled are like those who enter the Kingdom.' They said to him, 'Shall we then, as children, enter the Kingdom?' Jesus said to them, 'When you make the two one, and when you make the inside like the outside and the outside like the inside, and the above like the below, and when you make the male and the female one and the same, so that the male not be male nor the female female; and when you fashion eyes in place of an eye, and a hand in place of a hand, and a foot in place of a foot, and a likeness in place of a likeness, then will you enter the Kingdom.'"[3]

The first part of the saying sounds much like Matthew 18:1–4: "At that time the disciples came to Jesus, saying, 'Who is the greatest in the Kingdom of heaven?' And calling to him a child, he put him in the midst of them, and said, 'Truly, I say to you, unless you turn and become like children, you will never enter the kingdom of heaven. Whoever humbles himself like this child, he is the greatest in the kingdom of Heaven.'" (See also Mark 10:15, Luke 18:17.) However, the rest of Saying 22 takes the paradoxical quality of the canonical saying and expands it considerably beyond what the synoptic Jesus says. Indeed, by the end of the saying it is far from clear just what all the paradox and overcoming is supposed to mean. Generally, one senses that the author of Thomas has in mind a state, either original or terminal, in which the conflicts of present existence are overcome, but outside/inside, above/below, and male/female are susceptible of various interpretations. The implication is that those privy to the inner circles from which the Gospel of Thomas derived would know what this esoteric speech signified, but one can see why those who composed the canonical New Testament would be leery of such literature, since it could be made to signify whatever a given interpreter wished.

The other genres of apocryphal New Testament materials are interesting but not so significant as the apocryphal Gospels. The Acts include five grouped together in the so-called Leucian collection (attributed to Leucius Charinus, probably an early Gnostic): the Acts of John, the Acts of Peter, the Acts of Paul, the Acts of Andrew, and the Acts of Thomas. These works stress sexual asceticism, show a fascination with miraculous (for example, talking) animals, and are curious about the details of the deaths of the apostles. Other apocryphal Acts, many of them also attributed to apostles, are in the nature of Greek romances of the third and fourth centuries.

The apocryphal Epistles include letters attributed to Jesus, Paul, and Titus. There is also a Third Epistle to the Corinthians and an Epistle to the Laodiceans, but scholars generally consider none of these Epistles to add appreciably to our knowledge of Jesus or early orthodoxy.

Finally, the apocryphal Apocalypses purport to be divine revelations to an early Christian hero. Their favorite topics include the means to salvation and ethical teachings, and they provide graphic descriptions of heaven and hell.

Overall, the significance of the apocryphal New Testament materials is mainly the testimony they bear to options that the canonizers of the New Testament ruled out. As mentioned, many of these materials develop Gnostic themes, so they were specific cases in which orthodoxy could test its instincts about the full humanity of Jesus, his true death on the cross, and the traditional biblical conviction he expressed that the world, despite all of its imperfections, continued to be as Genesis depicted it: come from God and essentially good.

The apocryphal materials do suggest that the fund of oral materials on which the canonical Gospels drew may have been larger than scholars used to think, and they also suggest that sapiential interests may have been stronger than New Testament scholarship used to think. But the discernibly different tone of the apocryphal materials, when one contrasts them with the Synoptics and even the Gospel of John, shows that the canonizers rejected the degree of asceticism, spiritualizing, and esotericism that made many apocryphal texts suspect as Gnostic. As well, the different tone regarding miracles is significant. Where the miracles that the canonical Jesus regularly works are signs of the divine power and claims upon bystanders' faith, the miracles of the apocryphal sources often are simple prodigies or even foolish happenings such as making bed bugs obedient to God.

NOTES

[1] See Dennis R. MacDonald, "Apocryphal New Testament," in *Harper's Bible Dictionary*, ed. Paul J. Achtemeier. San Francisco: Harper & Row, 1985, pp. 38–39.

[2] Harold W. Attridge, "Gospel of Thomas," ibid., p. 355.

[3] Willis Barnstone, ed., *The Other Bible*. San Francisco: Harper & Row, 1984, p. 302.

Glossary

Abhidhamma: The thematic arrangement and logical development of the Buddha's teaching.

Ahimsa: Hindu term for noninjury or nonviolence.

Allegorical: Concerned with a symbolic or moral interpretation.

Anathemas: Condemnations (usually of doctrines deemed heretical).

Anthropology: The study of human nature.

Apocalypticism: Purportedly deriving from a revelation and usually pertaining to the approach of the end-time.

Apocrypha: Writings not accorded canonical status and so viewed as somewhat spurious.

Apollinarianism: The fourth-century christological heresy according to which the place of Christ's human mind was taken by the divine Logos.

Apologia: A defense of oneself or an intellectual position.

Apostolic: Related to the eyewitness disciples of Jesus.

Artha: Hindu term for wealth and worldly prosperity.

Avatar: In Hinduism, the form that a divinity takes to be present to a given historical age. For example, Krishna is an avatar of Vishnu.

Baptism: The Christian sacrament of initiation into divine and Church life.

Beatific vision: The sight of God that constitutes heaven.

Bhakti: Devotional love (mainly in Hinduism).

Brahmanism: The phase when Hinduism was dominated by priests and their sacrificial rituals.

Caliphs: The heads of the Muslim community.

Charismatic: Endowed with powerful spiritual gifts.

Christology: The study of the meaning of Jesus Christ.

Classic: Something that becomes a human norm or ideal.

Conciliar: Concerning the Church councils that dominated the early Christian centuries.

Daimon: An inner voice or inspiring spirit.

Dharma: Hindu and Buddhist term for Teaching; doctrine; Hindu term for caste responsibilities.

Dialectical: Having a struggling, back-and-forth character.

Docetists: Early heretics who denied Christ's full humanity.

Dogmas: Teachings declared official by Church authorities.

Dualistic: Having two somewhat unreconciled sides—for example, matter and spirit or good and evil.

Ecclesiological: Concerning the study of the Church (*ecclesia*).

Ecumenical: Concerning the whole, worldwide Church.

Epiphany: A manifestation (often of God).

Eschatology: Concerning the last things (death, judgment, heaven, and hell).

Essenes: Jewish sect of the late centuries B.C.E. and early centuries C.E. that withdrew from ordinary society to practice a purified religious life.

Eucharist: The Christian sacrament of the Lord's Supper.

Exegesis: Interpretation (usually of texts).

Exegetes: Interpreters.

Filioque: The Western Christian notion that the Spirit proceeds from the Son as well as the Father.

Gentiles: Non-Jews.

Gnostics: People claiming a special, secret, saving knowledge.

Halakah: Jewish legal lore.

Hellenistic: Concerning the Greek cultural ideals stimulated by Alexander the Great.

Hermeneutics: The study of the canons of interpretation.

Hur: The lovely maidens who populate the Muslim heaven.

Hypostasis: A personal substance.

Inspiration: The notion that something (usually Scripture) has been crucially influenced by God or a spiritual force.

Kairos: A time of crisis and special opportunity.

Karma: The Indian moral law of cause and effect.

Karmayoga: Hindu term for the discipline of purifying work by acting without desire.

Kerygma: The proclamation of the good news about Jesus.

Kingdom of God: Jesus' central symbol for the period of God's reign that he was announcing.

Margas: Hindu spiritual paths.

Messiahship: Christhood or status as God's anointed deliverer.

Moksha: Hindu term for deliverance from life's sufferings (for example, those due to karma) and for complete fulfillment and salvation.

Mystagogy: Stirring up of an appreciation of divine mystery.

Nirvana: Buddhist notion of unconditioned fulfillment.

Ontology: The study of being or existence.

Pantokrator: The Eastern Christian notion of Christ's universal Lordship.

Parables: Short, often paradoxical teaching stories.

Parousia: The return or second coming of Christ in full power that will consummate history.

Paschal: Concerning Passover or Easter.

Patristic: Relating to the age of the Fathers (early Christian centuries).

Penance: The Christian sacrament of forgiveness or the practice of trying to make reparation for sin.

Pentateuch: The first five books of the Hebrew Bible.

Pericopes: Textual units, bits of tradition.

Pleroma: A fullness or totality.

Pneumatic: Spirit-filled.

Polemical: Disputatious, warlike.

Prophetic: Inspired to call the times to account or predict future consequences.

Q: From the German "Quelle" or "source." The early Christian source that scholars hypothesize was used by Matthew and Luke to fashion the second and third synoptic Gospels.

Revelation: Disclosure, communication of what was hidden.

Satyagraha: Gandhi's notion that truth has invincible force.

Scholastics: Members of a school, especially the medieval university scholars.

Secular: Focused on this-worldly matters.

Servant songs: The poems of Second Isaiah (Isaiah 40–55) that Christians soon took as predictions of Jesus' suffering role.

Sophists: Pre-Christian Greek philosophers who taught rhetoric and have been considered careless about truth.

Soteriological: Concerning salvation.

Stoics: Greek philosophers of the late pre-Christian and early Christian eras who taught the sober endurance of pain and a theory of natural law.

Surahs: Chapters of the Qur'an.

Synodal: Concerning a meeting of Church leaders.

Synoptic: Being able to be taken in at a glance; having to do with the first three Gospels.

Tantra: Hindu or Buddhist symbolic exercises in pursuit of liberation.

Taoist: Concerning the Way, especially as described by the Chinese sage Lao-tzu.

Theophanies: Manifestations of God.

Theoria: The Greek notion of the contemplative or visionary pursuit of subsistent truth.

Theotokos: The Virgin Mary as the "God-bearer."

Torah: Jewish Teaching or Law.

Transmigration: The passage of a spirit from one body to another.

Types: Old Testament anticipations that Jesus fulfilled.

Wu-wei: The Taoist notion of active not-doing.

Annotated Bibliography

Abernathy, David. *Understanding the Teaching of Jesus.* New York: Seabury, 1983. A good survey of the main themes in Jesus' message, based on the lectures of the late Norman Perrin.

Ahlstrom, Sydney E. *A Religious History of the American People.* New Haven: Yale University Press, 1972. A comprehensive one-volume overview.

American Friends Service Committee. *A Compassionate Peace.* New York: Hill & Wang, 1982. A moving and persuasive specimen of Christian efforts at peacemaking.

Anderson, Gerald H., and Stransky, Thomas F., eds. *Christ's Lordship and Religious Pluralism.* Maryknoll, NY: Orbis, 1981. An excellent overview of the problems involved in the christology of universal salvation.

Barclay, William. *The Letters to the Philippians, Colossians, and Thessalonians.* Rev. ed. Philadelphia: Westminster, 1975. A rather traditional reading of these Pauline Epistles.

Barr, James. *The Scope and Authority of the Bible.* Philadelphia: Westminster, 1980. A balanced and well-informed study of basic issues in determining the status of the Bible.

Brown, Raymond E. *The Birth of the Messiah.* Garden City, NY: Doubleday, 1977. A close study of the infancy narratives of Matthew and Luke.

———. *The Community of the Beloved Disciple.* New York: Paulist, 1979. A fascinating hypothesis about the formation of the Johannine community and theology, by a leading scholar of the Johannine materials.

———. *The Epistles of John.* Garden City, NY: Doubleday, 1982. The major current study on this topic.

Brown, Robert McAfee. *Making Peace in the Global Village.* Philadelphia: Westminster, 1981. Readable but challenging reflections on Christian peacemaking.

———. *Unexpected News: Reading the Bible with Third World Eyes.* Philadelphia: Westminster, 1984. Liberation theology made concrete and tied to the biblical themes of justice.

Carmody, John. *Ecology and Religion.* Ramsey, NJ: Paulist, 1983. Applications of the theological method of Bernard Lonergan to the project of creating a new Christian theology of nature.

Carpenter, Humphrey. *Jesus.* New York: Oxford University Press, 1980. A small and helpful volume from a series on leading religious figures.

Cleage, Albert. *The Black Messiah.* New York: Sheed and Ward, 1968. A leading
early work in black theology that takes Jesus' blackness literally.

Collins, Adela Yarbro. *Crisis and Catharsis: The Power of the Apocalypse.* Philadelphia: Westminster, 1984. A sociologically oriented study of the motivations behind the Book of Revelation.

Collins, Raymond E. *Introduction to the New Testament.* Garden City, NY:
Doubleday, 1983. A solid, fairly technical survey of fundamental scholarly
issues.

Cragg, Kenneth, and Speight, Marston, eds. *Islam from Within.* Belmont, CA:
Wadsworth, 1980. A good collection of primary sources on central issues in
Islam.

Cunliffe-Jones, Hubert, ed. *A History of Christian Doctrine.* Philadelphia: Fortress, 1980. An excellent one-volume survey by leading historians of Christian doctrine.

Desrochers, John. *Christ the Liberator.* Bangalore, India: Center for Social Action, 1977. A somewhat abstract example of liberation christology done in
an Indian context.

Douglas, Mary, and Tipton, Steven, eds. *Religion and America: Spirituality in a
Secular Age.* Boston: Beacon Press, 1983. The reprint of an issue of *Daeda-
lus* with (often sociologically oriented) studies of contemporary American
religion by leading scholars.

Duling, Dennis C. *Jesus Christ through History.* New York: Harcourt, Brace,
Jovanovich, 1979. An interesting treatment of christological developments
within Western Christian history.

Dunn, James D. G. *Jesus and the Spirit.* Philadelphia: Westminster, 1975. A close
textual study of the pneumatic christology of the New Testament sources.

———. *Unity and Diversity in the New Testament.* Philadelphia: Westminster,
1977. A thorough analysis of the differences and likenesses in the theologies
of the New Testament sources.

Eliade, Mircea. *A History of Religious Ideas.* Vols. 1 and 2. Chicago: University
of Chicago Press, 1978, 1982. The synthetic masterwork by the leading
American historian of world religions.

Endo, Shusaku. *A Life of Jesus.* New York: Paulist, 1978. An intriguing "translation" of the New Testament portrait into Japanese cultural terms.

Erikson, Erik H. *Gandhi's Truth.* New York: W. W. Norton, 1969. A masterful
psychoanalytic study of the Mahatma as a prime specimen of middle-aged
generativity and as the creator of the instrument (nonviolent protest) offering the most hope for peace in a nuclear age.

Fingarette, Herbert. *Confucius: The Secular as Sacred.* New York: Harper &
Row, 1972. An illuminating study of ritual in Confucius' day and now.

Fitzmyer, Joseph A. *A Christological Catechism.* New York: Paulist, 1982. Questions and answers from a leading New Testament scholar on the hard issues
of New Testament christology.

———. *The Gospel According to Luke I–IX.* 2d ed. Garden City, NY: Doubleday,
1983. A massive and masterful study of Lukan theology.

Griffin, Emilie. *Turning: Reflections on the Experience of Conversion.* Garden
City, NY: Doubleday, 1980. A study that interweaves the author's own expe-
riences with those of such famous converts as C. S. Lewis and Thomas
Merton.

Grollenberg, Lucas. *Jesus.* Philadelphia: Westminster, 1978. A simple, very readable account that stresses the cultural context and the personality of the man Jesus.

———. *Paul.* Philadelphia: Westminster, 1978. A simple study of the main Pauline letters that makes good sense out of Paul's vision and personality.

Hayes, John H. *Son of God to Superstar.* Nashville: Abingdon, 1976. Chapters on the leading twentieth-century views of Jesus.

Hellwig, Monika K. *Jesus: The Compassion of God.* Wilmington, DE: Michael Glazier, 1983. Christology set in the context of a liberation theologian's desire to stress soteriology.

Henry, Patrick. *New Directions in New Testament Study.* Philadelphia: Westminster, 1979. An excellent survey of the scholarly trends and emphases.

Kee, Howard Clark. *Jesus in History.* 2d ed. New York: Harcourt, Brace, Jovanovich, 1977. Studies in the gospel presentations of Jesus.

———. *Understanding the New Testament.* 4th ed. Englewood Cliffs, NJ: Prentice-Hall, 1983. A respected undergraduate text.

Krodel, Gerhard, ed. *Ephesians, Colossians, 2 Thessalonians, the Pastoral Epistles.* Philadelphia: Fortress, 1978. Helpful textual analyses and commentary by competent New Testament scholars.

———. *Hebrews, James, 1 and 2 Peter, Jude, Revelation.* Philadelphia: Fortress, 1977. Solid studies of these theologies of the New Testament.

Küng, Hans. *On Being a Christian.* Garden City, NY: Doubleday, 1976. A massive popular work by a leading Roman Catholic theologian.

Machovec, Milan. *A Marxist Looks at Jesus.* Philadelphia: Fortress, 1976. An illuminating view from the perspective of a committed Marxist immersed in recent biblical scholarship.

McKenzie, John L. *The New Testament without Illusions.* Chicago: Thomas More, 1980. Crusty reflections on various New Testament problems and their bearing on current Christian life.

Miranda, José. *Marx against the Marxists.* Maryknoll, NY: Orbis, 1980. A defense of Marx against those who call him atheistic or antireligious.

———. *Marx and the Bible.* Maryknoll, NY: Orbis, 1974. Good textual studies on the theme that Marx and the biblical prophets share a similar passion for social justice.

Muggeridge, Malcolm. *Jesus: The Man Who Lives.* New York: Harper & Row, 1975. A lively, well-written interpretation by a convert from agnosticism to evangelical Christianity.

Nichols, Aiden. *The Art of God Incarnate.* New York: Paulist, 1980. Interesting reflections on the depiction of Christ in Christian and Western art.

Nolan, Albert. *Jesus before Christianity.* Maryknoll, NY: Orbis, 1978. Liberation christology from the perspective of South Africa.

Novak, Michael, ed. *Capitalism and Socialism: A Theological Inquiry.* Washington, DC: American Enterprise Institute for Public Policy Research, 1979. Conservative reflections on the interplay between religion and economics.

Panikkar, Raimundo. *The Unknown Christ of Hinduism.* Rev. ed. Maryknoll, NY: Orbis, 1981. An absorbing study of the relations between the Logos and Hindu theology.

Parrinder, Geoffrey. *A Dictionary of Non-Christian Religions.* Philadelphia: Westminster, 1971. A readable and reliable one-volume word-book.

————. *Jesus in the Qur'an*. New York: Oxford University Press, 1977. A thorough textual study of the image and understanding of Jesus in Islam's sacred book.

Paton, Alan. *Ah, but Your Land Is Beautiful*. New York: Charles Scribner's Sons, 1982. A very moving novel of life and religion in South Africa.

Pelikan, Jaroslav. *The Christian Tradition: A History of the Development of Doctrine*. Vols. 1 and 2. Chicago: University of Chicago Press, 1971, 1974. Good scholarly analyses of how Christian faith unfolded in conciliar times and in the classical era of Eastern theology.

Perkins, Pheme. *Reading the New Testament: An Introduction*. Ramsey, NJ: Paulist, 1978. A readable short undergraduate text.

Perrin, Norman, and Duling, Dennis C. *The New Testament: An Introduction*. 2d ed. New York: Harcourt, Brace, Jovanovich, 1982. A solid undergraduate textbook.

Ricoeur, Paul. *Essays on Biblical Interpretation*. Ed. Lewis S. Mudge. Philadelphia: Fortress, 1980. Important essays by one of the most important theoreticians of religious language.

Robinson, Richard H., and Johnson, Willard L. *The Buddhist Religion*. 3d ed. Belmont, CA: Wadsworth, 1982. An insightful undergraduate text.

Ruether, Rosemary Radford. *Sexism and God-Talk*. Boston: Beacon Press, 1983. A solid work on the thoroughgoing implications of feminist Christian theology.

————. *To Change the World: Christology and Cultural Criticism*. New York: Crossroad, 1981. A slim volume of lectures that illustrate the major liberational themes.

Sandmel, Samuel. *We Jews and Jesus*. New York: Oxford University Press, 1973. Sensitive yet forthright presentations of christological issues from a Jewish perspective.

Schillebeeckx, Edward. *Christ*. New York: Seabury, 1980. A massive study of the early Christian experience of the grace of Jesus' Lordship.

————. *God Is New Each Moment*. New York: Seabury, 1983. Conversations with Huub Oosterhuis that summarize much of Schillebeeckx's faith and political conviction.

————. *Jesus*. New York: Seabury, 1979. Detailed studies of the centrality of the historical Jesus to the early Christian convictions about definitive salvation.

Schüssler-Fiorenza, Elisabeth. *In Memory of Her*. New York: Crossroad, 1983. A pioneering feminist study of the place of women in earliest Christianity.

Sloyan, Gerard. *Jesus in Focus*. Mystic, CT: Twenty-Third Publications, 1983. An excellent and readable overview of the New Testament Christ.

Sobrino, Jon. *Christology at the Crossroads*. Maryknoll, NY: Orbis, 1978. The first major liberational christology and still one of the fullest.

Staniforth, Maxwell, trans. *Early Christian Fathers*. Baltimore: Penguin, 1968. A convenient and readable collection of the major texts of the early second century.

Tracy, David. *The Analogical Imagination*. New York: Crossroad, 1981. A massive study of how theology ought to address current American religious pluralism.

United States Catholic Bishops. "The Challenge of Peace." In *Catholics and Nuclear War*, ed. Philip J. Murnion. New York: Crossroad, 1983. The bishops' controversial yet much-praised pastoral letter on Christian ethics in an age of nuclear arms.

————. "Pastoral Letter on Social Teachings and the U.S. Economy." *The National Catholic Reporter*, November 23, 1984. The first draft of the bishops' study of the application of Christian ethical principles to current American economic and political life.

Vermes, Geza. *Jesus the Jew*. London: Collins, 1973. An excellent positioning of Jesus in his contemporary culture by a leading Jewish New Testament scholar.

Weitzman, Kurt, ed. *The Icon*. New York: Alfred A. Knopf, 1982. A handsome volume on Eastern Christian iconography with both beautiful plates and helpful historical studies.

Index